Martha Stewart's COOKIES

Martha Stewart's COOKIES

The Very Best Treats to Bake and to Share

From the Editors of
Martha Stewart Living

Photographs by Victor Schrager and others

Clarkson Potter/Publishers
New York

 Published in the United States by Clarkson Potter/Publishers, an imprint of the Crown Publishing Group, a division of Random House, Inc., New York.

www.crownpublishing.com
www.clarksonpotter.com
www.marthastewart.com

Clarkson N. Potter is a trademark and Potter and colophon are registered trademarks of Random House, Inc.

Library of Congress Cataloging-in-Publication Data
Martha Stewart's cookies: the very best treats to bake and to share / the editors of Martha Stewart Living.
1. Cookies. I. Stewart, Martha. II. Martha Stewart Living. III. Title: Cookies.
TX772.M29 2007
641.8'654—dc22 2007014927

ISBN 978-0-307-39454-5

Printed in the United States of America

Design by Barbara de Wilde

10 9 8 7 6 5 4 3 2 1

First Edition

Many people contributed to the creation of this wonderful book, including editors Ellen Morrissey, Amy Conway, and Christine Cyr; art directors William van Roden, Barbara de Wilde, and Eric A. Pike; food editor Jennifer Aaronson; and photographer Victor Schrager and his assistant Addie Juell. Others who provided ideas, guidance, and support include:

THE TALENTED TEAM AT MARTHA STEWART LIVING OMNIMEDIA
Isabel Abdai
Andrea Bakacs
Monita Buchwald
Alison Vanek Devine
James Dunlinson
Heloise Goodman
Elizabeth Gottfried
Allison Hedges
Pamela Morris
Lucinda Scala Quinn
Robb Riedel
Margaret Roach

OUR PARTNERS AT CLARKSON POTTER
Rica Allannic
Amy Boorstein
Doris Cooper
Jenny Frost
Derek Gullino
Sibylle Kazeroid
Craig Libman
Mark McCauslin
Lauren Shakely
Jane Treuhaft

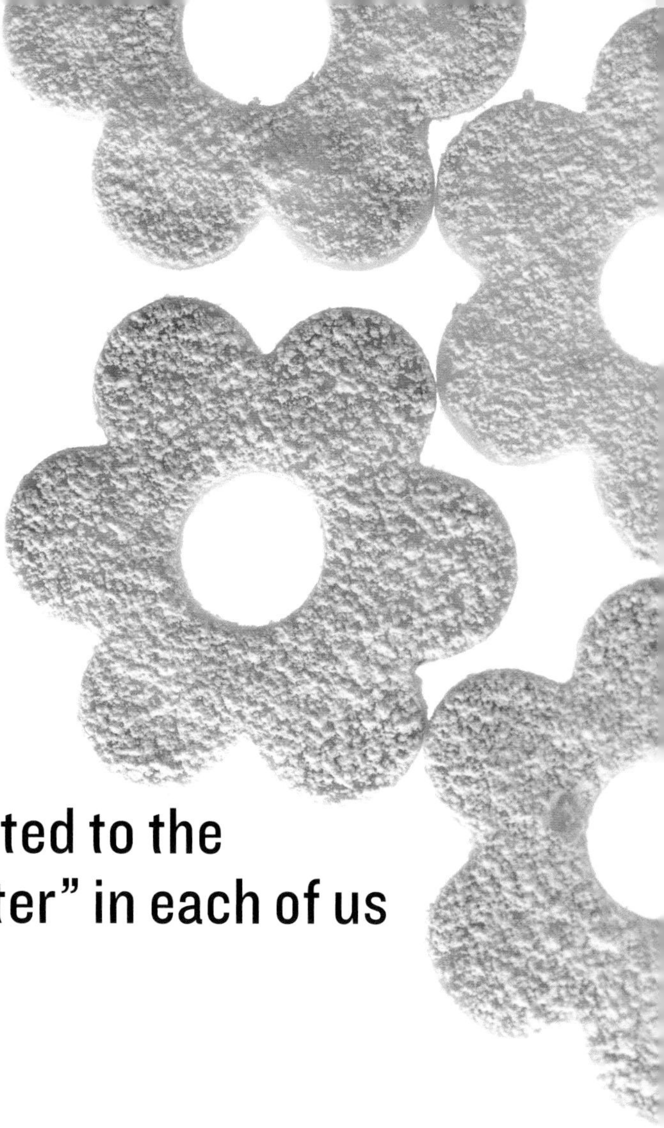

Dedicated to the
"cookie monster" in each of us

contents

light *and* delicate PAGE 20

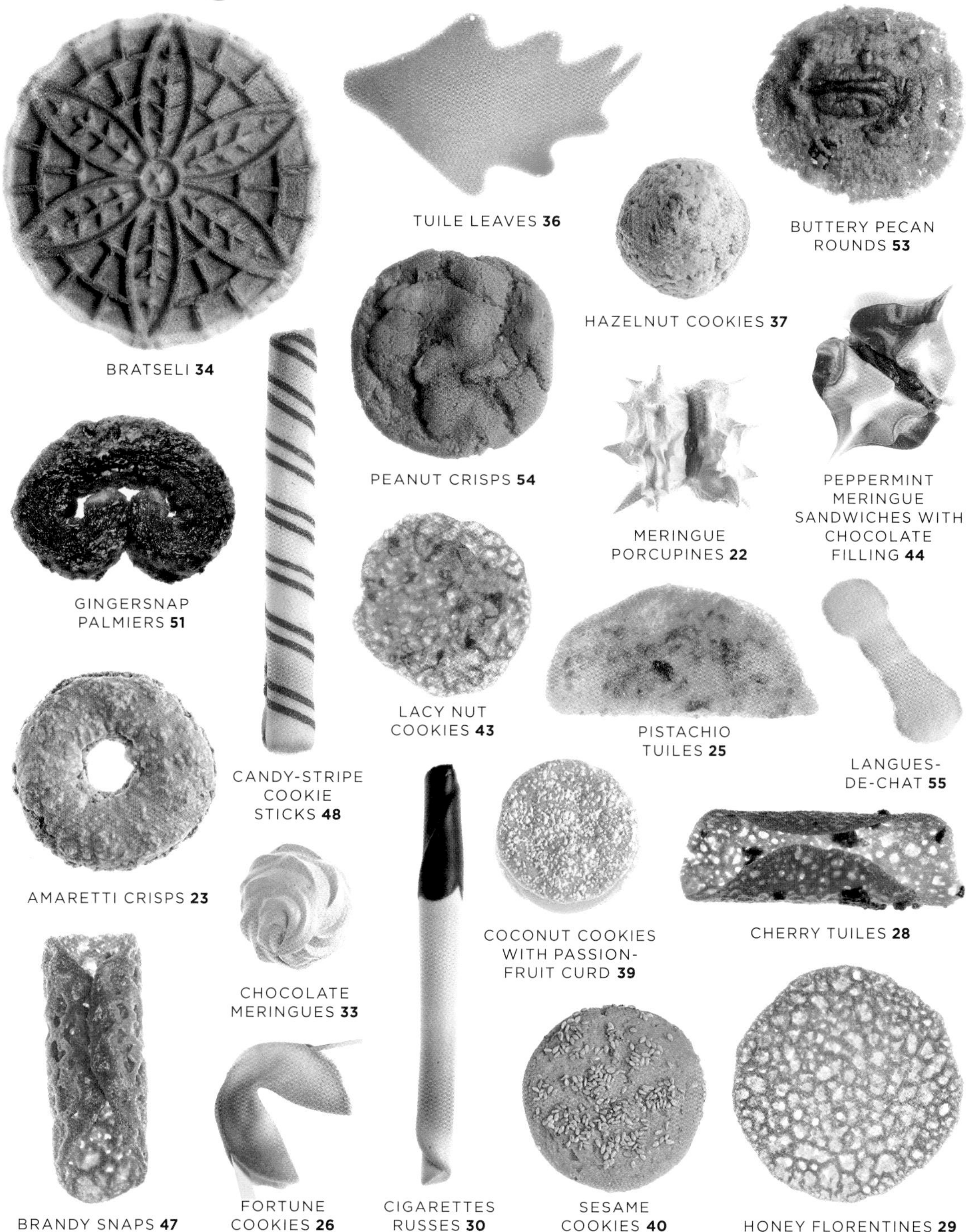

soft *and* chewy PAGE 56

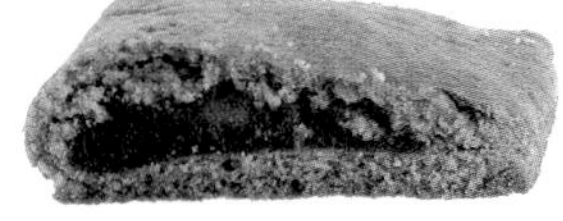

crumbly *and* sandy

PAGE 104

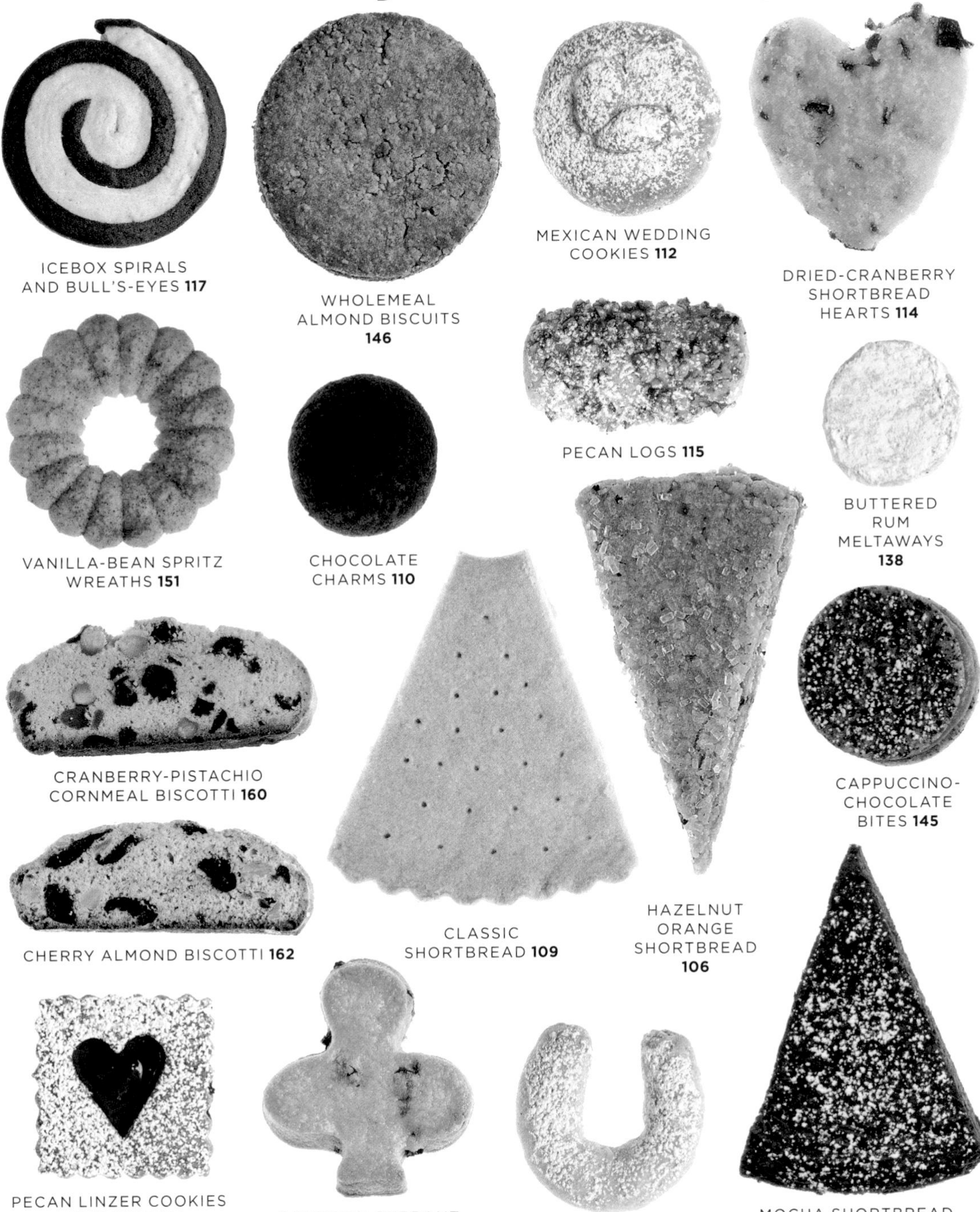

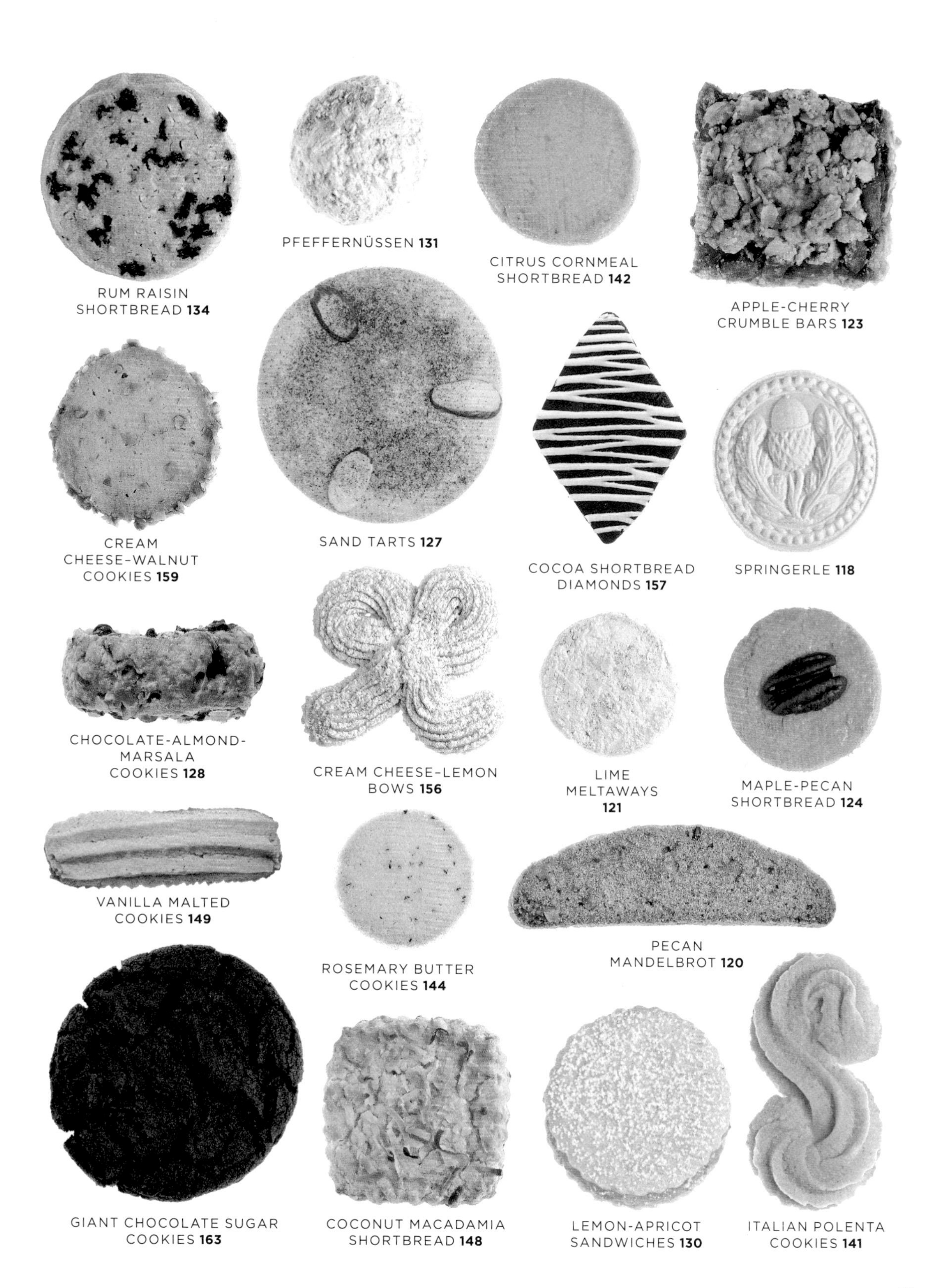

chunky *and* nutty PAGE 164

MACADAMIA-MAPLE STICKY BARS **174**

CHUNKY PEANUT, CHOCOLATE, AND CINNAMON COOKIES **179**

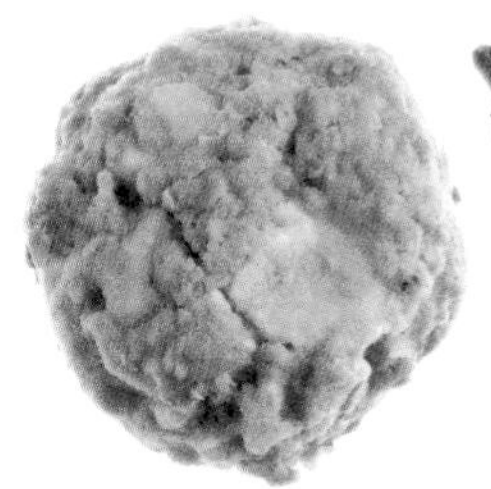
WHITE CHOCOLATE-CHUNK COOKIES **172**

ROCKY LEDGE BARS **166**

FRUIT AND NUT COOKIES **183**

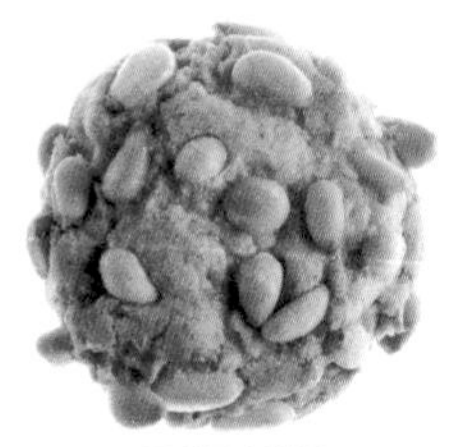
PINE NUT COOKIES **177**

BANANA-WALNUT CHOCOLATE-CHUNK COOKIES **170**

BLUEBERRY BONANZA BARS **186**

MAGIC BLONDIES **180**

CHOCOLATE CHIP COOKIES FOR PASSOVER **167**

TURTLE BROWNIES **187**

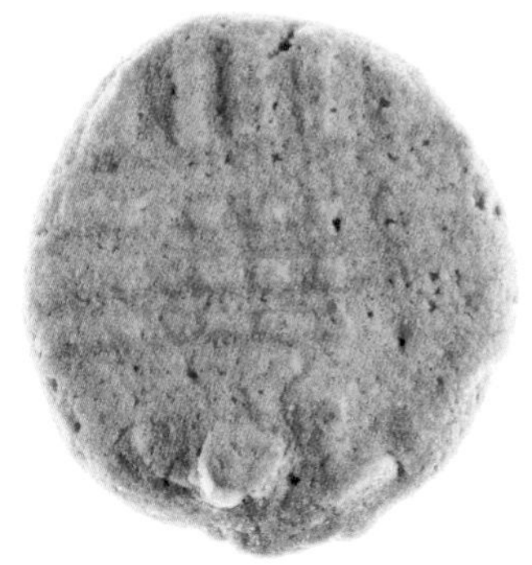
PEANUT BUTTER COOKIES **184**

DOUBLE CHOCOLATE COCONUT COOKIES **173**

NE PLUS ULTRA COOKIES **169**

cakey *and* tender PAGE 188

PUMPKIN COOKIES WITH BROWN-BUTTER ICING **197**

PEANUT BUTTER WHOOPIE PIES **207**

OATMEAL BARS WITH DATES AND WALNUTS **216**

CARROT CAKE COOKIES **202**

CHOCOLATE WAFFLES **214**

PEAR, PISTACHIO, AND GINGER BLONDIES **201**

BROWN-BUTTER TOFFEE BLONDIES **208**

LEMON MADELEINES **190**

SURPRISE COOKIES **195**

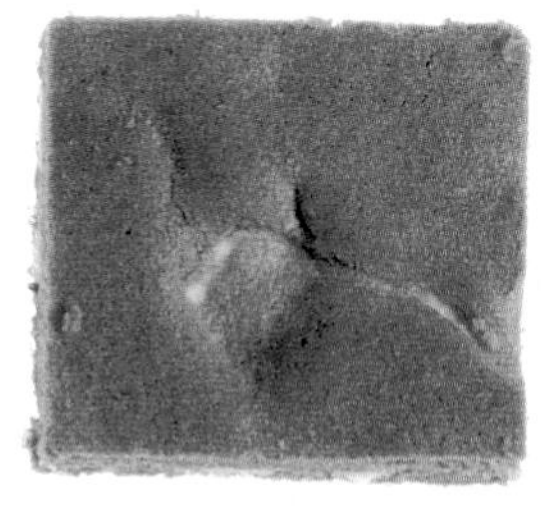

GINGERBREAD-WHITE CHOCOLATE BLONDIES **191**

FRESH-PEACH DROP COOKIES **217**

MINI BLACK-AND-WHITE COOKIES **213**

CAKEY CHOCOLATE CHIP COOKIES **198**

ORANGE-CARDAMOM MADELEINES **210**

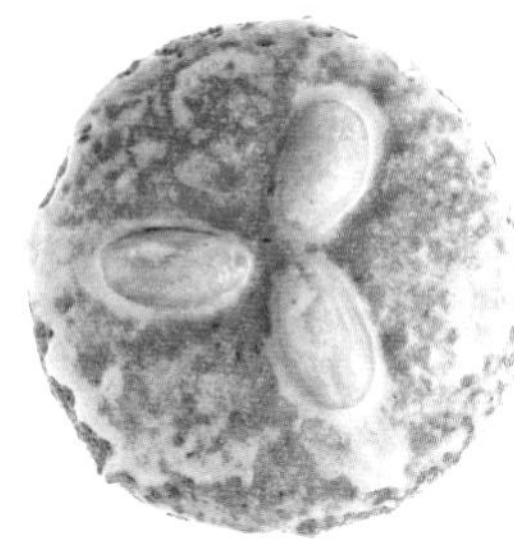

LEBKUCHEN **192**

RASPBERRY HONEY FINANCIERS **205**

RASPBERRY ALMOND BLONDIES **199**

crisp *and* crunchy

PAGE 218

ANZAC BISCUITS **238**

BUTTER TWISTS **248**

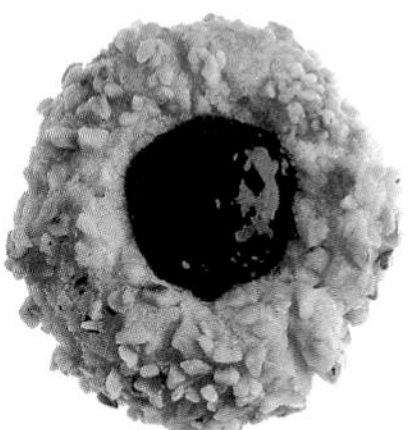

HAZELNUT JAM THUMBPRINTS **252**

COCONUT BISCUITS **249**

CASSIS CRISPS **253**

CHOCOLATE SANDWICHES **235**

GINGERBREAD SNOWFLAKES **259**

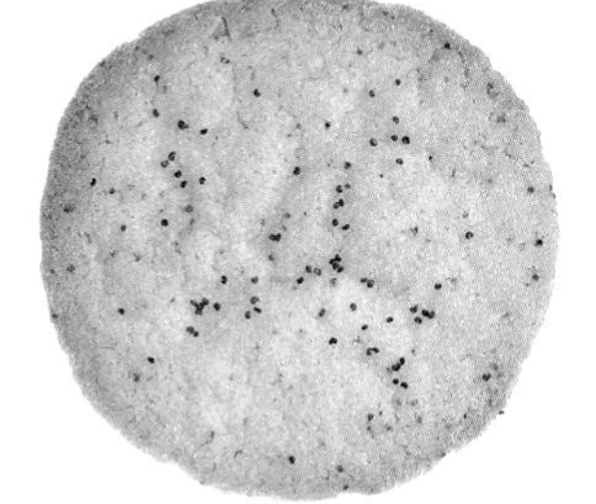

LEMON-POPPY SEED CRISPS **262**

CHOCOLATE PRETZELS **223**

CHOCOLATE-BLACK PEPPER COOKIES **245**

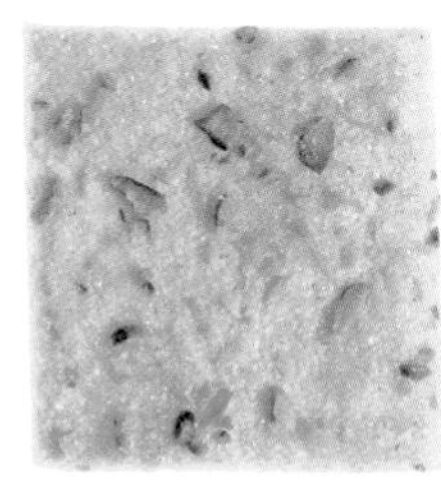

SWEET CARDAMOM CRACKERS **263**

HOMEMADE GRAHAM CRACKERS **255**

SUGAR COOKIE CUTOUTS **241**

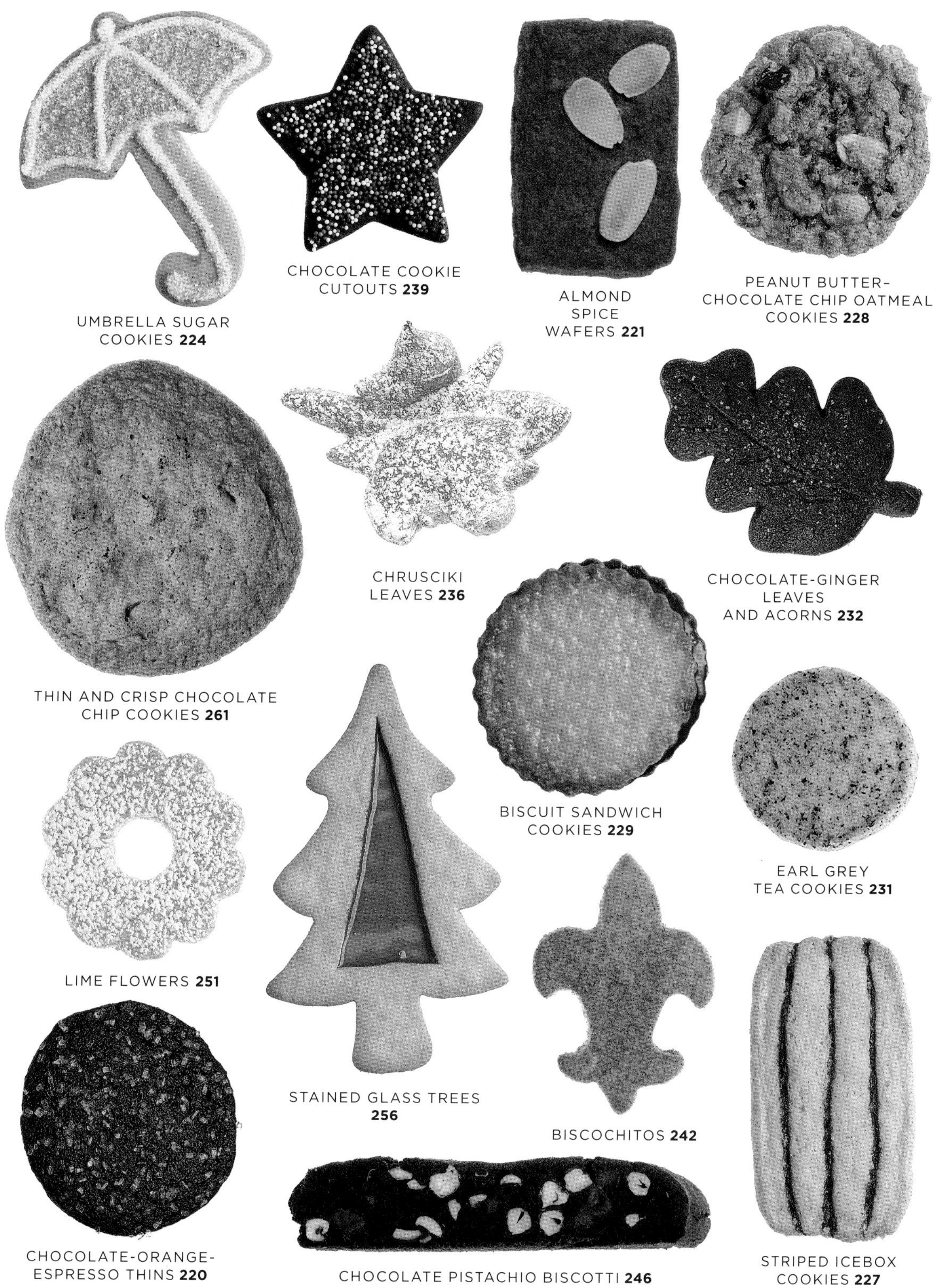

rich *and* dense PAGE 264

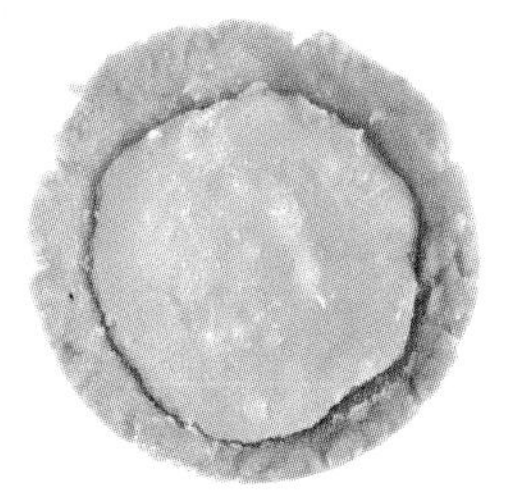

LEMON TASSIES **292**

BUTTERSCOTCH-CASHEW BLONDIES **277**

COCONUT SWIRL BROWNIES **274**

KEY LIME BARS **303**

PRUNE RUGELACH **298**

SARAH BERNHARDT COOKIES **282**

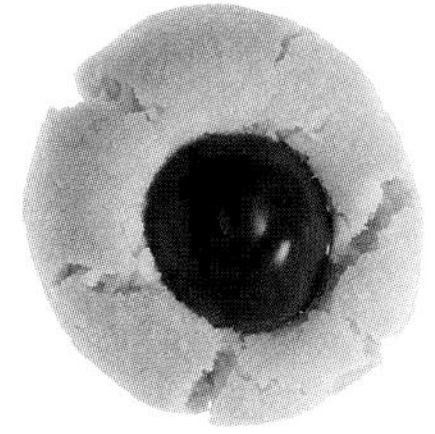

CHOCOLATE THUMBPRINTS **278**

RUGELACH FINGERS **288**

CHOCOLATE PISTACHIO COOKIES **294**

CHOCOLATE CHERRY CRUMB BARS **305**

GINGER CHEESECAKE BARS **272**

DOUBLE CHOCOLATE BROWNIES **287**

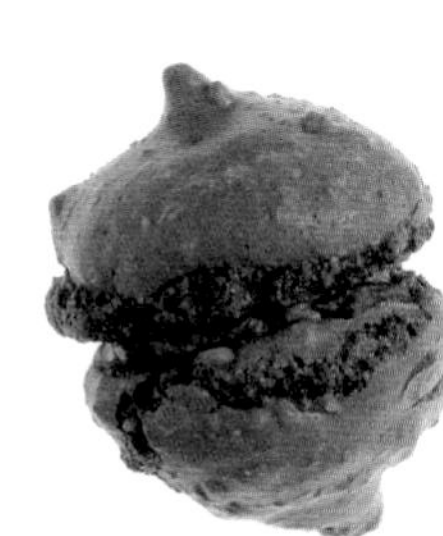

introduction

The instant I saw the photograph of these Chewy Chocolate Gingerbread Cookies (the recipe is on page 67), I knew I had to bake them that night. Cookies often spark a strong reaction in people, and you probably have your own favorites. Are they light and delicate, like classic meringues, rich and dense, like the lemon bars that I love, or crisp and crunchy, like the chocolate chip cookies that my daughter, Alexis, is partial to? At *Martha Stewart Living,* when we talk about cookies—which is often!—and invent new recipes for them, we've found that it's usually a certain texture, whether chunky or sandy or soft, that we crave, even before a particular flavor or ingredient. So when we gathered all of our best recipes into a book, that's how we decided to organize them.

You'll find 175 recipes here; most likely there's a version of those favorites of yours, along with dozens of others you've never imagined. Cookies, after all, are wonderfully versatile things. Depending on how you mix, form, and bake a few simple ingredients, you can create cookies that make the perfect anytime snack, an elegant dessert, or a lunch-box treat. They can be wholesome, indulgent, or anywhere in between. They can be familiar or surprising. And most of them are even easy to make. So go ahead and choose a recipe from these pages—try a new one each week, and you'll be baking for years! What could be better than that?

Martha Stewart

light *and* delicate

The ingredients list for most cookies includes butter, sugar, flour, and eggs, and usually a leavener such as baking soda or powder. Any number of mix-ins can alter flavors and textures—think spices, extracts, zests, nuts, chocolate chips, and such. To produce cookies that are light and delicate, however, the key is often in taking away ingredients, not adding. The meringue is a prime example: It consists almost entirely of sugar and egg whites—no butter, flour, or leaveners—that are whipped into cloudlike puffs before baking. Similarly, the batters for tuiles and brandy snaps rely on very little flour and no leavener, and our hazelnut cookies achieve their ethereal texture from a complete absence of butter. Each of the delightful cookies in this chapter is proof that less can indeed add up to more.

MERINGUE PORCUPINES, **page 22**

Meringue Porcupines

We spread apricot preserves between these meringues, but another filling, such as raspberry jam, would be delicious, too. The meringues should be baked no more than one day before sandwiching them.

MAKES 1 DOZEN

- Swiss Meringue (recipe follows)
- ½ cup heavy cream
- 1 drop pure almond extract
- 1 cup plus 2 tablespoons best-quality apricot preserves

1. Preheat oven to 200°F. Line two baking sheets with parchment.

2. Scoop a spoonful of meringue onto a large oval soupspoon, and use another soupspoon to form meringue into the shape of a small egg. Use second spoon to push meringue oval off first spoon and onto parchment. Spoon 12 ovals onto each prepared baking sheet. Using a small offset spatula, pull out spikes of meringue, creating a porcupine effect.

3. Bake cookies until they are crisp on outside but have marshmallow consistency inside, about 1 hour. Reduce oven to 175°F if meringue starts to brown. Remove from oven, and gently press bottom of each meringue so that it caves in and can be filled. Turn off oven, and return meringues to oven to dry, about 20 minutes. Let cool completely on parchment on wire racks before filling.

4. Put cream and almond extract in the chilled bowl of an electric mixer fitted with the whisk attachment, and mix on medium speed until just stiff, about 2 minutes. Fill half of the hollowed meringues with cream, and the remaining halves with preserves. Sandwich together. Serve immediately.

SWISS MERINGUE MAKES 4 CUPS

- 4 large egg whites
- 1 cup sugar
- Pinch of cream of tartar
- ½ teaspoon pure vanilla extract

Put egg whites, sugar, and cream of tartar in the heatproof bowl of an electric mixer set over a pan of simmering water. Cook, whisking constantly, until sugar has dissolved and mixture is warm to the touch, 3 to 3½ minutes. Transfer bowl to electric mixer fitted with the whisk attachment; beat, starting on low speed and gradually increasing to high, until stiff, glossy peaks form, about 10 minutes. Add vanilla; mix until combined. Use immediately.

HOW TO ASSEMBLE MERINGUE PORCUPINES
1. After scooping meringues onto a parchment paper–lined baking sheet, use an offset spatula to pull out little spikes. 2. Bake for one hour, then push in the bottoms of the baked cookies so you can fill them with whipped cream and preserves. Let dry and cool completely before sandwiching pairs together.

Amaretti Crisps

To achieve the most volume, whisk egg whites in a metal bowl set over a pot of simmering water until just warm to the touch. Toast the almond slices by placing them in a single layer on a rimmed baking sheet and baking at 325°F, stirring occasionally until fragrant, about 10 minutes.

MAKES ABOUT 1½ DOZEN

- 1¾ cups sliced almonds (about 5½ ounces), toasted
- 1 cup confectioners' sugar
- 2 large egg whites, room temperature
- ½ teaspoon pure almond extract

1. Preheat oven to 350°F. Process almonds and confectioners' sugar in a food processor until ground to a fine powder. Transfer to a bowl.

2. Put egg whites in the bowl of an electric mixer fitted with the whisk attachment; beat on medium-high speed until stiff peaks form. Fold egg whites into almond mixture; fold in almond extract.

3. Transfer mixture to a pastry bag fitted with a ½-inch plain round tip (such as Ateco #806). Pipe twenty 2-inch rings onto baking sheets lined with parchment paper, spacing about 1 inch apart. Bake cookies, rotating sheets halfway through, until golden brown and firm to the touch, about 25 minutes. Transfer cookies on parchment to wire racks; let cool completely. Cookies can be stored in an airtight container at room temperature up to 2 days.

Pistachio Tuiles

Tuile (pronounced "tweel") means "tile" in French. Once the cookies cool, their shape takes on the appearance of a curved roof tile. MAKES ABOUT 6 DOZEN

- ⅔ cup sugar
- 3 large egg whites
- ⅛ teaspoon salt
- 4 tablespoons (½ stick) unsalted butter, melted and cooled
- 2 tablespoons all-purpose flour
- ½ cup shelled unsalted pistachios, finely chopped in a food processor

1. Preheat oven to 350°F. Whisk sugar, egg whites, and salt in a bowl until sugar has dissolved. Whisk in butter, then flour. Stir in pistachios.

2. Line a baking sheet with a nonstick baking mat (such as Silpat). Place a long-handled wooden spoon on a clean work surface; prop up each end on a metal spoon to raise it slightly (you will use handle of wooden spoon to form tuiles).

3. Drop teaspoons of batter onto baking mat, spacing about 2 inches apart; using an offset spatula, flatten into 1½-inch rounds. Bake until pale golden, 8 to 10 minutes. Let cool on baking sheet 30 seconds.

4. Working quickly with one cookie at a time, use an offset spatula to lift cookies from sheet and drape them over spoon handle. (If cookies become too crisp to work with, return to oven until pliable, about 1 minute.) Let cookies cool slightly, 20 to 30 seconds, then remove from handle; press sides together to close. Let cool completely. Repeat with remaining batter. Cookies can be stored in an airtight container at room temperature up to 1 week.

Fortune Cookies

The key to success with these cookies is to bake no more than two to three on a sheet at one time. Shape them as quickly as possible after removing from the oven, because they begin to firm up as soon as they are lifted off the baking sheet. To avoid wasting cookies, try the shaping process with a circle of paper first. MAKES 45

- 4 large egg whites
- 1 cup superfine sugar
- 1 cup all-purpose flour, sifted
- Pinch of salt
- 5 tablespoons unsalted butter, melted
- 3 tablespoons heavy cream
- 1 teaspoon pure almond extract
- 45 paper fortunes, about 5 inches long
- Vegetable oil cooking spray

1. Preheat oven to 400°F. Coat a baking sheet liberally with cooking spray.

2. In the bowl of an electric mixer fitted with the paddle attachment, combine egg whites and sugar, and beat on medium speed until frothy, about 30 seconds. Add flour and salt, and beat until combined. Add butter, cream, and almond extract, and beat until combined, about 30 seconds.

3. Leaving space for one or two more cookies, spoon 1 teaspoon of batter onto the baking sheet, and spread with the back of the spoon into an even, thin 3- to 4-inch circle; repeat. Bake cookies until the edges turn golden brown, about 8 minutes, rotating pan halfway through.

4. Transfer baking sheet to a heat-resistant surface. Working as quickly as possible, slide an offset spatula under one of the cookies. Lift it up, and place it on a clean kitchen towel. Center a paper fortune on top of the cookie. Using your fingers, fold the cookie in half, pinching the top together to form a loose semicircle. Hold the cookie with your index fingers inserted at each open end, and slide your thumbs together along the bottom line. Press into the center while bending the two open ends together and down to form the shape of a fortune cookie. This whole process should take about 10 seconds. Once the cookie hardens, which begins to happen almost immediately, you cannot shape it.

5. Place the cookie on the kitchen towel to cool, and shape the second cookie. Repeat until all the batter is used up. To speed up the process, bake four cookies at a time, staggering two cookie sheets by 4 minutes to give you time to shape. Cookies can be stored in an airtight container at room temperature up to 1 week.

cookies are
happiness

Cherry Tuiles

While they're warm, these tuiles are draped over a cannoli mold or a narrow rolling pin to give them their shape. To make edible bowls for serving scoops of ice cream or sorbet, shape the warm cookie rounds over inverted muffin tins or ramekins instead. MAKES ABOUT 4 DOZEN

- ½ cup dried sour cherries
- ⅔ cup packed light brown sugar
- ½ cup (1 stick) unsalted butter
- ½ cup light corn syrup
- Pinch of coarse salt
- ⅔ cup cake flour (not self-rising), sifted

1. Put cherries in a small bowl, and add warm water to cover. Let stand until softened, about 20 minutes. Drain and coarsely chop cherries.

2. Heat brown sugar, butter, corn syrup, and salt in a saucepan over medium heat, stirring, until sugar dissolves and butter melts, about 5 minutes. Remove from heat. Whisk in flour. Fold in cherries. Transfer to a small bowl and cover with plastic wrap. Chill until firm, about 1 hour.

3. Preheat oven to 375°F. Roll dough into ¾-inch balls; space about 2 inches apart on baking sheets lined with parchment paper. Flatten slightly. Bake cookies, one baking sheet at a time, until golden brown, about 7 minutes. Let cool on sheet on a wire rack for about 10 seconds.

4. Using a small offset spatula, remove cookies one at a time and wrap around a cannoli mold or a 1½-inch rolling pin until set. Transfer to a wire rack. Tuiles need to be warm to shape; if they get cold, return them to the oven briefly until they are pliable. Cookies can be stored in a single layer in airtight containers at room temperature up to 2 days.

Honey Florentines

To ensure uniform cookies, scoop out this batter with a measuring spoon. Leave adequate space between dollops—the cookies will expand considerably while they bake. If desired, embellish the cooled cookies with melted chocolate: Sandwich two cookies with it, dip cookie halves in it, drizzle it over the tops, or spread it on the flat sides of each. MAKES 2 DOZEN

- 2 tablespoons unsalted butter
- 2 tablespoons packed light brown sugar
- 1½ tablespoons honey
- 2 tablespoons all-purpose flour
- Pinch of coarse salt

1. Preheat oven to 375°F. Melt butter, brown sugar, and honey in a small saucepan over medium-low heat. Transfer to a bowl. Whisk in flour and salt until smooth.

2. Working quickly, drop ½ teaspoons of batter onto large baking sheets lined with parchment paper, spacing at least 3 inches apart. Bake cookies until they spread and turn golden brown, about 6 minutes. Let cool on sheets on wire racks. Carefully remove cookies from sheets with your fingers. Cookies can be stored between layers of parchment in airtight containers at room temperature up to 2 days.

Cigarettes Russes

These cookies are soft and pliable when they first come out of the oven. You have to prepare these delicate wafers one sheet at a time so that you can quickly roll them around a dowel while they are still warm. Don't be discouraged if your first few attempts aren't perfect—just keep going and you'll soon get the hang of it. MAKES ABOUT 3 DOZEN

- 2 cups confectioners' sugar, sifted
- 1¼ cups all-purpose flour
- ⅛ teaspoon salt
- 10½ tablespoons unsalted butter, melted
- 6 large egg whites, lightly beaten
- 1 tablespoon heavy cream
- 1 teaspoon pure vanilla extract
- 4 ounces bittersweet chocolate, finely chopped
- 2 teaspoons vegetable oil
- Finely chopped toasted almonds, for rolling (optional)

1. Whisk together confectioners' sugar, flour, and salt in a large bowl; make a well in the center. Add butter, egg whites, cream, and vanilla. Stir until well combined. Refrigerate, covered, at least 2 hours or up to overnight.

2. Preheat oven to 425°F. Line two baking sheets with nonstick baking mats (such as Silpats).

3. Make four cookies at once: Spoon a heaping tablespoon of batter onto baking sheet. Using an offset spatula, spread batter into a very thin 6 by 3½-inch oval. Repeat, making two more ovals of batter on the sheet. Bake just until brown around edges, about 6 minutes.

4. When cookies come out of the oven, use a long offset spatula to quickly transfer cookies, one at a time, to a work surface; roll around a chopstick or a thin wooden dowel, forming a cylinder shape; transfer to a wire rack, and let cool completely. Repeat to roll remaining three cookies. If they harden too quickly, return baking sheet to oven for 30 seconds. Repeat with remaining batter.

5. Put chocolate into a heatproof bowl set over a pan of simmering water; stir often until smooth. Stir in oil. Let cool slightly. Dip about 2 inches of each cooled cookie into chocolate. Roll dipped edge in chopped nuts, if desired. Transfer to a wire rack, placing dipped section off the edge, to set. Cookies can be stored between layers of waxed paper in an airtight container at room temperature up to 3 days.

Chocolate Meringues

Loaded with a big cocoa flavor, these bonbons are surprisingly small in stature, each just larger than a quarter. This is a good cookie to bake in a pinch because it's likely you'll have the few ingredients on hand. But be aware that the cookies need about 2 hours in the oven. MAKES ABOUT 4½ DOZEN

- ¼ cup unsweetened Dutch-process cocoa powder
- Swiss Meringue (recipe follows)

1. Preheat oven to 175°F. Sift cocoa powder over meringue, and fold so that streaks of cocoa remain.

2. Transfer to a pastry bag fitted with a ½-inch star tip (such as Ateco #825). Pipe 1¼-inch cookies onto baking sheets lined with parchment paper, spacing about 1 inch apart.

3. Bake cookies until they can be lifted off parchment easily, about 2 hours. Cookies can be stored in a single layer in airtight containers at room temperature up to 2 days.

SWISS MERINGUE MAKES 4 CUPS

- 4 large egg whites
- 1 cup sugar
- Pinch of cream of tartar
- ½ teaspoon pure vanilla extract

Put egg whites, sugar, and cream of tartar in the heatproof bowl of an electric mixer set over a pan of simmering water. Cook, whisking constantly, until sugar has dissolved and mixture is warm to the touch, 3 to 3½ minutes. Transfer bowl to electric mixer fitted with the whisk attachment; beat, starting on low speed and gradually increasing to high, until stiff, glossy peaks form, about 10 minutes. Add vanilla; mix until combined. Use immediately.

Bratseli

These Swiss cookies, sometimes spelled Bräzeli or Bratzeli, are made with a specialty tool much like a waffle iron, but the results are thinner. You can also use a pizzelle iron. MAKES ABOUT 6 DOZEN

- 7 to 9 cups all-purpose flour, sifted
- 1 tablespoon ground cinnamon
- ¼ teaspoon coarse salt
- 1 cup (2 sticks) unsalted butter, room temperature
- 1½ cups sugar
- 1 tablespoon pure vanilla extract
- 1 tablespoon pure lemon extract
- Finely grated zest of 1 lemon (optional)
- 2 large eggs, room temperature, lightly beaten
- 1 cup heavy cream, room temperature
- Vegetable oil cooking spray

1. Whisk together 3 cups flour, the cinnamon, and salt in a medium bowl.

2. With an electric mixer, mix butter and sugar on medium speed until pale and fluffy. Add extracts and zest, if using; mix until combined. Add eggs; mix until combined.

3. Whisk cream in another medium bowl until just slightly thickened. Fold into butter mixture. Reduce mixer speed to low. Add flour mixture, and mix until just combined. Add remaining flour, 1 cup at a time, mixing until incorporated after each addition, until dough is just soft enough to handle but still slightly sticky. Roll tablespoons of dough into balls.

4. Coat a bratseli or pizzelle iron with cooking spray, and heat. Place one ball of dough in each grid, and press handle down tightly. Cook bratseli until golden (some machines have a green light that will illuminate when done), 1 to 1½ minutes. Trim edges, if needed. Let cool completely on wire racks. Cookies can be stored between layers of parchment in airtight containers at room temperature up to 1 week.

Tuile Leaves

A few leaves make a pretty garnish when scattered on top of a cake for Thanksgiving; you can also serve them anytime with bowls of ice cream or fresh fruit. You will need a leaf stencil, available at crafts-supply stores, to form these tuiles. MAKES ABOUT 1½ DOZEN

- 1 large egg white
- ¼ cup superfine sugar
- ¼ cup all-purpose flour, sifted
- Pinch of coarse salt
- 4 teaspoons unsalted butter, melted
- 2 teaspoons heavy cream
- ¼ teaspoon pure almond extract

1. Preheat oven to 350°F. Line a rimmed baking sheet with a nonstick baking mat (such as Silpat).

2. Put egg white and sugar in the bowl of an electric mixer fitted with the whisk attachment. Mix on medium speed until combined, about 30 seconds. Reduce speed to low. Add flour and salt; mix until just combined. Add butter, cream, and almond extract; mix 30 seconds.

3. Place a 4¼-inch leaf stencil in corner of baking sheet. Using a small offset spatula, spread batter in a thin layer over stencil. Carefully lift stencil. Repeat, filling sheet with leaves.

4. Bake until golden, 6 to 8 minutes. Lift cookies with a small offset spatula, and quickly drape over a rolling pin to cool. Repeat with remaining batter. Cookies can be stored between layers of parchment in an airtight container at room temperature up to 2 days.

Hazelnut Cookies

Combining beaten egg whites with a nut-and-sugar mix helps give these cookies their airy texture. MAKES 1½ DOZEN

- 1⅓ cups (about 6 ounces) hazelnuts
- ¾ cup sugar
- 2 large egg whites
- ¼ teaspoon coarse salt
- ¾ cup all-purpose flour
- ½ teaspoon pure vanilla extract

1. Preheat oven to 350°F. Place hazelnuts in a single layer on a rimmed baking sheet. Bake until skins crack, 10 minutes. Transfer to a clean kitchen towel and roll up. Let steam 5 minutes. Rub the nuts in the towel until most of the skin has come off. Let cool.

2. Process hazelnuts and ¼ cup sugar in a food processor until ground to a fine powder.

3. Put egg whites and salt in the bowl of an electric mixer fitted with the whisk attachment; mix on medium speed until soft peaks form. Add remaining ½ cup sugar, and mix until egg whites form stiff (but not dry) peaks. Add hazelnut mixture, flour, and vanilla; mix on medium-low speed until just combined. Refrigerate, covered, until cold, at least 1 hour or up to 1 day.

4. Preheat oven to 375°F. With cool, dampened hands, mold heaping tablespoons of dough into pyramids, each about 1½ inches wide and 1¼ inches high. Space about 2 inches apart on baking sheets lined with parchment paper. Bake cookies until edges and bottoms begin to brown, 15 to 18 minutes. Let cool on sheets on wire racks. Cookies can be stored in an airtight container at room temperature up to 3 days.

Coconut Cookies with Passion-Fruit Curd

For these sandwich cookies, tiny, delicate coconut wafers surround a creamy, sweet-tart, tropical-fruit filling. In a pinch, use prepared lemon curd instead of our homemade passion fruit version. MAKES ABOUT 3 DOZEN

for the curd:

- ½ cup store-bought passion-fruit puree
- 1½ tablespoons fresh lemon juice
- ½ cup granulated sugar
- Pinch of salt
- 2 tablespoons cornstarch
- 4 large egg yolks, lightly beaten
- 4 tablespoons (½ stick) cold unsalted butter, cut into small pieces

for the cookies:

- ½ cup all-purpose flour, plus more for work surface
- ½ teaspoon baking powder
- ⅛ teaspoon salt
- 4 tablespoons (½ stick) unsalted butter
- 1 cup granulated sugar
- 1 large egg
- ½ teaspoon pure vanilla extract
- 3½ ounces unsweetened medium-flake coconut (about 1½ cups)
- Confectioners' sugar, for dusting

1. Make curd: Bring passion-fruit puree, lemon juice, sugar, salt, and cornstarch to a simmer in a saucepan over medium heat. Slowly whisk in egg yolks. Cook, whisking constantly, until thick enough to coat the back of a spoon. Remove from heat. Add butter; whisk until melted. Pour through a fine sieve into a bowl. Place plastic wrap directly on surface of curd. Refrigerate until set, about 2 hours or up to overnight.

2. Make cookies: Whisk flour, baking powder, and salt in a bowl. Put butter and granulated sugar in the bowl of an electric mixer fitted with the paddle attachment. Mix on medium-high speed until pale and fluffy, about 2 minutes. Mix in the egg and vanilla. Reduce speed to low. Gradually mix in flour mixture. Stir in coconut. Shape dough into two disks; wrap each in plastic. Refrigerate until cold, about 30 minutes.

3. Preheat oven to 375°F. Turn out one disk of dough onto a lightly floured work surface; roll to a scant ¼ inch thick. Using a 1¼-inch cookie cutter, cut rounds of dough; place on parchment paper–lined baking sheets. Repeat with remaining dough. Freeze until firm, about 15 minutes.

4. Bake until edges of cookies just turn golden, 8 to 10 minutes. About 6 minutes into baking, flatten the cookies with the bottom of a measuring cup if they are puffing up. Let cool completely on sheets on wire racks.

5. Transfer curd to a pastry bag fitted with a medium round tip (such as Ateco #12). Pipe curd onto flat side of a cookie; sandwich with another cookie. Repeat with remaining curd and cookies. Dust with confectioners' sugar before serving. Sandwiches should be assembled just before serving, though the unfilled cookies can be stored between layers of parchment in an airtight container at room temperature up to 1 week.

Sesame Cookies

A relative of the Chinese almond cookie, this light sesame round makes a perfect companion to a strong cup of coffee. When preparing to grind toasted seeds, let them cool first: Hot seeds release too much of their essential oils and thus lose flavor. MAKES ABOUT 6 DOZEN

- 7 ounces unhulled sesame seeds (1¼ cups)
- 2¾ cups all-purpose flour, plus more for hands
- 1 teaspoon baking powder
- ½ teaspoon baking soda
- ¼ teaspoon salt
- 1½ cups (3 sticks) unsalted butter, room temperature
- 1½ cups sugar
- 2 large whole eggs
- 1 teaspoon pure vanilla extract
- 1 large egg yolk
- 1 teaspoon water

1. Preheat oven to 350°F. Line two baking sheets with parchment paper. Place sesame seeds in a large skillet over medium heat, stirring frequently until fragrant, 3 to 5 minutes, being careful not to burn them. Remove from heat; let cool. Reserve ½ cup of seeds, and set aside. Using a spice or coffee grinder, coarsely grind remaining seeds; set aside.

2. In a bowl, sift together flour, baking powder, baking soda, and salt. Whisk in ground sesame seeds.

3. In the bowl of an electric mixer fitted with the paddle attachment, beat butter and sugar on medium speed until light and fluffy, scraping down the bowl as necessary. Add eggs and vanilla; beat to combine. Gradually add the dry ingredients; mix on low speed until combined.

4. Transfer dough to a clean work surface, and knead until smooth. Using lightly floured hands, shape a tablespoon of dough into a slightly flattened ball about 2 inches in diameter. Repeat, placing cookies on prepared baking sheets 2 inches apart.

5. Combine egg yolk and water. Brush tops with egg mixture, and generously sprinkle with reserved sesame seeds. Gently press seeds into the dough. Place in freezer until firm, about 15 minutes.

6. Bake until lightly browned, 18 to 20 minutes, rotating sheets halfway through. Transfer cookies to wire rack until cool. Cookies can be stored between layers of parchment in airtight containers at room temperature up to 1 week.

Lacy Nut Cookies

These tuile-like cookies have a rich caramel flavor, but are packed with nuts. The addition of bread flour, which contains more gluten than all-purpose flour, makes them sturdier than traditional tuiles. MAKES ABOUT 2½ DOZEN

- 1 cup (2 sticks) plus 5 tablespoons unsalted butter, room temperature
- 2¼ cups confectioners' sugar
- ¼ cup corn syrup
- 1¼ cups bread flour
- 1¼ cups chopped nuts, such as almonds, blanched hazelnuts, or pecans (about 5⅓ ounces)

1. In the bowl of an electric mixer fitted with the paddle attachment, beat the butter and confectioners' sugar on medium speed until fluffy. With the mixer running, add the corn syrup. Reduce speed to low; add bread flour, and mix to combine. Add the nuts, and mix to combine.

2. Place a 12 by 16-inch piece of parchment on a clean work surface. Spoon the dough across the middle of the parchment. Fold parchment over dough, and using a ruler, press dough into a neat log, and roll until even. Chill log in refrigerator for at least 30 minutes.

3. Preheat oven to 350°F. Line two baking sheets with parchment.

4. Remove the parchment from the log, and slice log into ¼-inch-thick rounds. Place rounds on baking sheets, spacing 3½ inches apart. Bake until golden brown and lacy, 15 to 20 minutes, rotating halfway through. Transfer cookies to a wire rack to cool. Repeat with remaining dough. Cookies can be stored in an airtight container at room temperature up to 2 weeks.

Peppermint Meringue Sandwiches with Chocolate Filling

Rich chocolate ganache and cool peppermint make a merry combination, especially at holiday time. To get stripes on the meringues, you pipe the cookies with a pastry bag painted with red food coloring. MAKES ABOUT 5 DOZEN

for the meringues:

- 3 large egg whites
- ¾ cup sugar
- ½ teaspoon pure peppermint extract
- Red gel-paste food coloring

for the ganache:

- 1 cup heavy cream
- 6 ounces good-quality semisweet chocolate, finely chopped

1. Preheat oven to 175°F. Line two baking sheets with parchment paper. Fit a pastry bag with a small open-star tip (such as Ateco #22).

2. Make meringues: Put egg whites and sugar in the heatproof bowl of an electric mixer. Set bowl over a pan of simmering water, and stir gently until sugar has dissolved and mixture is warm to the touch, 2 to 3 minutes. Transfer bowl to an electric mixer fitted with the whisk attachment. Mix on medium-high speed until stiff peaks form. Mix in peppermint extract.

3. Using a new small paintbrush, paint two or three stripes of red gel-paste food coloring inside the pastry bag. Fill bag with 1 to 2 cups meringue. Pipe small (¾-inch high) star shapes onto prepared baking sheets. Refill bag as necessary, adding food coloring each time. Bake cookies until crisp but not brown, about 1 hour 40 minutes. Let cool completely on sheets on wire racks.

4. Meanwhile, make ganache: Heat cream in a small saucepan over medium-low heat until just simmering. Pour over chocolate in a small bowl. Let stand 5 minutes. Gently stir until smooth, about 5 minutes. Let ganache cool at room temperature, stirring every 5 to 10 minutes, until thick enough to hold its shape, about 45 minutes. (If ganache sets before using, reheat in a heatproof bowl set over a pan of simmering water; repeat the cooling process.)

5. Fill a pastry bag fitted with a small plain round tip (such as Ateco #5) with ganache. Pipe a small amount onto bottom of one meringue. Sandwich with another. Repeat with remaining ganache and meringues. Transfer to wire racks; let set 30 minutes. Cookies can be stored in a single layer in airtight containers at room temperature up to 2 days.

HOW TO PIPE PEPPERMINT MERINGUES
Use a new small paintbrush to brush two or three evenly spaced stripes of gel-paste food coloring along the length of the inside of a pastry bag fitted with an open-star tip. Fill the bag with meringue, and pipe star shapes onto a parchment paper–lined baking sheet. Each time you refill the bag with meringue, paint new stripes inside.

Brandy Snaps

Made from a batter rich in golden syrup, these cookies rarely contain brandy anymore, although some cooks fill them with freshly whipped cream flavored with a splash of brandy. Lyle's Golden Syrup, popular in England, is a liquid sweetener made from evaporated cane sugar. Look for it in specialty food shops and large supermarkets. MAKES 1½ DOZEN

- ½ cup all-purpose flour
- ½ teaspoon ground ginger
- 5 tablespoons unsalted butter
- ⅓ cup sugar
- ¼ cup Lyle's Golden Syrup

1. Preheat oven to 350°F. Line a baking sheet with parchment paper.

2. In a small bowl, combine flour and ginger with a whisk. Melt butter in a small saucepan over medium heat. Add sugar and golden syrup; cook, stirring with a wooden spoon, until sugar is dissolved. Remove from heat; stir in flour mixture.

3. Drop six even tablespoons of batter onto prepared baking sheet, about 2 inches apart. Bake until flat and golden brown, about 10 minutes, rotating halfway through.

4. Let cookies cool until slightly firm, about 2 minutes; immediately wrap them, one at a time, around a wide round whisk handle (about ¾-inch wide); let set 30 seconds. Transfer from whisk handle to a wire rack to cool. Repeat with remaining batter. If cookies get too cool to shape, return them to the oven for a few seconds until they soften. Cookies can be stored in single layers in airtight containers at room temperature up to 2 days.

Candy-Stripe Cookie Sticks

Just a few of these striped showstoppers make a festive and memorable holiday gift; be sure to package them carefully, as they are very fragile. Bake the cookies two or three at a time, then roll them as they come out of the oven, while they're still pliable. MAKES 2½ DOZEN

- 8 large egg whites
- 2 cups sugar
- 2 cups all-purpose flour
- Pinch of coarse salt
- 10 tablespoons (1¼ sticks) unsalted butter, melted and cooled
- ¼ cup plus 2 tablespoons heavy cream
- 1 teaspoon pure vanilla extract
- Red gel-paste food coloring

1. Preheat oven to 400°F. Put egg whites and sugar in the bowl of an electric mixer fitted with the whisk attachment, and beat on medium speed until foamy. Reduce speed to low. Add flour and salt; mix until just combined. Add butter, cream, and vanilla, and beat until combined.

2. Transfer 1 cup batter to a bowl (set remaining batter aside). Stir in red coloring until desired color is reached. Transfer tinted batter to a pastry bag fitted with a small plain round tip (such as Ateco #2). Secure end of pastry bag with rubber band. Set aside.

3. Put a 3 by 6-inch rectangle stencil on a baking sheet lined with a nonstick baking mat (such as Silpat). Spoon a heaping tablespoon of plain batter into the rectangle, and spread with a small offset spatula. Repeat with stencil and more batter. Pipe evenly spaced diagonal tinted stripes onto each rectangle. Bake until pale golden, 6 to 8 minutes.

4. Immediately loosen edges with a spatula, and flip cookie over. Starting from one long side, roll cookie into a thin cylinder. Place seam side down on a clean work surface; let cool until set. Quickly repeat with second cookie. Repeat process, tinting and baking two or three cookies at a time. Cookies can be stored between layers of parchment in airtight containers at room temperature up to 1 week.

HOW TO FORM COOKIE STICKS 1. Cut a 3 by 6-inch rectangle from cardboard as a template. Position template on baking sheet, and spoon on a tablespoon of batter. Spread it to fill template with an offset spatula. 2. Pipe evenly spaced diagonal stripes over batter. Repeat a second time on same baking sheet. 3. Bake flat, and roll cookies while they're still warm, then set aside to cool.

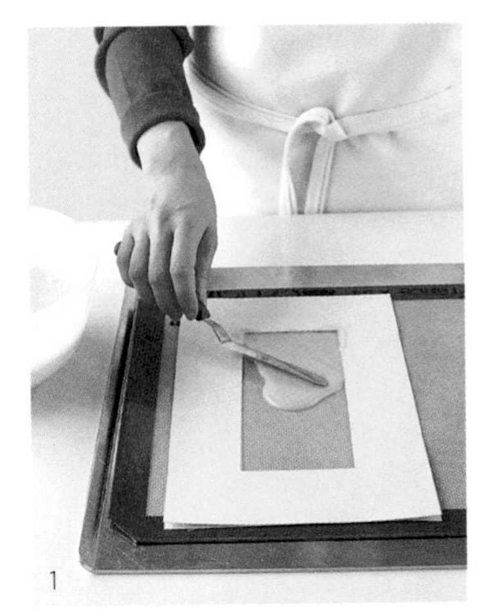

Gingersnap Palmiers

Palmiers, sometimes called palm leaves, are made with puff pastry folded several times, then sliced, to create a distinctive heart-shaped coil design. Ginger syrup and spiced sugar make these crisp French cookies festive and fragrant. MAKES ABOUT 3½ DOZEN

- ½ cup packed light brown sugar
- ¼ cup dark unsulfured molasses
- 2 teaspoons finely grated fresh ginger
- ¼ cup water
- ⅔ cup granulated sugar
- ½ teaspoon coarse salt
- ½ teaspoon ground cinnamon
- ½ teaspoon freshly grated nutmeg
- ¼ teaspoon ground allspice
- ¼ teaspoon freshly ground pepper
- 14 ounces good-quality thawed frozen puff pastry, such as Dufour

1. Bring brown sugar, molasses, ginger, and water to a simmer in a saucepan, whisking until sugar has dissolved. Simmer until slightly thickened, 1 to 2 minutes. Pour syrup into a bowl; let cool.

2. Whisk granulated sugar, salt, and spices in a bowl. Lightly sprinkle some sugar mixture over a clean work surface; place puff pastry on top. Cut into two 10 by 7-inch pieces. Sprinkle generously with some sugar mixture; press into pastry with a rolling pin. Brush generously with syrup. Working with one piece of dough at a time, roll from both long sides, meeting in the center; brush with syrup to seal. Sprinkle generously with sugar mixture. Wrap in plastic; freeze until firm, at least 3 hours or up to overnight.

3. Cut each piece of frozen dough crosswise into ½-inch-thick slices. Dip slices in sugar mixture. Space 2 inches apart on a parchment paper–lined baking sheet. Flatten with your palm. Freeze 30 minutes.

4. Preheat oven to 425°F. Bake 10 minutes. Flip, and brush with syrup. Reduce oven temperature to 400°F. Bake until darkened, 10 minutes more. Let cool completely on wire racks. Cookies can be stored in an airtight container at room temperature up to 3 days.

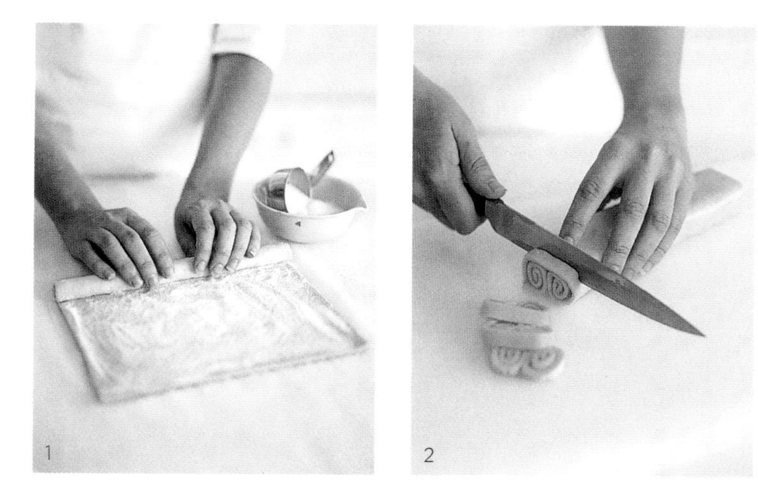

HOW TO FORM PALMIERS 1. After rolling out the puff pastry to a rectangle and topping with sugar filling, roll up one side of pastry along the edges lengthwise, halfway to center; repeat with the other side. 2. Use a sharp knife to cut the dough into ½-inch-thick slices.

BUTTERY PECAN ROUNDS, **opposite**

PEANUT CRISPS, **page 54**

Buttery Pecan Rounds

The virtues of this cookie recipe are many: It relies on just a few basic ingredients, the dough is remarkably easy to prepare, and as the cookies bake, they fill the kitchen with the most magnificent scent. MAKES ABOUT 3 DOZEN

- 1 cup all-purpose flour
- ½ teaspoon coarse salt
- 1 cup (2 sticks) unsalted butter, room temperature
- ¾ cup packed dark brown sugar
- 1 large egg yolk
- ⅔ cup finely chopped toasted pecans (about 2 ounces)
- Pecan halves, for decorating

1. Preheat oven to 325°F. Sift together flour and salt into a bowl.

2. Put butter and brown sugar in the bowl of an electric mixer fitted with the paddle attachment; mix on medium speed until smooth, about 3 minutes. Mix in egg yolk until combined. Reduce speed to low. Add flour mixture; mix until combined. Mix in chopped pecans.

3. Using a 1¼-inch ice cream scoop, drop batter onto baking sheets lined with parchment paper, spacing about 3 inches apart. Press one pecan half into the center of each. Bake cookies, rotating sheets halfway through, until golden brown, 12 to 15 minutes. Let cool completely on sheets on wire racks. Cookies can be stored between layers of parchment in airtight containers at room temperature up to 2 days.

Peanut Crisps

The addition of whole, salted peanuts in this super-crunchy cookie imparts the perfect balance of salty and sweet. And the light-as-air texture of the crisps themselves contrasts quite nicely with the chunkiness of the peanuts. MAKES 3½ DOZEN

- 1 cup all-purpose flour
- ¼ teaspoon coarse salt
- ¼ teaspoon baking soda
- 4 tablespoons (½ stick) unsalted butter, room temperature
- 1¼ cups packed light brown sugar
- 1 large egg
- 1 teaspoon pure vanilla extract
- 1 cup salted whole peanuts

1. Preheat oven to 350°F. Stir together flour, salt, and baking soda in a small bowl.

2. Put butter and brown sugar in the bowl of an electric mixer fitted with the paddle attachment; mix on medium speed until pale and fluffy, about 2 minutes. Mix in egg and vanilla. Reduce speed to low. Gradually add flour mixture; mix until combined. Stir in peanuts.

3. Drop 2 teaspoons of dough on baking sheets lined with parchment paper, spacing about 3 inches apart. Lightly flatten to 1½ inches in diameter. Bake cookies, rotating sheets halfway through, until edges are just golden, about 13 minutes. Let cool on sheets on wire racks. Cookies can be stored in airtight containers at room temperature up to 1 week.

Langues-de-Chat

The long, thin shape of these cookies accounts for their distinctive name in many languages: *langues-de-chat* in French, *lingue di gatto* in Italian, and cat's tongues in English. Serve them as an accompaniment to fruit compote or ice cream. MAKES ABOUT 5 DOZEN

- ⅔ cup plus 1 tablespoon all-purpose flour
- ¼ teaspoon salt
- 7 tablespoons unsalted butter, room temperature
- ¾ cup confectioners' sugar, sifted
- 2 large eggs
- 2 teaspoons pure vanilla extract

1. Preheat oven to 375°F. Sift together flour and salt in a bowl.

2. Put butter into the bowl of an electric mixer fitted with the paddle attachment; mix on medium speed until pale and creamy. Mix in confectioners' sugar. Add eggs one at a time, mixing well after each addition. Mix in vanilla. Fold in flour mixture.

3. Transfer batter to a pastry bag fitted with a ⅜-inch plain round tip (such as Ateco #802). Pipe 2¾-inch lengths about ⅜ inch wide (the ends should be slightly wider than the center) onto baking sheets lined with parchment, spacing about 1 inch apart. (Batter should be refrigerated if not being used immediately.)

4. Bake until just golden around edges, 10 to 12 minutes, rotating sheets halfway through. Let cool on sheets 3 minutes. Transfer to wire racks; let cool completely. Cookies can be stored in airtight containers at room temperature up to 3 days.

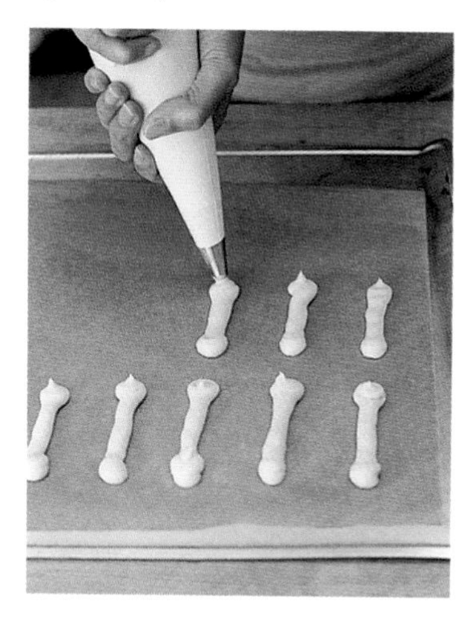

HOW TO PIPE LANGUES-DE-CHAT Use a pastry bag fitted with a plain round tip to pipe lengths of batter in rows; squeeze a bit of extra dough on the ends of each, so that the ends are slightly wider than the centers.

soft and chewy

Think back to the cookies of your childhood, and you're sure to conjure images of soft favorites, eaten straight from the jar—if not warm from the oven. This chapter contains the undisputed champs of the cookie world: chocolate chip, oatmeal raisin, snickerdoodles, and old-fashioned sugar cookies, as well as a few less expected varieties. Many are drop style, which are easy to make in large batches. Some are sweetened with brown sugar, which absorbs moisture after baking and helps maintain softness. For bar cookies or icebox pinwheels, shredded coconut or pureed fig filling can lend a chewy bite. Taking cookies out of the oven a few minutes before they're done, and leaving them on the baking sheet before transferring them to a wire rack, also helps give them this distinct texture.

SOFT AND CHEWY CHOCOLATE CHIP COOKIES, **page 58**

Soft and Chewy Chocolate Chip Cookies

A sugar- and butter-rich batter is the foundation for these cookie-jar classics. Just baked, they make a perfect snack on a chilly winter night—or any time. MAKES ABOUT 3 DOZEN

- 2¼ cups all-purpose flour
- ½ teaspoon baking soda
- 1 cup (2 sticks) unsalted butter, room temperature
- ½ cup granulated sugar
- 1 cup packed light brown sugar
- 1 teaspoon coarse salt
- 2 teaspoons pure vanilla extract
- 2 large eggs
- 2 cups semisweet or milk chocolate chips, or a combination (about 12 ounces)

1. Preheat oven to 350°F. Whisk together flour and baking soda in a bowl. Put butter and sugars in the bowl of an electric mixer fitted with the paddle attachment. Mix on medium speed until pale and fluffy, about 2 minutes. Reduce speed to low. Add salt, vanilla, and eggs; mix until well blended, about 1 minute. Mix in flour mixture. Stir in chocolate chips.

2. Drop heaping tablespoons of dough onto baking sheets lined with parchment paper, spacing 2 inches apart. Bake cookies, rotating sheets halfway through, until edges turn golden but centers are still soft, 10 to 12 minutes. Let cool on sheets on wire racks 2 minutes. Transfer cookies to wire racks; let cool completely. Cookies can be stored between layers of parchment in airtight containers at room temperature up to 1 week.

Peanut Butter and Jelly Bars

This version of a well-loved combination from childhood concentrates the flavors into a sweet dessert that appeals to all ages. We like strawberry jam, but feel free to substitute any flavor you prefer. MAKES ABOUT 3 DOZEN

- 1 cup (2 sticks) unsalted butter, room temperature, plus more for pan
- 3 cups all-purpose flour, plus more for pan
- 1½ cups sugar
- 2 large eggs
- 2½ cups smooth peanut butter
- 1½ teaspoons salt
- 1 teaspoon baking powder
- 1 teaspoon pure vanilla extract
- 1½ cups strawberry jam, or other flavor
- 1 cup salted peanuts (5 ounces), roughly chopped

1. Preheat oven to 350°F. Butter a 9 by 13-inch baking pan, and line the bottom with parchment paper. Butter the parchment, dust with flour, and tap out excess.

2. Place butter and sugar in the bowl of an electric mixer fitted with the paddle attachment. Beat on medium speed until fluffy, about 2 minutes. With mixer running, add eggs and peanut butter; beat until combined, about 2 minutes. Whisk together flour, salt, and baking powder. Add to the butter mixture, and beat on low speed until combined. Add vanilla.

3. Transfer two-thirds of mixture to prepared pan; spread evenly with an offset spatula. Using offset spatula, spread jam on top of peanut-butter mixture. Crumble remaining third of peanut butter mixture on top of jam. Sprinkle evenly with peanuts.

4. Bake until golden, 45 to 60 minutes, rotating halfway through. Tent loosely with foil if bars are getting too dark. Transfer to a wire rack to cool. Run knife around edges and refrigerate, 1 to 2 hours. Cut into about thirty-six bars (about 1½ by 2 inches). Cookies can be stored in airtight containers at room temperature up to 3 days.

Coconut-Cream Cheese Pinwheels

Rich cream cheese dough, coconut-cream cheese filling, and a topper of jam make these pinwheels complex—chewy on the outside, creamy in the center. Create a variety of flavors by substituting different fruit jams for the strawberry. MAKES ABOUT 2½ DOZEN

for the dough:

- 2 cups all-purpose flour, plus more for work surface
- ⅔ cup sugar
- ½ teaspoon baking powder
- ½ cup (1 stick) unsalted butter, room temperature
- 3 ounces cream cheese, room temperature
- 1 large egg
- 1 teaspoon pure vanilla extract

for the filling:

- 3 ounces cream cheese, room temperature
- 3 tablespoons granulated sugar
- 1 cup unsweetened shredded coconut
- ¼ cup white chocolate chips

for the glaze:

- 1 large egg, lightly beaten
- Fine sanding sugar, for sprinkling
- ⅓ cup strawberry jam

1. Make dough: Whisk together flour, sugar, and baking powder in a bowl. Put butter and cream cheese into the bowl of an electric mixer fitted with the paddle attachment; mix on medium-high speed until fluffy, about 2 minutes. Mix in egg and vanilla. Reduce speed to low. Add flour mixture, and mix until just combined. Divide dough in half, and pat into disks. Wrap each piece in plastic, and refrigerate until dough is firm, 1 to 2 hours.

2. Preheat oven to 350°F. Line baking sheets with nonstick baking mats (such as Silpats).

3. Make filling: Put cream cheese and sugar into the bowl of an electric mixer fitted with the paddle attachment; mix on medium speed until fluffy. Fold in coconut and chocolate chips.

4. Remove one disk of dough from refrigerator. Roll about ⅛ inch thick on a lightly floured surface. With a fluted cookie cutter, cut into fifteen 2½-inch squares. Transfer to prepared baking sheets, spacing about 1½ inches apart. Refrigerate 15 minutes. Repeat with remaining dough.

5. Place 1 teaspoon filling in center of each square. Using a fluted pastry wheel, cut 1-inch slits diagonally from each corner toward the filling. Fold every other tip over to cover filling, forming a pinwheel. Press lightly to seal. Use the tip of your finger to make a well in the top.

6. Make glaze: Using a pastry brush, lightly brush tops of pinwheels with beaten egg. Sprinkle with sanding sugar. Bake 6 minutes. Remove and use the lightly floured handle of a wooden spoon to make the well a little deeper. Fill each well with about ½ teaspoon jam. Return to oven, and bake, rotating sheets halfway through, until edges are golden and cookies are slightly puffed, about 6 minutes more. Transfer sheets to wire racks; let cool 5 minutes. Transfer cookies to rack; let cool completely. Cookies can be stored in single layers in airtight containers at room temperature up to 3 days.

Coconut Macaroons

Unsweetened shredded coconut is available in health food stores. You can also use sweetened shredded coconut (reduce the sugar in the recipe from ¾ cup to 1 tablespoon). For the variations, pair the coconut with chocolate—chips or cocoa powder—to create rich combinations reminiscent of a candy bar. MAKES ABOUT 1½ DOZEN

- ¾ cup sugar
- 2½ cups unsweetened shredded coconut
- 2 large egg whites
- 1 teaspoon pure vanilla extract
- Pinch of salt

1. Preheat oven to 325°F. Line a baking sheet with parchment paper.

2. In a large bowl, combine sugar, coconut, egg whites, vanilla, and salt. Using your hands, mix well, completely combining ingredients.

3. Dampen hands with cold water. Use 1½ tablespoons to form mounds; place on prepared baking sheet, spacing about 1 inch apart.

4. Bake until golden brown, 16 to 17 minutes, rotating halfway through. Let cool on a wire rack. Cookies can be stored in an airtight container at room temperature up to 3 days.

CHOCOLATE CHUNK MACAROONS

Follow the recipe for Coconut Macaroons, adding ½ cup coarsely chopped semisweet chocolate to the other ingredients. Use 1½ tablespoons of mixture to form loose haystacks; place on prepared baking sheet, spacing about 1 inch apart. Bake until golden brown, 15 to 20 minutes, rotating sheets halfway through.

CHOCOLATE MACAROONS

Place 4 ounces semisweet chocolate, chopped into small pieces, in a heatproof bowl or the top of a double boiler set over a pan of simmering water. Stir until chocolate has melted; set aside to cool. Follow instructions for Coconut Macaroons, increasing coconut to 2⅔ cups and combining all ingredients with cooled chocolate and ¼ cup unsweetened cocoa powder, sifted. The baking time should be about the same; you will know the cookies are done when they are just firm to the touch but still soft in the middle.

CHOCOLATE CHUNK
COCONUT
CHOCOLATE

Anise Drops

The dough for these cookies develops into two distinct textures as it bakes—a soft, chewy center surrounded by a wafer-like shell. MAKES ABOUT 4 DOZEN

- 1½ cups all-purpose flour
- ½ teaspoon baking powder
- ½ teaspoon coarse salt
- 3 large eggs
- 1¼ cups sugar
- 1 teaspoon anise extract

1. Preheat oven to 350°F. Sift together flour, baking powder, and salt into a bowl.

2. Put eggs in the bowl of an electric mixer fitted with the whisk attachment. Mix on medium speed until eggs are fluffy, about 3 minutes. Gradually beat in sugar until incorporated, about 3 minutes. Mix in anise extract. Reduce speed to low; mix in flour mixture. Transfer to a pastry bag fitted with a coupler or a ½-inch plain tip (such as an Ateco #806). Pipe 1¾-inch rounds onto baking sheets lined with parchment paper, spacing ½ inch apart.

3. Bake cookies, rotating sheets halfway through, until tops crack and cookies are very pale, 8 to 9 minutes. Transfer to wire racks; let cool completely. Cookies can be stored in airtight containers at room temperature up to 3 days.

Cornmeal Thyme Cookies

Thyme serves as a savory counterpoint to these sweet, soft, and chewy tea cookies. Cornmeal and dried currants add additional texture—and flavor.

MAKES ABOUT 3 DOZEN

- 1¾ cups all-purpose flour
- 1 cup yellow cornmeal
- 1 teaspoon baking soda
- ½ teaspoon coarse salt
- 1 cup (2 sticks) unsalted butter, room temperature
- 1¼ cups sugar
- 2 large eggs
- ¾ cup dried currants
- 1 tablespoon plus ½ teaspoon finely chopped fresh thyme

1. Preheat oven to 350°F. Whisk together flour, cornmeal, baking soda, and salt in a bowl.

2. Put butter and sugar in the bowl of an electric mixer fitted with the paddle attachment. Mix on medium speed until pale and fluffy, about 3 minutes. Mix in eggs one at a time. Reduce speed to low; mix in flour mixture until just combined. Mix in currants and thyme.

3. Drop rounded tablespoons of dough onto baking sheets lined with parchment paper, spacing 2 inches apart. Bake until pale golden, 10 to 12 minutes. Transfer cookies on parchment to wire racks; let cool. Cookies can be stored in airtight containers at room temperature up to 3 days.

Chewy Chocolate Gingerbread Cookies

To say these are memorable is an understatement. A combination of fresh and ground ginger, molasses, and chunks of semisweet chocolate makes the cookies sophisticated enough for adults but chocolaty enough for children. MAKES 2 DOZEN

- 1½ cups plus 1 tablespoon all-purpose flour
- 1¼ teaspoons ground ginger
- 1 teaspoon ground cinnamon
- ¼ teaspoon ground cloves
- ¼ teaspoon freshly grated nutmeg
- 1 tablespoon unsweetened Dutch-process cocoa powder
- ¼ pound (1 stick) unsalted butter, room temperature
- 1 tablespoon freshly grated peeled ginger
- ½ cup packed dark brown sugar
- ½ cup unsulfured molasses
- 1 teaspoon baking soda
- 1½ teaspoons boiling water
- 7 ounces best-quality semisweet chocolate, cut into ¼-inch chunks
- ¼ cup granulated sugar

1. Line two baking sheets with parchment paper.

2. In a bowl, sift together flour, ground ginger, cinnamon, cloves, nutmeg, and cocoa. In the bowl of an electric mixer fitted with the paddle attachment, beat butter and fresh ginger on medium speed until lightened, about 4 minutes. Add brown sugar; beat until combined. Add molasses; beat until combined.

3. In a small bowl, dissolve baking soda in boiling water. Beat half of flour mixture into butter mixture. Beat in baking soda mixture, then remaining half of flour mixture. Mix in chocolate; turn onto plastic wrap. Pat out to a 1-inch thickness; seal with wrap. Refrigerate until firm, 2 hours or overnight.

4. Preheat oven to 325°F. Roll dough into 1½-inch balls; place 2 inches apart on prepared baking sheets. Chill 20 minutes. Roll in granulated sugar. Bake until surfaces just begin to crack, 10 to 12 minutes, rotating halfway through. Let cool 5 minutes. Transfer to a wire rack and cool completely. Cookies are best the day they are made, but can be stored in airtight containers at room temperature up to 5 days.

Chocolate Crackles

A variegated pattern of deep dark chocolate and pure white powdered sugar makes these crinkly cookies a striking study in contrast. Roll balls of the rich dough first in granulated sugar, then in confectioners' sugar. The first layer ensures that the second one retains its snowy white appearance.

MAKES ABOUT 5 DOZEN

- 8 ounces bittersweet chocolate, finely chopped
- 1¼ cups all-purpose flour
- ½ cup unsweetened Dutch-process cocoa powder
- 2 teaspoons baking powder
- ¼ teaspoon coarse salt
- ½ cup (1 stick) unsalted butter, room temperature
- 1½ cups packed light brown sugar
- 2 large eggs
- 1 teaspoon pure vanilla extract
- ⅓ cup whole milk
- 1 cup granulated sugar
- 1 cup confectioners' sugar

1. Melt chocolate in a heatproof bowl set over a pan of simmering water, stirring. Set aside and let cool. Sift together flour, cocoa powder, baking powder, and salt in a bowl.

2. With an electric mixer, beat butter and brown sugar on medium speed until pale and fluffy, 2 to 3 minutes. Mix in eggs and vanilla, and then the melted chocolate. Reduce speed to low; mix in flour mixture in two batches, alternating with the milk. Divide dough into four equal pieces. Wrap each in plastic; refrigerate until firm, about 2 hours.

3. Preheat oven to 350°F. Divide each piece into sixteen 1-inch balls. Roll in granulated sugar to coat, then in confectioners' sugar to coat. Space 2 inches apart on baking sheets lined with parchment paper.

4. Bake until surfaces crack, about 14 minutes, rotating sheets halfway through. Let cool on sheets on wire racks. Cookies can be stored between layers of parchment in airtight containers at room temperature up to 3 days.

Chocolate Malt Sandwiches

Malted-milk powder, a combination of powdered milk, wheat flour, and malted barley, adds a rich component to both these cookies and their filling. A double dose of chocolate (chopped semisweet and lots of cocoa powder) makes these sandwich cookies extra decadent. MAKES ABOUT 1½ DOZEN

for the cookies:

- 2 cups plus 2 tablespoons all-purpose flour
- ½ cup unsweetened Dutch-process cocoa powder
- ¼ cup plain malted milk powder
- 1 teaspoon baking soda
- ½ teaspoon coarse salt
- 1 cup (2 sticks) unsalted butter, room temperature
- 1¾ cups sugar
- 1 large egg
- 2 teaspoons pure vanilla extract
- ¼ cup crème fraîche
- 3 tablespoons hot water

for the filling:

- 10 ounces semisweet chocolate, coarsely chopped
- 4 tablespoons (½ stick) unsalted butter, cut into small pieces
- 1 cup plain malted milk powder
- 3 ounces cream cheese, room temperature
- ¼ cup plus 2 tablespoons half-and-half
- 1 teaspoon pure vanilla extract

1. Preheat oven to 350°F. Make cookies: Sift together flour, cocoa powder, malted milk powder, baking soda, and salt. With an electric mixer, beat butter and sugar on medium-high speed until pale and fluffy. Mix in egg, vanilla, crème fraîche, and hot water. Reduce speed to low; mix in flour mixture.

2. Space tablespoon-size balls of dough 3½ inches apart on parchment paper–lined baking sheets. Bake until flat and just firm, 10 to 12 minutes. Let cool on parchment on wire racks.

3. Make filling: Melt chocolate and butter in a heatproof bowl set over a pan of simmering water, stirring. Let cool. With an electric mixer, beat malted milk powder and cream cheese on medium speed until smooth. Gradually mix in half-and-half, chocolate mixture, and vanilla. Refrigerate, covered, until thick, about 30 minutes. Mix on high speed until fluffy, about 3 minutes.

4. Assemble cookies: Spread a heaping tablespoon filling on the bottom of one cookie. Sandwich with another cookie. Repeat. Cookies can be refrigerated between layers of parchment in airtight containers at room temperature up to 3 days.

CASHEW CARAMEL COOKIES, **opposite**

WHOLE-WHEAT DATE BARS, **page 74**

Cashew Caramel Cookies

Salted cashews—both ground into a butter and chopped—give these cookies deep flavor. Soft caramel candies are melted and drizzled over the tops of the baked cookies for an easy embellishment. MAKES ABOUT 3 DOZEN

- 1⅔ cups all-purpose flour
- ½ teaspoon coarse salt
- 2½ cups roasted salted cashews
- 2 tablespoons plus 1 teaspoon canola oil
- ½ cup (1 stick) unsalted butter, room temperature
- ¾ cup packed light brown sugar
- ½ cup granulated sugar
- 1 large egg
- 1 teaspoon pure vanilla extract
- 24 soft caramel candy cubes (7 ounces)
- ¼ cup heavy cream

1. Preheat oven to 350°F. Sift together flour and salt. Coarsely chop 1 cup cashews; set aside. Process remaining 1½ cups cashews in a food processor until finely chopped. Pour in oil; process until creamy, about 2 minutes.

2. Put cashew mixture, butter, and sugars in the bowl of an electric mixer fitted with the paddle attachment. Mix on medium speed until pale and fluffy, about 2 minutes. Mix in egg and vanilla. Reduce speed to low; gradually mix in flour mixture and reserved chopped cashews.

3. Using a 1½-inch ice cream scoop, drop dough onto baking sheets lined with parchment paper, spacing 2 inches apart. Bake 6 minutes; gently flatten cookies. Bake until bottoms are golden, 6 to 7 minutes more. Let cool on sheets on wire racks.

4. Melt caramels with cream in a saucepan over low heat, stirring. Let cool. Using a spoon, drizzle caramel over cookies; let set. Cookies can be stored in airtight containers at room temperature in single layers up to 3 days.

Whole-Wheat Date Bars

These date-filled cookies get their soft texture from applesauce; wheat flour and bran add wholesome notes. MAKES ABOUT 2½ DOZEN

for the filling:

- 2¼ cups pitted dates (about 11 ounces), preferably Medjool
- ¾ cup apple cider

for the dough:

- 1¼ cups whole wheat flour
- 1 cup all-purpose flour, plus more for parchment
- ¼ cup wheat bran
- ¼ teaspoon coarse salt
- ¼ teaspoon baking soda
- ⅔ cup packed dark brown sugar
- 1 teaspoon finely grated lemon zest
- 10 tablespoons (1¼ sticks) unsalted butter, room temperature
- 1 large egg
- ¼ cup smooth unsweetened applesauce

1. Make filling: Bring dates and cider to a boil in a saucepan over medium-high heat. Reduce heat to medium; simmer until dates are soft and almost all liquid has reduced, about 10 minutes. Let cool completely. Transfer to a food processor. Puree date mixture until smooth.

2. Make dough: Whisk together both flours, bran, salt, and baking soda in a bowl. Put brown sugar and zest in the bowl of an electric mixer fitted with the paddle attachment. Mix on medium speed 30 seconds. Add butter; mix until combined, about 1 minute. Add egg; mix until fluffy. Add flour mixture in three batches, alternating with two batches of applesauce. Divide dough in half. Wrap each half in plastic; shape into a rectangle. Refrigerate until firm, about 2 hours.

3. Preheat oven to 375°F. Roll out one piece of dough between two lightly floured sheets of parchment paper to a 9½ by 13-inch rectangle. Dust with more flour, if needed. Remove top piece of parchment. Trim dough to a 9 by 12-inch rectangle. Transfer rectangle on parchment to a baking sheet.

4. Cut rectangle in half lengthwise. Spread a heaping ¼ cup filling down half of each length, leaving a ¼-inch border. Fold dough over; pinch to seal. Refrigerate until firm, about 20 minutes. Repeat with remaining chilled dough and filling.

5. Bake until golden brown, about 20 minutes. Let cool on sheets on wire racks 5 minutes. Cut into 1½-inch bars. Transfer bars to wire racks using a spatula; let cool. Bars can be stored in airtight containers at room temperature up to 3 days.

Grammy's Chocolate Cookies

A hefty dose of cocoa powder makes these old-fashioned drop cookies perfect for fans of dark chocolate. The recipe is so simple, it's a natural for preparing with children; they especially love forming the dough into balls and rolling them in sanding sugar. MAKES ABOUT 3½ DOZEN

- 2 cups plus 2 tablespoons all-purpose flour
- ¾ cup unsweetened Dutch-process cocoa powder
- 1 teaspoon baking soda
- ½ teaspoon salt
- 1¼ cups (2½ sticks) unsalted butter, room temperature
- 2 cups granulated sugar
- 2 large eggs
- 2 teaspoons pure vanilla extract
- Sanding sugar, for rolling

1. Sift together flour, cocoa powder, baking soda, and salt into a bowl.

2. In the bowl of an electric mixer fitted with the paddle attachment, beat butter and sugar on medium speed until light and fluffy, about 2 minutes. Add eggs and vanilla, and beat to combine. Reduce speed to low, and gradually add flour mixture; beat to combine. Form dough into a flattened disk, wrap with plastic wrap, and chill until firm, about 1 hour.

3. Preheat oven to 350°F. Shape dough into 1¼-inch balls. Roll each ball in sanding sugar. Place on baking sheets lined with parchment paper, about 1½ inches apart. Bake until set, 10 to 12 minutes, rotating halfway through. Transfer to a rack to cool for 5 minutes. Transfer cookies from baking sheet to wire rack. Cookies can be stored between layers of parchment in an airtight container at room temperature up to 1 week.

ICED OATMEAL
APPLESAUCE COOKIES, **opposite**

FIG BARS, **page 78**

Iced Oatmeal Applesauce Cookies

The applesauce in this recipe keeps the cookies moist; maple syrup flavors the simple white icing that gets drizzled over the tops. MAKES ABOUT 2½ DOZEN

for the cookies:

- 4 tablespoons (½ stick) unsalted butter, melted
- 1 cup packed light brown sugar
- ½ cup granulated sugar
- 1 large egg
- ½ cup chunky-style applesauce
- 1½ cups old-fashioned rolled oats
- 1¼ cups all-purpose flour
- ½ teaspoon baking soda
- ¼ teaspoon baking powder
- ¼ teaspoon coarse salt
- 1 cup golden raisins

for the icing:

- 1¾ cups confectioners' sugar
- 3 tablespoons pure maple syrup
- 3 tablespoons water

1. Preheat oven to 350°F. Make cookies: Put butter and sugars in the bowl of an electric mixer fitted with the paddle attachment. Mix on low speed until combined. Add egg and applesauce; mix until well blended, 2 to 3 minutes. Mix in oats, flour, baking soda, baking powder, and salt. Mix in raisins.

2. Using a 1½-inch ice cream scoop, drop dough onto baking sheets lined with parchment paper, spacing 2 inches apart. Bake cookies until golden and just set, 13 to 15 minutes, rotating halfway through. Let cool on sheets 5 minutes. Transfer cookies to a wire rack set over parchment paper; let cool completely.

3. Make icing: Whisk confectioners' sugar, maple syrup, and water until smooth. Drizzle over cookies; let set. Cookies can be stored in single layers in airtight containers at room temperature up to 3 days.

Fig Bars

If you're a fan of store-bought fig cookies, just wait until you taste these—they're well worth the time spent making them. MAKES 2 DOZEN

- 1 cup (2 sticks) unsalted butter, room temperature
- ½ cup sugar
- 1 large whole egg plus 2 large egg yolks
- 1 teaspoon pure vanilla extract
- Finely grated zest of 1 lemon
- 2½ cups all-purpose flour, plus more for parchment
- ¼ teaspoon salt
- Fig Filling (recipe follows)
- 1 teaspoon whole milk

1. In the bowl of an electric mixer fitted with the paddle attachment, beat butter and sugar on medium speed until light and fluffy. Add egg, 1 egg yolk, vanilla, and zest; mix well. Add flour and salt; mix on low just until dough comes together. Divide dough in half; wrap each half in plastic wrap. Chill until firm, about 1 hour.

2. Dust a large piece of parchment paper with flour, and roll out half of the dough to slightly larger than a 9 by 14-inch rectangle, chilling as necessary if dough gets too soft. Remove excess flour with a dry pastry brush, and trim to even edges. Pick up dough by wrapping it around a rolling pin; unroll it onto a baking sheet lined with parchment. Spread filling evenly over pastry. Roll remaining dough; cover filling. Trim excess pastry to make a rectangle. Chill 1 hour.

3. Preheat oven to 375°F. In a small bowl, beat together the remaining egg yolk and the milk. Use a paring knife to score dough lightly into 1¼ by 3-inch bars. Lightly brush with egg wash. Bake until golden brown, 25 to 30 minutes, rotating sheet halfway through. Transfer to a wire rack until cool. Cut into bars. Bars can be stored between layers of parchment in an airtight container at room temperature up to 3 days.

FIG FILLING

For best results, use moist, plump dried figs.

- 3 cups roughly chopped dried Calimyrna figs (about 1 pound)
- ¼ cup honey
- 1 cup red wine
- 1 cup water
- ¼ teaspoon ground cinnamon
- ½ teaspoon finely ground pepper

Combine all ingredients in a nonstick frying pan, and cook over low heat, stirring often, until reduced to a thick paste, 10 to 15 minutes. After mixture cools, pulse until smooth in food processor. Spread mixture on a baking sheet to cool. Filling can be stored, covered, in the refrigerator up to 1 week. Bring to room temperature before using.

Milk-Chocolate Cookies

Oversized and ever-so-slightly underbaked, these cookies feature milk chocolate in two forms—melted and mixed into the dough, and chopped into big chunks. MAKES ABOUT 3 DOZEN

- 1 cup all-purpose flour
- ½ cup unsweetened Dutch-process cocoa powder
- ½ teaspoon baking soda
- ½ teaspoon coarse salt
- 8 ounces good-quality milk chocolate (4 ounces coarsely chopped, 4 ounces cut into ¼-inch chunks)
- ½ cup (1 stick) unsalted butter
- 1½ cups sugar
- 2 large eggs
- 1 teaspoon pure vanilla extract

1. Preheat oven to 325°F. Whisk together flour, cocoa powder, baking soda, and salt in a bowl.

2. Melt 4 ounces coarsely chopped chocolate with the butter in a small heatproof bowl set over a pan of simmering water; let cool slightly.

3. Put chocolate mixture, sugar, eggs, and vanilla in the bowl of an electric mixer fitted with the paddle attachment. Mix on medium speed until combined. Reduce speed to low; gradually mix in flour mixture. Fold in chocolate chunks.

4. Using a 1½-inch ice cream scoop, drop dough onto parchment paper–lined baking sheets, spacing 2 inches apart. Bake until cookies are flat and surfaces crack, about 15 minutes (cookies should be soft). Let cool on parchment on wire racks. Cookies can be stored between layers of parchment in airtight containers at room temperature up to 3 days.

Coconut Cream-Filled Macaroons

Tropical-fruit lovers get a double dose of a favorite flavor in these bite-size sandwiches—coconut macaroons surround a creamy coconut filling. Unsalted butter can be used in place of the cream of coconut in the filling, but the flavor will not be the same. MAKES ABOUT 2 DOZEN

for the cookies:

- 3 cups unsweetened finely shredded coconut
- ¾ cup granulated sugar
- 2 large egg whites
- 1 teaspoon coconut extract
- ⅛ teaspoon coarse salt

for the filling:

- 2 tablespoons unsalted butter, room temperature
- 2 tablespoons cream of coconut or unsalted butter, room temperature
- ¼ cup vegetable shortening
- ¾ cup confectioners' sugar
- 1 teaspoon coconut extract

1. Make cookies: Stir together coconut, granulated sugar, egg whites, coconut extract, and salt in a large bowl. Refrigerate, covered, until cold, at least 1 hour or overnight.

2. Preheat oven to 325°F. Form heaping teaspoons of dough into balls; space 1½ inches apart on baking sheets lined with parchment paper. Gently flatten to about 1½ inches in diameter. Bake cookies, rotating sheets halfway through, until edges begin to turn golden, 9 to 10 minutes. Transfer cookies to wire racks; let cool completely.

3. Make filling: Put butter, cream of coconut, and shortening in the bowl of an electric mixer fitted with the paddle attachment. Mix on medium speed until smooth, about 1 minute. Add confectioners' sugar and coconut extract; mix until pale and fluffy, about 2 minutes.

4. Assemble cookies: Place a heaping teaspoon of filling on the bottom of one cookie. Sandwich with another cookie. Repeat with remaining cookies and filling. Transfer to a platter; cover with plastic wrap. Refrigerate until filling is firm, about 30 minutes. Let stand at room temperature 10 minutes before serving. Cookies can be stored between layers of parchment in airtight containers at room temperature up to 3 days.

COCONUT CREAM-FILLED MACAROONS, **opposite**

SNICKERDOODLES, **page 82**
CHEWY MOLASSES CRINKLES, **page 83**

Snickerdoodles

The origin of the name of these homey, drop-style cookies is unclear, but recipes for them appear in early-twentieth-century American cookbooks and newspapers. After rolling balls of dough in cinnamon sugar, give them ample room on baking sheets; they spread quite a bit. MAKES ABOUT 1½ DOZEN

- 2¾ cups all-purpose flour
- 2 teaspoons baking powder
- ½ teaspoon coarse salt
- 1 cup (2 sticks) unsalted butter, room temperature
- 1½ cups plus 2 tablespoons sugar
- 2 large eggs
- 2 teaspoons ground cinnamon

1. Preheat oven to 350°F. Sift together flour, baking powder, and salt into a bowl. Put butter and 1½ cups sugar in the bowl of an electric mixer fitted with the paddle attachment. Mix on medium speed until pale and fluffy, about 3 minutes. Mix in eggs. Reduce speed to low; gradually mix in flour mixture.

2. Stir together cinnamon and remaining 2 tablespoons sugar in a small bowl. Shape dough into twenty 1¾-inch balls; roll in cinnamon sugar. Space 3 inches apart on baking sheets lined with parchment paper.

3. Bake cookies, rotating sheets halfway through, until edges are golden, 12 to 15 minutes. Let cool on sheets on wire racks. Cookies can be stored between layers of parchment in airtight containers at room temperature up to 3 days.

Chewy Molasses Crinkles

Though they have all the flavors of gingerbread, these cookies are softer and chewier than cutout varieties, such as the Gingerbread Snowflakes on page 259. They are as easy to prepare as Grammy's Chocolate Cookies (page 75), with a similar old-fashioned appeal. MAKES ABOUT 2 DOZEN

- ½ cup (1 stick) unsalted butter, room temperature
- 1 cup packed light brown sugar
- ½ cup granulated sugar, plus ¼ cup for rolling
- 2 large eggs
- ½ cup unsulfured molasses
- 2 tablespoons vegetable oil
- 2 cups all-purpose flour
- 1 teaspoon baking soda
- 1 teaspoon ground cinnamon
- 1 teaspoon ground ginger
- 1 teaspoon ground allspice
- ½ teaspoon coarse salt

1. Put butter, brown sugar, and ½ cup granulated sugar in the bowl of an electric mixer fitted with the paddle attachment. Mix on medium speed until smooth, about 3 minutes. Mix in eggs one at a time, followed by the molasses and oil.

2. Reduce speed to low; gradually mix in flour, baking soda, cinnamon, ginger, allspice, and salt. Cover dough with plastic wrap; refrigerate until firm, about 1 hour or overnight.

3. Preheat oven to 325°F. Put remaining ¼ cup granulated sugar in a bowl. Using a 1¾-inch ice cream scoop, form balls of dough. Roll balls in sugar to coat, and space 3 inches apart on baking sheets lined with parchment paper. Bake, rotating sheets halfway through, until cookies are flat and centers are set, about 17 minutes. Let cool completely on sheets on wire racks. Cookies can be stored between layers of parchment in airtight containers at room temperature up to 5 days.

Apricot Windows

With sweet apricot jam atop a thin, buttery dough and a piped lattice topping, this bar cookie is as lovely to look at as it is to eat.

MAKES 4 DOZEN BARS OR 2 DOZEN SQUARES

- 2¼ cups apricot jam, room temperature
- 3½ cups all-purpose flour
- 1⅓ cups yellow cornmeal
- ¾ teaspoon salt
- 2¼ cups (4½ sticks) unsalted butter, room temperature
- 1½ cups sugar
- 3 large eggs, room temperature
- Vegetable oil cooking spray

1. Preheat oven to 375°F. Lightly coat an 11 by 17-inch rimmed baking sheet with cooking spray, and line bottom with parchment paper.

2. Spoon jam into a bowl, and beat with a rubber spatula to smooth out texture; set aside. In another bowl, whisk together flour, cornmeal, and salt.

3. In the bowl of an electric mixer fitted with the paddle attachment, beat butter and sugar on medium speed until light and fluffy, 2 to 3 minutes. Add eggs one at a time, beating until smooth after each addition. Reduce speed to low, add reserved flour mixture, and beat until thoroughly combined. Remove 1¾ cups of the dough; use it to fill a pastry bag fitted with a plain round tip (such as Ateco #11). Fold the end over to keep dough from drying out.

4. Using an offset spatula, spread the remaining dough into prepared pan as evenly and smoothly as possible. Bake until golden brown, about 20 minutes.

5. Remove pan from oven, and transfer to a heatproof surface. Using an offset spatula, spread jam on top in an even layer. Using a prepared pastry bag, pipe parallel lines of dough spaced 1 inch apart over the jam. Pipe perpendicular lines of dough at 1-inch intervals over first lines. Place in oven and bake until golden, 20 to 25 minutes, rotating sheet halfway through. Transfer to a wire rack to cool. Cut into 1½ by 3-inch bars or 3-inch squares. Cookies can be stored in single layers in airtight containers at room temperature up to 3 days.

Old-Fashioned Sugar Cookies

These big cookies have two coats of sanding sugar, which create a delicate crust that sparkles. The crunchy coating gives way to a soft cookie with bright, lemony flavor in each bite. MAKES ABOUT 1½ DOZEN

- 3 cups all-purpose flour
- 1 teaspoon baking soda
- ¼ teaspoon coarse salt
- 1¾ cups granulated sugar
- ¼ cup packed light brown sugar
- 1 tablespoon finely grated lemon zest
- 1 cup (2 sticks) unsalted butter, room temperature
- 2 large eggs
- 1 tablespoon fresh lemon juice
- Sanding sugar, for sprinkling

1. Preheat oven to 350°F. Sift together flour, baking soda, and salt.

2. Put sugars and zest in the bowl of an electric mixer fitted with the paddle attachment. Mix on medium speed 30 seconds. Add butter; mix until pale and fluffy, about 1 minute. Mix in eggs one at a time, and then the lemon juice. Reduce speed to low; gradually mix in flour mixture.

3. Using a 2-inch ice cream scoop, drop dough onto parchment paper–lined baking sheets, spacing 3 inches apart. Flatten cookies slightly; sprinkle with sanding sugar. Lightly brush with a wet pastry brush; sprinkle with more sanding sugar.

4. Bake cookies until golden, about 15 minutes, rotating sheets halfway through. Transfer cookies to wire racks using a spatula; let cool completely. Cookies can be stored in airtight containers at room temperature up to 3 days.

RAISIN BARS, **opposite**

OATMEAL RAISIN COOKIES, **page 90**

Raisin Bars

These bars are more rustic than traditional dried fruit bars, since they are covered with a crumbly oat topping before baking. You can substitute chopped dried figs or dates for the raisins. MAKES ABOUT 3 DOZEN

Unsalted butter, room temperature, for baking sheet

for the filling:

- 2 cups raisins (about 13 ounces)
- 1 cup granulated sugar
- 1 teaspoon cornstarch
- 1 cup cold water
- ½ cup apple cider

for the dough:

- 2½ cups all-purpose flour
- 1¼ teaspoons baking soda
- 1¼ teaspoons coarse salt
- 1¼ cups vegetable shortening
- 1¼ cups packed light brown sugar
- 1 large egg
- 1¼ teaspoons pure vanilla extract
- 2½ cups old-fashioned rolled oats

1. Preheat oven to 350°F. Butter a 10 by 15-inch rimmed baking sheet. Line bottom with parchment paper, and butter parchment.

2. Make filling: Pulse raisins and sugar in a food processor until almost pureed. Transfer to a saucepan. Whisk cornstarch into cold water; whisk into raisin mixture. Stir in cider. Simmer over medium-low heat, stirring occasionally, until mixture thickens and sugar has dissolved, about 6 minutes. Let cool completely.

3. Make dough: Whisk together flour, baking soda, and salt in a bowl. Put shortening in the bowl of an electric mixer fitted with the paddle attachment. Mix on medium speed until smooth. Add brown sugar and mix until pale and fluffy, 2 to 3 minutes. Add egg and vanilla, and mix until combined. Reduce speed to low. Add flour mixture; mix until just combined. Mix in oats.

4. Press half the dough into prepared baking sheet. Using an offset spatula, spread raisin filling evenly over top of dough. Crumble remaining dough on top of filling using your fingers, gently pressing down so that topping covers filling. Bake, rotating sheet halfway through, until top is golden brown, about 35 minutes. Let cool completely in sheet on a wire rack. Cut into 2-inch squares. Bars can be stored between layers of parchment in airtight containers at room temperature up to 5 days.

Oatmeal Raisin Cookies

Toasted wheat germ and a generous amount of raisins make these cookies hearty. You can substitute an equal measure of dried cranberries, sour cherries, or chopped apricots for the raisins. To make oatmeal-chocolate chunk cookies, substitute 12 ounces good-quality chocolate, coarsely chopped, for the raisins. MAKES ABOUT 5 DOZEN

- 3 cups old-fashioned rolled oats
- 1 cup plus 2 tablespoons all-purpose flour
- ½ cup toasted wheat germ
- 1 teaspoon baking soda
- 1 teaspoon baking powder
- ½ teaspoon ground cinnamon
- ½ teaspoon coarse salt
- 1 cup (2 sticks) unsalted butter, room temperature
- 1 cup granulated sugar
- 1 cup packed light brown sugar
- 2 large eggs
- 1 teaspoon pure vanilla extract
- 1½ cups raisins

1. Preheat oven to 350°F. Stir together oats, flour, wheat germ, baking soda, baking powder, cinnamon, and salt in a large bowl.

2. Put butter and sugars in the bowl of an electric mixer fitted with the paddle attachment. Mix on medium speed until pale and fluffy, about 5 minutes. Mix in eggs and vanilla. Reduce speed to low. Add oat mixture; mix until just combined. Mix in raisins.

3. Using a 1½-inch ice cream scoop, drop dough onto baking sheets lined with parchment paper, spacing 2 inches apart. Flatten slightly.

4. Bake until golden and just set, about 14 minutes, rotating halfway through. Let cool on sheets on wire racks 5 minutes. Transfer cookies to wire racks; let cool completely. Cookies can be stored in airtight containers at room temperature up to 3 days.

Almond Macaroons

Some claim that macaroons were first made in Venice during the Renaissance, gaining their name from the Italian *maccherone*, or "fine paste." Others say that the original recipe came from a monastery in France. Whatever its origin, the combination of almond paste, sugar, and egg whites produces a cookie with a crackly outer layer and a chewy center. MAKES 1 DOZEN

- 4 ounces almond paste (about 5½ tablespoons)
- ½ cup confectioners' sugar, plus more for dusting
- Pinch of coarse salt
- 1 large egg white
- ¼ teaspoon pure vanilla extract
- ¼ cup sliced almonds

1. Preheat oven to 300°F. Put almond paste, sugar, and salt in the bowl of an electric mixer fitted with the paddle attachment. Mix on medium speed until crumbly, about 3 minutes. Add egg white and vanilla. Mix until smooth and thickened, about 3 minutes.

2. Drop batter by tablespoons onto baking sheets lined with parchment paper, spacing 2 inches apart. Place two almond slices on each mound of dough. Bake until cookies are golden brown, 20 to 25 minutes, rotating sheets halfway through.

3. Let cool completely on a wire rack. Just before serving, lightly dust cookies with confectioners' sugar. Cookies can be stored between layers of parchment in airtight containers at room temperature up to 3 days.

RASPBERRY CREAM SANDWICHES, **opposite**

PISTACHIO LEMON DROPS, **page 94**

Raspberry Cream Sandwiches

A filling made with sweetened pureed berries, heavy cream, and white chocolate is tucked between two vanilla-bean cookies. MAKES 3 DOZEN

for the cookies:

- 1¾ cups all-purpose flour
- 1 teaspoon baking soda
- ½ teaspoon coarse salt
- 10 tablespoons (1¼ sticks) unsalted butter, room temperature
- 1½ cups sugar
- 1 large egg
- 2 teaspoons pure vanilla extract
- 1 vanilla bean, halved lengthwise, seeds scraped and reserved

for the filling:

- 1⅓ cups fresh raspberries (½ pint)
- 2 teaspoons sugar
- 7½ ounces best-quality white chocolate, coarsely chopped
- ⅓ cup heavy cream

1. Preheat oven to 350°F. Make cookies: Whisk together flour, baking soda, and salt. Put butter and sugar in the bowl of an electric mixer fitted with the paddle attachment. Mix on medium-high speed until pale and fluffy, about 2 minutes. Add egg, vanilla extract, and vanilla seeds; reserve bean for another use. Mix until smooth. Reduce speed to low; gradually mix in flour mixture.

2. Using a 1-inch ice cream scoop, drop dough onto baking sheets lined with parchment paper, spacing 2 inches apart. Bake, rotating sheets halfway through until golden and just set, 8 to 10 minutes. Let cool on parchment on wire racks.

3. Make filling: Puree raspberries and sugar in a food processor. Pour mixture through a fine sieve into a small bowl, pressing to extract juice; discard seeds.

4. Melt white chocolate in a heatproof bowl set over a pan of simmering water. Remove from heat; whisk in cream in a slow, steady stream. Add reserved raspberry mixture; slowly whisk until pale, about 3 minutes. Refrigerate 30 minutes.

5. Assemble cookies: Spread 1 tablespoon filling onto the bottom of one cookie; sandwich with another. Repeat. Cookies can be refrigerated between layers of parchment in airtight containers at room temperature up to 2 days.

Pistachio Lemon Drops

The six ingredients called for here come together in a delightful cookie. Pistachios and lemon juice make a great flavor combination, and the egg white gives a soft texture. MAKES ABOUT 2 DOZEN

- 1 large egg white
- Pinch of coarse salt
- 1 cup toasted salted pistachios, finely chopped (about 4½ ounces)
- 1 cup packed light brown sugar
- 1 tablespoon all-purpose flour
- ½ teaspoon fresh lemon juice

1. Preheat oven to 325°F. Put egg white and salt in the bowl of an electric mixer fitted with the whisk attachment, and mix on medium-high speed until stiff peaks form. Reduce speed to medium; mix in nuts and brown sugar, then flour and lemon juice.

2. Using a 1¼-inch ice cream scoop, drop dough onto baking sheets lined with parchment paper, spacing 2 inches apart. Bake cookies, rotating sheets halfway through, until edges are golden, 10 to 12 minutes. Let cool on sheets on wire racks. Cookies can be stored between layers of parchment in airtight containers at room temperature up to 3 days.

Cream-Filled Chocolate Sandwiches

If you like, roll the sides of the filled cookies in crushed candy canes or finely chopped nuts. The dough can be made ahead and chilled, wrapped well in plastic, for up to one week or frozen for up to one month; let thaw completely before proceeding with the recipe. MAKES ABOUT 2½ DOZEN

- 1¼ cups all-purpose flour
- ¾ cup unsweetened Dutch-process cocoa powder
- 1 teaspoon baking soda
- ¼ teaspoon baking powder
- ¼ teaspoon salt
- 1½ cups sugar, plus more for flattening cookies
- 10 tablespoons (1¼ sticks) unsalted butter, room temperature
- 1 large egg, room temperature
- Vanilla Cream Filling (recipe follows)

1. Preheat oven to 375°F. Into a bowl, sift together flour, cocoa powder, baking soda, baking powder, and salt.

2. In the bowl of an electric mixer fitted with the paddle attachment, cream sugar and butter until light and fluffy, about 2 minutes. Add egg; beat to combine. With mixer on low speed, gradually add flour mixture; continue beating until dough is well combined.

3. Using a 1¼-inch ice cream scoop, drop dough onto parchment-lined baking sheets about 2 inches apart. Dip bottom of a glass in sugar; press to flatten cookies to about ⅛ inch thick. (You may need to carefully remove dough from glass with a thin metal spatula.)

4. Transfer to oven and bake until cookies are firm, 10 to 12 minutes, rotating sheets halfway through. Transfer baking sheets to wire racks to cool completely.

5. Place cream filling in a pastry bag fitted with a coupler, and pipe about 1 tablespoon filling onto the flat side of half the cookies. Place remaining cookies on top, and gently press on each to squeeze filling to edges. Filled cookies can be stored in airtight containers at room temperature up to 2 days.

VANILLA CREAM FILLING

MAKES ABOUT 1 CUP

- ½ cup (1 stick) unsalted butter, room temperature
- ½ cup solid vegetable shortening
- 3½ cups confectioners' sugar
- 1 tablespoon pure vanilla extract

With an electric mixer, cream butter and shortening until well combined. On low speed, gradually add confectioners' sugar and continue beating until light and fluffy, about 2 minutes. Add vanilla and beat to combine. Set aside at room temperature until ready to use.

Date Triangles

Pastry-like in texture and appearance, these cookies pair the intense sweetness of dates with the delicate flavor of almonds. The filling is enhanced by fresh orange zest and juice, as well as orange-flower water; look for the latter in specialty foods shops and Middle Eastern markets. MAKES ABOUT 1½ DOZEN

- 1¼ cups all-purpose flour
- ¼ cup sugar
- Pinch of salt
- 1 tablespoon finely grated orange zest
- ½ cup (1 stick) unsalted butter, cut in small pieces
- 2 teaspoons orange-flower water (optional)
- 3 tablespoons ice water
- ¾ cup dates, preferably Medjool, pitted
- ⅓ cup sliced almonds, plus more for garnish
- 2 tablespoons fresh orange juice
- ½ teaspoon whole milk
- 2 tablespoons honey

1. In a food processor, combine flour, sugar, salt, and half the zest; pulse to combine. Add butter; pulse until mixture is crumbly. Combine orange-flower water, if using, and ice water; drizzle over mixture. Pulse until dough just comes together. Chill, covered, for 20 minutes.

2. In the clean bowl of a food processor, combine dates, almonds, remaining zest, and orange juice; pulse to coarsely chop.

3. Heat oven to 350°F. Form dough into 1½-inch-diameter balls; flatten into 3½-inch circles. Place 1 heaping teaspoon date filling on each. Fold sides toward centers, making triangles; press to flatten slightly. Place pastries 2 inches apart on baking sheets lined with parchment paper; press again.

4. In a small bowl, whisk to combine milk and honey; brush on pastries. Arrange 3 sliced almonds on each pastry. Bake until golden, 30 to 40 minutes, rotating sheets halfway through. Transfer pastries to a wire rack; brush with glaze again. Let stand 15 minutes before serving. Cookies can be kept in an airtight container at room temperature up to 3 days.

Dark Chocolate Cookies with Sour Cherries

We can't seem to get enough of the flavor of sour cherries in our test kitchen. Here they are generously added to a dough rich with bittersweet chocolate and cocoa. The result is a deep, dark, utterly delicious cookie with unexpected tartness in every bite. MAKES ABOUT 3 DOZEN

- 1¾ cups all-purpose flour
- 1¼ cups unsweetened Dutch-process cocoa powder
- 2 teaspoons baking soda
- ¼ teaspoon salt
- 1¼ cups (2½ sticks) unsalted butter, room temperature
- 1¼ cups granulated sugar
- ¾ cup firmly packed dark brown sugar
- 2 large eggs
- ¼ teaspoon pure vanilla extract
- 12 ounces bittersweet chocolate, coarsely chopped
- 1½ firmly packed cups dried sour cherries (9 ounces)

1. Preheat oven to 350°F. Line two baking sheets with parchment paper.

2. In a bowl, sift together the flour, cocoa powder, baking soda, and salt.

3. In the bowl of an electric mixer fitted with the paddle attachment, cream the butter and sugars until fluffy. Add eggs and vanilla; beat until well combined. Add the flour mixture, and beat on low speed until just combined. Do not overbeat. With a wooden spoon, fold in chocolate and cherries. (Dough can be frozen at this point, wrapped well in plastic, up to 1 month; thaw completely before baking.)

4. Form balls of dough, each about ¼ cup; place balls on prepared baking sheets about 3 inches apart. Bake until puffed and cracked, 9 to 11 minutes, rotating sheets halfway through. Transfer to a wire rack to cool completely. Cookies can be stored in an airtight container at room temperature up to 3 days.

FIG PINWHEELS, **opposite**

ICED HERMITS, **page 102**

Fig Pinwheels

If you're in a hurry, you can simplify this recipe by using a high-quality, chunky store-bought jam in place of the homemade fig filling.

MAKES ABOUT 6½ DOZEN

for the dough:

- 2½ cups all-purpose flour, plus more for dusting
- 1 teaspoon coarse salt
- ½ teaspoon baking soda
- 1 cup (2 sticks) unsalted butter, room temperature
- ½ cup granulated sugar
- ½ cup packed light brown sugar
- 2 large eggs

for the filling:

- 1¾ cups dried figs, stemmed (about 8 ounces)
- 1 cup golden raisins (about 4 ounces)
- 1 cup apple juice
- 1 cup fresh orange juice

1. Make dough: Sift together flour, salt, and baking soda into a large bowl. Put butter and sugars in the bowl of an electric mixer fitted with the paddle attachment. Mix on medium speed until smooth, about 3 minutes. Mix in eggs. Reduce speed to low; gradually mix in flour mixture. Divide dough in half; wrap each half in plastic. Refrigerate until firm, about 1 hour or overnight.

2. Transfer one of the dough halves to a lightly floured piece of parchment paper. Roll out to a 10 by 12-inch rectangle; trim edges with a knife. Repeat with remaining dough half. Transfer each rectangle on parchment to a baking sheet. Refrigerate 30 minutes.

3. Make filling: Bring figs, raisins, and juices to a simmer in a saucepan over medium-high heat. Reduce heat to medium. Cook, stirring often, until fruit has softened and only a few tablespoons of liquid remain, about 25 minutes. Let cool completely. Transfer fig mixture to a food processor and puree until smooth.

4. Spread half the filling over each rectangle. Starting with a long side, roll dough into a log. Wrap each log in plastic; refrigerate until firm, about 1 hour or overnight.

5. Preheat oven to 350°F. Cut logs into ¼-inch-thick slices using a sharp knife, transferring to baking sheets lined with parchment paper (and reshaping into rounds, if needed) as you work. Bake cookies, rotating sheets halfway through, until edges turn golden brown, about 15 minutes. Let cool on sheets on wire racks. Cookies can be stored between layers of parchment in airtight containers at room temperature up to 3 days.

HOW TO ROLL PINWHEELS After spreading filling over chilled dough, gently but tightly roll the dough, starting with a long side, into a log. Wrap in plastic; chill 1 hour or overnight. To keep pinwheels from flattening on one side, remove the log from the refrigerator from time to time, and roll it again on a flat surface. Then cut the log into ¼-inch-thick rounds, rerolling it as needed to retain shape.

Iced Hermits

Hermits, which originated in colonial New England, supposedly gained their name because the flavor of the cookie improves after being stowed away—like a hermit—for a few days. These bars, topped with brown sugar icing and candied ginger, are best eaten a day or two after they're baked so the flavors have a chance to deepen. MAKES ABOUT 3 DOZEN

for the cookies:

- ½ cup (1 stick) unsalted butter, room temperature, plus more for baking sheet
- 1¾ cups all-purpose flour
- ¾ teaspoon baking powder
- ¾ teaspoon baking soda
- 1 tablespoon ground ginger
- 1 teaspoon ground cinnamon
- ½ teaspoon freshly grated nutmeg
- ¼ teaspoon coarse salt
- ¼ teaspoon freshly ground pepper
- Pinch of ground cloves
- 1¼ cups packed dark brown sugar
- 1 large egg plus 1 large egg yolk
- ¼ cup unsulfured molasses
- 1 cup chopped candied ginger, cut into ¼-inch pieces
- ¾ cup raisins

for the icing:

- ¼ cup packed light brown sugar
- 2 tablespoons whole milk, plus more if needed
- 2 tablespoons unsalted butter
- 1 teaspoon pure vanilla extract
- 1 cup sifted confectioners' sugar, plus more if needed

1. Preheat oven to 350°. Butter a 10 by 15-inch rimmed baking sheet. Line bottom with parchment paper and butter parchment.

2. Make cookies: Whisk flour, baking powder, baking soda, ground ginger, cinnamon, nutmeg, salt, pepper, and cloves in a bowl.

3. Put butter in the bowl of an electric mixer fitted with the paddle attachment. Beat on medium speed until smooth. Add brown sugar; mix until pale and fluffy, about 2 minutes. Mix in whole egg and yolk, and molasses. Reduce speed to low; gradually mix in flour mixture. Mix in ½ cup candied ginger and the raisins.

4. Spread dough evenly onto prepared baking sheet. Bake, rotating sheet halfway through, until firm, 18 to 22 minutes. Cool completely in baking sheet on a wire rack.

5. Make icing: Put brown sugar, milk, and butter in a saucepan over medium heat. Cook, stirring constantly, until butter has melted and sugar has dissolved. Remove from heat; whisk in vanilla and confectioners' sugar. If icing is too thick to drizzle, stir in more milk, a teaspoon at a time. If icing is too thin, stir in more confectioners' sugar, a teaspoon at a time. Let cool slightly.

6. Drizzle bars with icing; sprinkle with remaining ½ cup candied ginger. Let stand until icing has set, about 15 minutes. Cut into 2-inch squares. Bars can be stored in single layers in airtight containers at room temperature up to 5 days.

Gingersnap-Raspberry Sandwiches

The subtle but distinct taste of ginger pairs well with raspberry jam. Apricot makes an equally delicious filling. Or, try sandwiching the cookies with rich chocolate ganache (recipe on page 44). MAKES 2 DOZEN

- ½ cup (1 stick) unsalted butter, room temperature
- ¼ cup vegetable shortening
- 2 cups sugar
- 2 cups all-purpose flour
- 2 teaspoons baking soda
- 1 teaspoon ground cinnamon
- 1 tablespoon ground ginger
- ¼ cup pure maple syrup
- 1 large egg, beaten
- 1 cup raspberry jam

1. Position rack in center of oven, and preheat oven to 375°F. Line a baking sheet with parchment paper.

2. In the bowl of an electric mixer fitted with the paddle attachment, cream butter, shortening, and 1 cup sugar on medium speed. In a bowl, sift together the flour, baking soda, cinnamon, and ginger.

3. Add maple syrup to butter mixture; beat to combine. Beat in egg until well combined. Reduce speed to low; slowly add the reserved flour mixture, a little at a time, until well blended.

4. Place remaining cup sugar in a bowl. Measure 2 teaspoons dough; roll into a ball. Roll dough in sugar; transfer to prepared baking sheet. Repeat, spacing balls 3 inches apart. Bake until golden, about 12 minutes, rotating halfway through. Transfer cookies to a wire rack to cool. Form and bake the remaining dough.

5. Spread about 2 teaspoons jam over half of the cookies; place a second cookie on top of jam-covered ones, making sandwiches. Filled cookies are best eaten the same day; unfilled cookies can be stored in an airtight container at room temperature up to 1 week.

crumbly *and* sandy

When it comes to texture, cookies with just the right amount of crumble are an old-world classic. In Scotland there's shortbread; in Italy, twice-baked biscotti; and in France, the sablé—which literally means "sandy." The success of many of these recipes depends on a large amount of butter, which interrupts gluten formation. (Gluten is produced when liquids mix with the protein in flour, creating the framework for dough.) Coating these proteins with fat shortens the gluten strands (thus the name "shortbread"), which in turn keeps the cookies crumbly. Many of the delicacies in this section keep well—and, in some cases, taste even better a few days after they are baked—making them the perfect treat to have on hand when guests pop in for a visit.

HAZELNUT ORANGE SHORTBREAD, **page 106**

Hazelnut Orange Shortbread

Here a free-form dough wheel is scored, baked, and cut into generous wedges. We love the combination of hazelnut and orange, but you can use this dough as a building block for other flavorful add-ins—such as ground almonds and lemon zest. MAKES 2 DOZEN

- 1½ cups hazelnuts (about 6 ounces), toasted, skins removed (see page 37)
- 1¼ cups all-purpose flour, plus more for dusting
- ½ cup plus 2 tablespoons granulated sugar
- 10 tablespoons (1¼ sticks) unsalted butter, melted and cooled
- 1½ teaspoons finely grated orange zest
- ¼ teaspoon coarse salt
- 2 tablespoons sanding sugar

1. Preheat oven to 350°F with racks in upper and lower thirds. Process nuts in a food processor until finely chopped, about 20 seconds (do not overprocess). Transfer nuts to a large bowl; add flour, granulated sugar, butter, zest, and salt. Mix with hands until dough just comes together and forms a ball.

2. Halve dough; shape each into a disk. Transfer to a baking sheet lined with parchment paper. With lightly floured hands, shape one disk into a 7-inch round and score to mark 12 equal wedges (do not cut all the way through). Sprinkle with 1 tablespoon sanding sugar. Repeat with remaining disk and sanding sugar.

3. Bake, rotating halfway through, until golden brown, 15 to 20 minutes. While shortbread is warm, cut wedges to separate completely. Let wedges cool slightly on sheets, then transfer to a rack to cool completely. Cookies can be stored in an airtight container at room temperature up to 1 week.

Almond Horns

This confectioners' sugar-dusted butter cookie gets its crunchy, crumbly texture from finely ground toasted almonds—and its name from its characteristic curve. Take care not to overprocess the almonds.

MAKES ABOUT 3 DOZEN

- 2½ cups all-purpose flour
- ½ teaspoon baking powder
- 1½ teaspoons coarse salt
- 1 cup (2 sticks) unsalted butter, room temperature
- 1¼ cups confectioners' sugar, sifted, plus more for dusting
- 1 large egg
- 2 teaspoons pure vanilla extract
- ¼ teaspoon pure almond extract
- 1 cup whole raw almonds, toasted (see page 112) and finely ground in a food processor

1. Whisk together flour, baking powder, and salt in a bowl.

2. Put butter and confectioners' sugar in the bowl of an electric mixer fitted with the paddle attachment. Mix on medium speed until pale and fluffy, about 2 minutes. Mix in egg and extracts. Reduce speed to low. Mix in flour mixture and almonds until just combined. Wrap dough in plastic; refrigerate until firm, about 30 minutes.

3. Preheat oven to 350°F. Roll 1 tablespoon of dough into a 4-inch-long log; gently shape into a horseshoe. Repeat with remaining dough. Transfer to baking sheets lined with parchment.

4. Bake cookies until pale golden, about 20 minutes, rotating sheets halfway through. Transfer cookies to wire racks; let cool completely. Sift confectioners' sugar over cookies. Cookies can be stored in an airtight container at room temperature up to 3 days.

Classic Shortbread

Shortbread is the ultimate expression of four building blocks of baking: butter, sugar, flour, and salt. In this variation, the dough is pressed into a fluted tart pan to form petticoat tails, which got their name either from their likeness to frilly underskirts or a mispronunciation of the French *petites gatelles* (little cakes). MAKES 8

- 2 cups all-purpose flour
- 1¼ teaspoons coarse salt
- 1 cup (2 sticks) unsalted butter, room temperature, plus more for pan
- ¾ cup confectioners' sugar

1. Sift together flour and salt into a bowl. Put butter into the bowl of an electric mixer fitted with the paddle attachment. Mix on medium-high speed until fluffy, 3 to 5 minutes, scraping down sides of bowl. Gradually add confectioners' sugar; beat until pale and fluffy, about 2 minutes. Reduce speed to low. Add flour mixture all at once; mix until just combined.

2. Preheat oven to 300°F, with rack in upper third.

3. Using plastic wrap, press dough into a buttered 10-inch fluted tart pan with a removable bottom. With plastic on dough, refrigerate 20 minutes. Remove plastic wrap. Cut out a round from center using a 2¼-inch cookie cutter; discard. Put cutter back in center. Cut dough into eight wedges with a paring knife. Using a wooden skewer, prick all over at ¼-inch intervals.

4. Bake until golden brown and firm in center, about 1 hour. Transfer pan to a wire rack. Recut shortbread into wedges; let cool completely in pan. Cookies can be stored in an airtight container at room temperature up to 2 weeks.

Chocolate Charms

The dusting of cocoa on these little cookies, much like that on a chocolate truffle, may seem to promise a similar velvety interior, but the illusion is fleeting. One bite reveals the unmistakable crumbly texture of shortbread. If giving as a gift, enclose about three tablespoons of cocoa powder in a small bag, along with instructions for dusting. MAKES ABOUT 3 DOZEN

- 2 cups all-purpose flour
- ¼ cup unsweetened cocoa powder, plus more for dusting
- ¼ teaspoon salt
- 1 cup (2 sticks) unsalted butter, room temperature
- ¾ cup sugar
- 1 teaspoon pure vanilla extract (optional)

1. Sift together flour, cocoa, and salt into a bowl.

2. Place butter in the bowl of an electric mixer fitted with the paddle attachment. Beat on medium speed until fluffy, about 5 minutes. Add sugar, and beat about 2 minutes more, until very light in color and fluffy, occasionally scraping down the sides of the bowl with a spatula. Add vanilla, if using. Add flour mixture, and combine on low speed, scraping with spatula if necessary, until flour is just incorporated and dough sticks together when squeezed with fingers. Form dough into a flattened disk; wrap in plastic. Chill until firm, at least 1 hour.

3. Preheat oven to 325°F. Line two baking sheets with parchment paper.

4. Using a spoon, form dough into 1-inch balls; place on prepared baking sheet. Bake until firm, 20 to 25 minutes, rotating halfway through. Cool completely on wire rack. Dust with cocoa powder just before serving. Cookies can be stored in an airtight container at room temperature up to 1 week.

Mexican Wedding Cookies

Variations on the Mexican wedding cookie show up among the foods of other countries, including Greece and Russia. All are formed from butter- and nut-rich dough; once baked the cookies are completely covered in confectioners' sugar. MAKES ABOUT 1½ DOZEN

- 5 ounces whole blanched almonds (1 cup), plus 40 more for decorating
- 2 cups plus 2 tablespoons all-purpose flour
- ¼ teaspoon salt
- ½ teaspoon ground cinnamon
- 1 cup (2 sticks) unsalted butter, room temperature
- 2¼ cups sifted confectioners' sugar
- 1 teaspoon pure vanilla extract
- ½ teaspoon pure almond extract
- 1 large egg white, beaten

1. Preheat oven to 350°F. Spread 1 cup almonds on a rimmed baking sheet; toast until fragrant, about 12 minutes, stirring occasionally. Transfer to a shallow bowl and set aside to cool.

2. Place toasted almonds, flour, salt, and cinnamon in the bowl of a food processor; process until nuts are finely chopped, about 1 minute.

3. In the bowl of an electric mixer fitted with the paddle attachment, mix the butter and 1 cup confectioners' sugar on medium speed until light and fluffy, about 4 minutes. Add vanilla and almond extracts; beat until combined. Add the chopped-almond mixture; beat on low speed until dough just comes together.

4. Roll dough into twenty 1½-inch-diameter balls; place on two clean baking sheets, spacing 2 inches apart. Flatten each ball slightly.

5. Place the 40 remaining whole almonds and 1 tablespoon beaten egg white in a small bowl; toss to coat. Press two almonds into top of each cookie.

6. Bake cookies until lightly browned around the edges, about 25 minutes, rotating halfway through. Transfer sheets to a wire rack; let rest until cookies are cool enough to handle.

7. Place remaining 1¼ cups confectioners' sugar in a fine-mesh sieve. Sift sugar over cookies, reserving any remaining sugar. Return cookies to baking sheets. Let cookies cool 15 minutes, and coat with sugar again. Cookies can be stored in an airtight container at room temperature up to 1 week.

MEXICAN WEDDING COOKIES, **opposite**

DRIED-CRANBERRY SHORTBREAD HEARTS, **page 114**

Dried-Cranberry Shortbread Hearts

This simple shortbread is first baked in a square pan and then cut into heart shapes. For variation, other dried fruits or mini chocolate chips can be substituted for the cranberries. MAKES ABOUT 1 DOZEN

- 1 cup (2 sticks) unsalted butter, room temperature
- ¾ cup sifted confectioners' sugar
- 1 teaspoon pure vanilla extract
- 2 cups sifted all-purpose flour
- ½ teaspoon coarse salt
- ½ cup finely chopped dried cranberries

1. Preheat oven to 325°F with rack in center. Put butter, confectioners' sugar, vanilla, flour, and salt in a large mixing bowl. Stir together with a wooden spoon until combined but not too creamy. Stir in dried cranberries.

2. Press dough evenly into an 8-inch square baking pan. Bake until firm and pale golden, about 30 minutes. Let cool on a wire rack, about 20 minutes.

3. Run a knife around edges; remove shortbread and transfer, right side up, to a work surface. Cut out hearts with a 2-inch heart-shape cookie cutter. Trim any stray bits of cranberry from edges with a paring knife. Cookies can be stored in an airtight container at room temperature up to 5 days.

Pecan Logs

To toast the pecans, spread them out in a single layer on a rimmed baking sheet and bake at 350°F, stirring occasionally, until fragrant, about 10 minutes. Take care not to overprocess the nuts in step 1; you want them to be finely ground, not paste-like. If desired, sift confectioners' sugar over cookies just before serving. MAKES ABOUT 4 DOZEN

- 2 cups pecans (about 5¼ ounces), toasted
- 2½ cups all-purpose flour
- ½ teaspoon baking powder
- 1½ teaspoons coarse salt
- 1 cup (2 sticks) unsalted butter, room temperature
- 1¼ cups confectioners' sugar, sifted
- 1 large egg
- 2 teaspoons pure vanilla extract

1. Process pecans in a food processor until finely ground; set aside.

2. Whisk together flour, baking powder, and salt in a bowl. Put butter and confectioners' sugar in the bowl of an electric mixer fitted with the paddle attachment; mix on medium speed until pale and fluffy, about 2 minutes. Add egg and vanilla; mix until well combined. Reduce speed to low. Add flour mixture and half of the ground pecans; mix until just combined. Wrap dough in plastic; refrigerate until cold, about 30 minutes.

3. Preheat oven to 350°F. Roll tablespoons of dough into 2-inch-long logs. Roll logs in remaining pecans. Place on baking sheets lined with parchment paper, spacing about 1 inch apart. Bake cookies, rotating sheets halfway through, until pale golden and slightly cracked, 14 to 15 minutes. Transfer logs to wire racks to cool. Cookies can be stored in airtight containers at room temperature up to 3 days.

Icebox Spirals and Bull's-Eyes

Half a batch of vanilla dough has cocoa powder added; the way the doughs are shaped and cut showcases the two distinct flavors with two designs. Kids particularly enjoy making—and eating—these cookies.

MAKES 34 BULL'S-EYES AND 28 SPIRALS

- 1½ cups (3 sticks) unsalted butter, room temperature
- 1¾ cups sugar
- 2 eggs plus 1 large egg white, lightly beaten
- 1 teaspoon coarse salt
- ⅔ cup whole milk
- 1 tablespoon pure vanilla extract
- 5 cups all-purpose flour, plus more for work surface
- ¼ cup unsweetened cocoa powder (not Dutch-process)

1. Make dough: Put butter and sugar in the bowl of an electric mixer fitted with the paddle attachment; mix on medium speed until creamy. Add whole eggs and the salt, and mix until combined. Mix in milk and vanilla. Reduce speed to medium-low. Add flour a little at a time, and mix until just combined.

2. Remove half of the dough from mixer; set aside. Add cocoa powder to remaining dough. Mix on low speed until combined.

3. Form bull's-eyes: Roll out one-quarter of the chocolate dough on a lightly floured surface to a 12-inch rod about ¾ inch thick. Transfer to a baking sheet; refrigerate until firm, about 20 minutes.

4. Roll out half of vanilla dough on lightly floured parchment to a 12 by 4-inch rectangle about ½ inch thick. (It should be as long as the chocolate rod and just wide enough to wrap around the rod.) Transfer to a baking sheet, and refrigerate until firm, about 20 minutes. Brush top of vanilla dough with egg white, then place chocolate rod along length of vanilla dough. Roll vanilla dough with your hands to enclose the chocolate rod. Trim excess. Gently pinch dough to seal. Refrigerate until firm, about 20 minutes.

5. Form spirals: Roll out remaining chocolate dough on a lightly floured piece of parchment paper to ¼ inch thick. Roll out remaining vanilla dough on a lightly floured piece of parchment paper to ½ inch thick. Trim doughs to two 9 by 6-inch rectangles. Refrigerate until firm, about 20 minutes.

6. Brush egg white onto top of each rectangle, then place vanilla dough on top of chocolate dough. Starting at one long side, roll up dough. Gently pinch and press the edge of the roll to seal it. Refrigerate until firm, about 20 minutes.

7. Bake cookies: Preheat oven to 350°F. Cut logs crosswise into ¼-inch-thick rounds. Space 1 inch apart on baking sheets lined with parchment paper. Bake until firm but not browned, 12 to 15 minutes, rotating sheets halfway through. Let cool on sheets 3 minutes, then transfer to wire racks to cool completely. Cookies can be stored in airtight containers at room temperature up to 3 days.

Springerle

These anise-flavored molded cookies originated hundreds of years ago; today, replicas of the traditional European molds are available in hundreds of designs. The cookies are made with lots of eggs, whose leavening effect may have given them the name *springerle*, which means "little jumper" in German. MAKES 4 TO 5 DOZEN

- ½ teaspoon baking powder
- 2 tablespoons whole milk
- 6 large eggs, at room temperature
- 6 cups sifted confectioners' sugar, plus more for dusting
- ½ cup (1 stick) unsalted butter, room temperature
- ½ teaspoon salt
- 1 teaspoon anise extract
- 1 teaspoon finely grated lemon zest
- 9 cups sifted cake flour, plus more for work surface if necessary

1. Dissolve baking powder in milk in a small bowl. Put the eggs in the bowl of an electric mixer fitted with the whisk attachment. Beat eggs on high speed until very thick and lemon colored, about 10 minutes. Gradually beat in sugar until creamy and smooth.

2. Add butter, 1 tablespoon at a time, beating on high speed, until creamy. Add baking powder and milk, salt, anise extract, and lemon zest; beat to combine.

3. Add 6 cups flour, 1 cup at a time, mixing on medium-low speed after each addition. Remove from mixer and stir in 3 more cups of flour, 1 cup at a time, until dough is stiff and well combined.

4. Transfer dough to a floured surface; knead by hand until dough is smooth and not sticky, adding more flour if necessary. Divide dough into 4 pieces; wrap well in plastic wrap.

5. Dust a work surface with confectioners' sugar; roll out 1 piece of dough ⅜ inch thick. Using a pastry brush, coat a springerle mold with confectioners' sugar. Press mold into the dough; lift off. Using a pizza cutter or knife, cut out cookie and slide it onto parchment-lined baking sheets; repeat, arranging cookies by size, about 1 inch apart. Let stand uncovered for 24 hours.

6. Preheat oven to 220°F. Bake cookies, 1 sheet at a time, until completely dry, about 1 hour. They will not take on any color. Transfer to wire racks to cool. Cookies can be stored in airtight containers at room temperature up to 3 weeks.

HOW TO FORM SPRINGERLE To make springerle, dough is rolled out on a work surface dusted with confectioners' sugar, a mold is pressed into the dough, and the excess is trimmed away.

Pecan Mandelbrot

Mandelbrot comes from the German words for "almond" (*Mandel*) and "bread" (*Brot*). Our variation contains pecans instead of almonds. As with biscotti, the dough is partially baked, sliced, and baked again. MAKES 3½ DOZEN

- ¾ cup vegetable oil
- 1¼ cups sugar
- 3 large eggs
- ¾ teaspoon coarse salt
- 1 teaspoon pure vanilla extract
- 3 cups all-purpose flour
- 1 teaspoon baking powder
- 1 teaspoon baking soda
- 1 cup chopped pecans (about 4 ounces), toasted
- 1 teaspoon ground cinnamon

1. Preheat oven to 350°F. Put oil, 1 cup sugar, eggs, salt, and vanilla in the bowl of electric mixer fitted with the paddle attachment, and mix on medium-low speed until combined.

2. Sift together flour, baking powder, and baking soda into a bowl. Reduce mixer speed to low. Add flour mixture; mix until combined. Stir in pecans.

3. Divide dough into three equal parts; shape each into a long log about 3 inches wide and 1 inch high. Space logs 4 inches apart on a baking sheet lined with parchment paper. Bake logs until golden, puffed, and just firm to the touch, about 35 minutes. Let cool slightly, 3 to 5 minutes.

4. Transfer logs to a cutting board. With a serrated knife, gently cut logs into ½-inch-thick slices. The cookies should still be slightly doughy inside. Work quickly, as slices will crumble if allowed to cool. Transfer slices to baking sheets lined with parchment paper.

5. Mix remaining ¼ cup sugar and the cinnamon in a small bowl. Sprinkle cookies with cinnamon-sugar mixture. Bake slices until golden brown and dry, about 15 minutes. Cookies can be stored in airtight containers at room temperature up to 1 week.

Lime Meltaways

The refreshing sweet-tart flavor of these crumbly cookies is just right after a spicy meal. Other citrus juices and zests can be substituted for the lime juice and zest. MAKES ABOUT 5 DOZEN

- ¾ cup (1½ sticks) unsalted butter, room temperature
- 1 cup confectioners' sugar
- Finely grated zest of 2 limes
- 2 tablespoons fresh lime juice
- 1 tablespoon pure vanilla extract
- 1¾ cups plus 2 tablespoons all-purpose flour
- 2 tablespoons cornstarch
- ¼ teaspoon coarse salt

1. Put butter and ⅓ cup confectioners' sugar in the bowl of an electric mixer fitted with the whisk attachment, and mix on medium speed until pale and fluffy. Add the lime zest and juice and the vanilla, and mix until fluffy.

2. Whisk together flour, cornstarch, and salt in a bowl. Add to butter mixture, and mix on low speed until just combined.

3. Divide dough in half. Place each log on an 8 by 12-inch sheet of parchment. Roll in parchment to form a log 1¼ inches in diameter, pressing a ruler along edge of parchment at each turn to narrow log. Refrigerate logs until cold and firm, at least 1 hour.

4. Preheat oven to 350°F. Remove parchment from logs; cut into ¼-inch-thick rounds. Space rounds 1 inch apart on baking sheets lined with parchment paper. Bake cookies until barely golden, about 13 minutes, rotating sheets halfway through. Transfer cookies to wire racks to cool slightly, 8 to 10 minutes. While still warm, toss cookies with remaining ⅔ cup sugar in a resealable plastic bag. Cookies can be stored in airtight containers at room temperature up to 2 weeks.

Apple-Cherry Crumble Bars

To heighten the flavor of apples in these crumbly fruit bars, we steeped dried apple slices in cider; dried cherries lend hints of color and tartness. And the bars are a cinch to make: Some of the dough is first pressed into the pan and covered with softened fruit; the remaining dough is then sprinkled over the top before baking. MAKES 2 DOZEN

- 1 cup (2 sticks) cold unsalted butter, cut into pieces, plus more for pan
- 3 cups dried apples (about 7 ounces)
- ¾ cup dried cherries (about 4½ ounces)
- 1¾ cups apple cider
- ¾ cup plus 2 tablespoons packed light brown sugar
- 1 teaspoon ground cinnamon
- 2 cups old-fashioned rolled oats
- 1½ cups all-purpose flour
- ½ teaspoon baking soda
- ½ teaspoon salt

1. Preheat oven to 375°F. Butter a 9 by 13-inch baking dish. Simmer apples, cherries, and cider in a covered saucepan, stirring occasionally, until fruits are softened, about 5 minutes. Reduce heat to low and simmer, covered, 5 minutes more. Drain, reserving 2 tablespoons liquid. Let cool.

2. Coarsely chop fruit. Combine with 2 tablespoons brown sugar, ¼ teaspoon cinnamon, and reserved cooking liquid in a bowl.

3. Whisk together oats, flour, baking soda, salt, remaining ¾ teaspoon cinnamon, and remaining ¾ cup brown sugar. Cut in cold butter with a pastry blender or 2 knives until mixture resembles coarse meal with a few larger clumps remaining.

4. Press 4 cups of oat mixture evenly into bottom of prepared dish. Spread fruit filling on top, leaving a ¼-inch border on all sides. Sprinkle remaining oat mixture evenly on top.

5. Bake until golden brown, about 35 minutes. Let cool completely in dish on a wire rack. Cut into 24 bars. Bars can be stored at room temperature in an airtight container up to 3 days.

Maple-Pecan Shortbread

Grade B maple syrup, which is darker and more strongly flavored than Grade A, adds a robust flavor to this nut-studded shortbread.

MAKES ABOUT 2 DOZEN

- 2¼ cups all-purpose flour, plus more for work surface
- ½ cup cake flour (not self-rising)
- ½ teaspoon salt
- ½ cup pecan halves (about 2¼ ounces), finely chopped, plus 24 whole pecan halves, for decorating
- 1 cup (2 sticks) unsalted butter, room temperature
- ¾ cup granulated sugar
- ¼ cup pure maple syrup, preferably Grade B
- 1 large egg yolk
- ¼ teaspoon pure maple extract
- 1 large egg, lightly beaten
- Turbinado sugar, for sprinkling

1. Sift flours and salt into a bowl. Whisk in chopped pecans.

2. In the bowl of an electric mixer fitted with the paddle attachment, beat butter and granulated sugar on medium-high speed until smooth and light, about 1 minute. Add maple syrup, egg yolk, and extract; beat on medium speed until well combined. On low speed, gradually add flour mixture, beating until just combined. Dough should be smooth and pliable. Flatten into a disk. Wrap in plastic; refrigerate until firm, 1½ hours or overnight.

3. Preheat oven to 350°F. Line a baking sheet with parchment paper.

4. On a lightly floured work surface, roll out dough to ¼ inch thick. Cut out rounds using a 2-inch cookie cutter; place 1 inch apart on prepared baking sheet. Brush tops with beaten egg; place pecan half in the center of each cookie. Sprinkle the entire surface with turbinado sugar.

5. Bake cookies, rotating sheet halfway through, until golden around the edges, 10 to 12 minutes. Transfer to a wire rack to cool. Cookies can be stored in airtight containers at room temperature up to 4 days.

Sand Tarts

Crisp sugar wafers are decorated with sliced almonds to resemble sand dollars. For a summertime treat, sandwich two cookies with softened ice cream; wrap sandwiches well in plastic and freeze until firm before serving.

MAKES 2 DOZEN

- ½ cup (1 stick) unsalted butter, softened
- 1¾ cups sugar
- 2 large eggs, 1 separated
- 1 teaspoon pure vanilla extract
- 1 teaspoon finely grated lemon zest
- 2½ cups sifted all-purpose flour, plus more for rolling
- ¼ teaspoon salt
- 1 teaspoon water
- ½ teaspoon ground cinnamon
- Sliced almonds, for decoration

1. In the bowl of an electric mixer fitted with the paddle attachment, beat butter on medium speed until creamy. Gradually add 1 cup sugar and beat until pale.

2. Beat in whole egg, egg yolk, vanilla, and lemon zest. Sift flour with salt, and add to butter mixture. Mix on low speed just until dough comes together. Shape into disk and wrap well in plastic; refrigerate several hours or overnight.

3. Preheat oven to 400°F. Whisk egg white and the water in a small bowl. Combine cinnamon and remaining ¾ cup sugar in another small bowl.

4. Roll out dough to ⅛-inch thickness between two sheets of lightly floured parchment paper. Cut with a 3½-inch round cutter, and place on ungreased baking sheet. Brush with egg-white mixture, decorate with 3 sliced almonds, and sprinkle with cinnamon-sugar mixture. Bake until golden brown, 8 to 10 minutes, rotating halfway through. Remove from oven; transfer to a wire rack to cool completely. Cookies can be stored in airtight containers at room temperature up to 1 week.

Chocolate-Almond-Marsala Cookies

Marsala wine, traditionally used in zabaglione and sometimes served as an apéritif, flavors these Italian goodies. Look for candied orange peel in specialty foods stores; do not substitute supermarket candied-fruit mixes.

MAKES ABOUT 2 DOZEN

- 1¼ cups all-purpose flour, plus more for work surface
- 2 teaspoons baking powder
- 1¼ teaspoons ground cinnamon
- 1 teaspoon coarse salt
- 2 large eggs
- ⅓ cup Marsala wine
- ½ cup whole raw almonds with skins, toasted and coarsely chopped
- ½ cup finely chopped candied orange peel
- 4 ounces semisweet chocolate, chopped
- 3 tablespoons honey

1. Stir together flour, baking powder, cinnamon, and salt in a large bowl. Beat 1 egg with the wine in a small bowl; stir into flour mixture. Stir in almonds, orange peel, and chocolate. Stir in honey.

2. Knead dough on a generously floured work surface just until it holds its shape. Divide dough in half; pat each half into a 10½ by 1½ by 1-inch rounded log. Refrigerate logs until cold, about 45 minutes.

3. Preheat oven to 250°F. Cut each log crosswise into ¾-inch-thick slices. Gently press edges of each slice to flatten. Lightly beat remaining egg. Stand cookies upright 1 inch apart on a baking sheet lined with parchment paper. Brush tops with beaten egg.

4. Bake 20 minutes. Raise oven temperature to 350°F. Bake until cookies are deep golden brown, 10 to 12 minutes more. Let cool on sheets on wire racks. Cookies can be stored in airtight containers at room temperature up to 2 days.

CHOCOLATE-ALMOND-MARSALA COOKIES, **opposite**

LEMON-APRICOT SANDWICHES, **page 130**

Lemon-Apricot Sandwiches

If you're looking for something to offer with tea or coffee, look no further—these dainty little sandwich cookies are the quintessential afternoon treat. They're also ideal for bridal and baby showers. MAKES ABOUT 1½ DOZEN

- ½ cup almond flour
- ½ cup all-purpose flour
- ¼ cup cornstarch
- ½ teaspoon salt
- ½ cup (1 stick) unsalted butter, room temperature
- ¼ cup confectioners' sugar, plus more for dusting
- 2 tablespoons granulated sugar
- Finely grated zest of 2 lemons
- 2 tablespoons fresh lemon juice
- ½ cup apricot jam

1. Whisk together both flours, cornstarch, and salt in a bowl.

2. Put butter, sugars, lemon zest, and 1 tablespoon lemon juice into the bowl of an electric mixer fitted with the paddle attachment. Beat on medium speed until fluffy, about 3 minutes. Reduce speed to low. Add flour mixture in three batches, mixing well after each addition. Cover dough with plastic wrap; refrigerate 30 minutes.

3. Preheat oven to 350°F. Place cold dough between two pieces of parchment paper and roll out to ⅛ inch thick. Transfer dough on parchment to a baking sheet; freeze 10 minutes.

4. Using a fluted 1⅛-inch round cutter, cut out dough; transfer to parchment-lined baking sheets. Reroll scraps, and cut out (you should have 40 rounds). Bake until pale golden, 10 to 11 minutes, rotating sheets halfway through. Let cool slightly on sheets on wire racks. Transfer cookies to racks to cool completely.

5. Using a rubber spatula, press the jam through a fine sieve into a small bowl. Stir in remaining tablespoon lemon juice. Spread 1 teaspoon jam mixture on flat side of half of the cookies, and sandwich with the remaining cookies. Dust with confectioners' sugar. Unfilled cookies can be stored in an airtight container at room temperature up to 3 days; filled ones are best eaten the day you assemble them.

Pfeffernüssen

The snowy sugar surface contrasts with the peppery flavor of these German spice cookies. *Pfeffer* means "pepper" in German; *Nuss* means "nut," and refers more to the shape than to the ingredients. MAKES 3 DOZEN

- 1¼ cups confectioners' sugar
- 2¼ cups all-purpose flour
- ¼ teaspoon freshly ground pepper
- ¾ teaspoon ground cinnamon
- ½ teaspoon ground allspice
- ¼ teaspoon freshly grated nutmeg
- ¼ teaspoon ground cloves
- ¼ teaspoon baking soda
- ½ cup (1 stick) unsalted butter, room temperature
- ¾ cup packed light brown sugar
- ¼ cup unsulfured molasses
- 1 large egg
- ½ teaspoon pure vanilla extract

1. Preheat oven to 350°F. Line two baking sheets with parchment paper. Place the confectioners' sugar in a brown paper bag.

2. In a bowl, combine flour, pepper, cinnamon, allspice, nutmeg, cloves, and baking soda.

3. Place butter, brown sugar, and molasses in the bowl of an electric mixer fitted with the paddle attachment. Beat on medium speed until fluffy, about 3 minutes. Beat in egg and vanilla. With mixer on low speed, add flour mixture; beat until just combined. Pinch off tablespoons of dough; roll into 1¼-inch balls. Arrange balls 1½ inches apart on prepared baking sheets. (Dough can be frozen at this point, covered tightly with plastic wrap, up to 1 month.)

4. Bake until golden and firm to the touch with slight cracking, about 15 minutes, rotating sheets halfway through. Transfer sheets to a wire rack to cool slightly, about 10 minutes. Working in batches, place cookies in paper bag; shake until well coated. Let cool completely on wire rack. Cookies can be stored in an airtight container at room temperature up to 1 week.

Mocha Shortbread Wedges

Baking this shortbread in a round cake pan and then cutting it while it's warm make it quite easy to prepare. The only trick is to make sure you don't overbake the shortbread, so keep an eye on it as the suggested baking time draws near. MAKES 8

- ½ cup plus 3 tablespoons all-purpose flour
- ¼ cup unsweetened Dutch-process cocoa powder
- Pinch of salt
- 2 teaspoons good-quality instant espresso powder
- ½ cup (1 stick) unsalted butter, room temperature
- ½ cup confectioners' sugar, plus more for sprinkling

1. Preheat oven to 350°F. Line an 8-inch round cake or springform pan with parchment paper.

2. Sift together flour, cocoa powder, and salt. Stir in espresso.

3. In an electric mixer fitted with the paddle attachment, beat butter on medium speed until pale and creamy. Add confectioners' sugar, and beat well. Add flour mixture, and beat on low speed until well combined.

4. Pat dough evenly into pan. Bake 20 to 25 minutes, or until puffed at the edges and dark all over the top. Remove from oven, and let sit 5 minutes; then cut into 8 wedges. Let cool completely on a rack. Sprinkle with confectioners' sugar just before serving. Cookies can be stored in an airtight container at room temperature up to 1 week.

Rum Raisin Shortbread

This crumbly shortbread is studded with dried currants, which are tiny raisins made from Zante grapes. The currants must be soaked overnight, so you'll need to plan your craving a day in advance. MAKES ABOUT 4½ DOZEN

- ½ cup dark rum
- 1 cup currants
- 1 cup (2 sticks) unsalted butter, room temperature
- ¾ cup confectioners' sugar
- ½ teaspoon finely grated orange zest
- 1 teaspoon pure vanilla extract
- 1½ cups all-purpose flour
- ¾ cup finely shredded unsweetened coconut
- 1 teaspoon coarse salt

1. Combine rum and currants in an airtight container; let sit at room temperature overnight. Drain; reserving 2 tablespoons rum.

2. Put butter, confectioners' sugar, and zest in the bowl of an electric mixer fitted with the paddle attachment. Beat until creamy and smooth, about 2 minutes. Add vanilla and reserved rum. Beat well, scraping down the sides of the bowl as necessary. Reduce speed to low. Add flour, coconut, and salt, and beat for 3 minutes. Stir in currants by hand. Divide dough in half and form each into a log about 1½ inches in diameter; wrap in parchment, and refrigerate 1 hour (or up to 3 days).

3. Preheat oven to 325°F. Remove dough from parchment; slice into ¼-inch-thick rounds. Place on parchment paper–lined baking sheets, spacing about 1 inch apart. Bake until pale golden, about 20 minutes, rotating sheets halfway through. Transfer to wire racks to cool completely. Cookies can be stored in airtight containers at room temperature up to 1 week.

Pecan Linzer Cookies with Cherry Filling

To make our linzer sandwiches, we substituted pecans for more traditional almonds, and cherry jam for the classic raspberry filling. The crumbly cookies with heart-shaped windows make delectable gifts for Valentine's Day.

MAKES ABOUT 2 DOZEN

- 2 cups all-purpose flour, plus more for dusting
- ½ teaspoon baking powder
- ¾ cup pecan halves, toasted (see page 115)
- 2 tablespoons confectioners' sugar, plus more for sprinkling
- ⅛ teaspoon salt
- ⅛ teaspoon ground cinnamon
- ½ cup (1 stick) cold unsalted butter, cut into small pieces
- ¼ cup granulated sugar
- 1 teaspoon pure vanilla extract
- 1 large egg
- ½ cup cherry jam, strained

1. Sift flour and baking powder together into a bowl. Pulse pecans, confectioners' sugar, salt, and cinnamon in a food processor until finely ground; transfer to the bowl of an electric mixer fitted with the paddle attachment.

2. Add butter and granulated sugar; beat on medium speed until fluffy. Mix in vanilla and egg. Reduce speed to low. Add flour mixture; mix until combined. Halve dough; shape into disks. Wrap each in plastic; refrigerate until firm, at least 2 hours.

3. Preheat oven to 375°F. Working with one disk at a time, roll out dough on a lightly floured surface to ⅛ inch thick. Refrigerate 20 minutes. Cut out squares with a 2-inch fluted cutter. Cut out centers of half the squares with a ½-inch heart cutter; reroll scraps. Space 2 inches apart on parchment paper–lined baking sheets. Bake squares and hearts until pale golden, 8 to 10 minutes. Transfer to racks to cool.

4. Meanwhile, heat jam in a small saucepan over medium heat until reduced and thickened, about 7 minutes; let cool.

5. Sprinkle cutout cookies with confectioners' sugar. Spread jam onto uncut squares; top with cutout ones. Cookies can be stored in an airtight container at room temperature up to 2 days.

Buttered Rum Meltaways

These melt-in-your-mouth treats are fragrant with warm spices of cinnamon, nutmeg, clove, and vanilla. They are also infused with a healthy dash of dark rum. The dough can be made up to one month in advance, frozen, and sliced to bake as needed. MAKES ABOUT 4 DOZEN

- 1¾ cups plus 2 tablespoons all-purpose flour
- 2 tablespoons cornstarch
- 2 teaspoons ground cinnamon
- 2 teaspoons freshly grated nutmeg
- ¼ teaspoon ground cloves
- ¾ teaspoon coarse salt
- ¾ cup (1½ sticks) unsalted butter, room temperature
- 1 cup confectioners' sugar
- ¼ cup dark rum
- 1 teaspoon pure vanilla extract

1. Whisk together flour, cornstarch, spices, and salt in a bowl. Put butter and ⅓ cup confectioners' sugar into the bowl of an electric mixer fitted with the paddle attachment. Beat on medium speed until pale and fluffy. Mix in rum and vanilla. Reduce speed to low, and gradually mix in flour mixture.

2. Divide dough in half. Place each on a piece of parchment paper; shape dough into logs. Fold parchment over dough; using a ruler, roll and press into a 1¼-inch-thick log. Wrap in parchment. Chill in freezer at least 30 minutes or up to 1 month.

3. Preheat oven to 350°F. Remove parchment. Cut logs into ¼-inch-thick rounds; space 1 inch apart on parchment paper–lined baking sheets. Bake until just golden, about 15 minutes. Transfer cookies to wire racks; let cool 10 minutes. Gently toss warm cookies with remaining ⅔ cup confectioners' sugar in a resealable plastic bag. Cookies can be stored in airtight containers at room temperature up to 2 weeks.

Italian Polenta Cookies

Polenta, which is made from cornmeal, is a staple in northern Italy. To achieve an authentic texture, use imported polenta; look for it in Italian markets and specialty foods stores. MAKES ABOUT 2½ DOZEN

- 1¾ cups all-purpose flour
- 1 cup Italian polenta or coarse yellow cornmeal
- ½ teaspoon salt
- 1 cup (2 sticks) unsalted butter, room temperature
- ⅔ cup sugar
- 1 tablespoon finely grated lemon zest
- 1 large egg plus 1 large egg yolk
- 1 teaspoon pure vanilla extract

1. Preheat oven to 350°F. Whisk together flour, polenta, and salt in a bowl.

2. Put butter, sugar, and lemon zest in the bowl of an electric mixer fitted with the paddle attachment; beat on medium-high speed until pale and fluffy, about 2 minutes, scraping down the sides of the bowl as needed. Add egg and egg yolk, one at a time, beating after each addition to combine. Mix in vanilla. Gradually add flour mixture, and beat until just combined. Transfer batter to a pastry bag fitted with a 7/16-inch star tip (such as Ateco #825).

3. Pipe S shapes about 3 inches long and 1 inch wide, spacing 1½ inches apart on baking sheets lined with parchment. Chill in freezer until dough is firm, about 30 minutes. Bake cookies until edges are golden, 15 to 18 minutes, rotating sheets halfway through. Transfer cookies on parchment to wire racks; let cool about 10 minutes. Remove cookies from parchment, and transfer to racks to cool completely. Cookies can be stored in an airtight container at room temperature up to 1 week.

Citrus Cornmeal Shortbread

Coating the outside of the dough with cornmeal gives the cookies a lovely bit of crunch and a texture reminiscent of many Italian pastries. MAKES 3 DOZEN

- 1 cup (2 sticks) unsalted butter, room temperature
- ¾ cup confectioners' sugar
- 2 teaspoons pure vanilla extract
- 1½ teaspoons finely grated orange zest
- 2 cups all-purpose flour
- ¼ cup plus 2 tablespoons yellow cornmeal
- 1 teaspoon coarse salt

1. Put butter and confectioners' sugar in the bowl of an electric mixer fitted with the paddle attachment; mix on medium speed until pale and creamy, about 2 minutes. Add vanilla and zest. Mix until combined, scraping down sides of bowl as needed.

2. Reduce speed to low. Add flour, 2 tablespoons cornmeal, and the salt; mix until well combined, about 3 minutes. Halve dough; shape each into a log about 1½ inches in diameter. Wrap each in plastic, and refrigerate until cold, at least 1 hour.

3. Preheat oven to 300°F. Place remaining ¼ cup cornmeal on a sheet of parchment paper. Roll logs in cornmeal to coat. Cut into ¼-inch-thick rounds, and space rounds 1 inch apart on a baking sheet lined with parchment paper. Bake until pale golden, 30 to 35 minutes. Cool on sheet on a wire rack. Cookies can be stored in an airtight container at room temperature up to 1 week.

CITRUS CORNMEAL SHORTBREAD,
opposite

ROSEMARY BUTTER COOKIES,
page 144

Rosemary Butter Cookies

These were originally developed as favors in *Martha Stewart Weddings* magazine. Rosemary, which denotes remembrance, love, loyalty, and friendship, has long held a place of honor in wedding ceremonies.

MAKES ABOUT 4 DOZEN

- 1 cup (2 sticks) unsalted butter, room temperature
- ¾ cup granulated sugar
- 1 large egg plus 1 egg white, beaten
- 1 teaspoon pure vanilla extract
- 2½ cups sifted all-purpose flour
- 1 tablespoon finely chopped fresh rosemary
- 1 teaspoon coarse salt
- ½ cup fine sanding sugar

1. Put butter and granulated sugar in the bowl of an electric mixer fitted with the paddle attachment; beat on medium speed until pale and fluffy, about 2 minutes. Mix in whole egg and vanilla. Reduce speed to low. Add flour, rosemary, and salt, and mix until combined.

2. Halve dough; shape each half into a log. Place each log on a 12 by 16-inch sheet of parchment. Roll in parchment to 1½ inches in diameter, pressing a ruler along edge of parchment at each turn to narrow log. Transfer to paper-towel tubes to hold shape, and freeze until firm, about 1 hour.

3. Preheat oven to 375°F. Brush each log with beaten egg white; roll in sanding sugar. Cut into ¼-inch-thick rounds. Space 1 inch apart on baking sheets lined with parchment. Bake until edges are golden, 18 to 20 minutes. Let cool on sheets on wire racks. Cookies can be stored in airtight containers at room temperature up to 3 days.

Cappuccino-Chocolate Bites

Flecks of espresso are dotted throughout these petite cookies, which are sandwiched together with creamy milk-chocolate ganache.

MAKES ABOUT 2½ DOZEN

- ⅔ cup all-purpose flour
- 1 tablespoon finely ground espresso beans
- ⅛ teaspoon coarse salt
- 6 tablespoons unsalted butter, room temperature
- ¼ cup confectioners' sugar, plus more for dusting
- ¼ teaspoon pure vanilla extract
- ⅓ cup heavy cream
- 2½ ounces milk chocolate, finely chopped
- Unsweetened cocoa powder, for dusting

1. Whisk flour, espresso, and salt in a bowl. Put butter and sugar in the bowl of an electric mixer fitted with the paddle, and mix on medium-high speed until pale and fluffy. Mix in vanilla. Add flour mixture; mix on medium-low until dough comes together. Shape into a disk, and wrap in plastic. Refrigerate 30 minutes.

2. Preheat oven to 350°F. Let dough stand at room temperature 10 minutes. Roll between sheets of parchment to ⅛ inch thick. Cut out rounds with a 1⅛-inch cutter; space ½ inch apart on baking sheets lined with parchment. Reroll scraps; cut out. Freeze 10 minutes.

3. Bake until set but not browned, about 9 minutes. Let cool on sheets 5 minutes. Transfer to wire racks; cool completely.

4. Bring cream to a simmer. Pour over chocolate; stir until smooth. Press plastic wrap onto surface; refrigerate at least 4 hours or up to overnight. Whisk to soft peaks; transfer to a pastry bag fitted with a ¼-inch plain round tip. Pipe about 1 teaspoon filling on bottoms of half the cookies; sandwich with remaining cookies. Dust with cocoa and confectioners' sugar. Cookies can be refrigerated in an airtight container up to 1 day.

Wholemeal Almond Biscuits

Fresh fruit and tangy soft cheeses make perfect partners for these salty-sweet wheatmeal cookies. Or, try using them in place of risen biscuits for strawberry shortcake: Top a biscuit with a dollop of sweetened ricotta cheese and some macerated berries. MAKES 15

- 1 cup blanched whole almonds, toasted
- ¾ cup whole wheat flour
- ½ cup all-purpose flour, plus more for work surface
- ⅓ cup packed light brown sugar
- ½ teaspoon coarse salt
- ¼ teaspoon ground cinnamon
- ½ cup (1 stick) unsalted butter, cold, cut into pieces
- 2 tablespoons ice water, plus more if needed

1. Pulse almonds in a food processor until coarsely ground. Add both flours, brown sugar, salt, and cinnamon, and pulse to combine. Add butter, and pulse until mixture resembles coarse meal. With machine running, pour in enough water until dough just starts to come together on the sides of the bowl. Shape dough into a ball, and wrap in plastic. Refrigerate until cold and slightly firm, no longer than 30 minutes.

2. Preheat oven to 350°F. Roll out dough on a lightly floured work surface to an 11-inch round just more than ¼ inch thick. Cut out 3-inch circles. Carefully gather scraps of dough, reroll, and cut out remaining biscuits. Place on baking sheets lined with parchment paper, spacing 1½ inches apart. Bake until edges are golden brown, about 30 minutes, rotating halfway through. Let cool on baking sheets on wire racks. Cookies can be stored in an airtight container at room temperature up to 5 days.

WHOLEMEAL
ALMOND BISCUITS, **opposite**

COCONUT
MACADAMIA SHORTBREAD, **page 148**

Coconut Macadamia Shortbread

This recipe combines a buttery Scottish tradition with the flavors of the Hawaiian Islands. If you don't have a fluted square cutter, use whatever other shape you have on hand. To toast macadamias, place them in a single layer on a rimmed baking sheet in a 350°F oven until lightly golden, about 10 minutes, stirring occasionally. MAKES ABOUT 2½ DOZEN

- 1 cup macadamia nuts (about 3 ounces), toasted
- ¾ cup plus 2 tablespoons sugar
- 1½ cups sweetened shredded coconut
- ¾ cup (1½ sticks) plus 1 tablespoon unsalted butter, room temperature
- 4 tablespoons cream of coconut or unsalted butter
- 2 teaspoons pure coconut extract
- 2 cups all-purpose flour, plus more for work surface
- ½ teaspoon coarse salt
- 1 large egg white, lightly beaten

1. Process nuts and 2 tablespoons sugar in a food processor until finely ground; set aside. Process 1 cup coconut until coarsely ground; set aside.

2. Put butter, cream of coconut, and remaining ¾ cup sugar in the bowl of an electric mixer fitted with the paddle attachment; beat on medium until pale and fluffy, about 2 minutes. Mix in coconut extract. Reduce speed to low. Add flour, salt, nut mixture, and ground coconut; mix until combined.

3. Halve dough. Shape halves into disks, and wrap well in plastic. Refrigerate until firm, about 1 hour.

4. Let dough soften before rolling. Roll out each disk on lightly floured parchment to ¼ inch thick. Cover with plastic; refrigerate until firm, 30 minutes.

5. Preheat oven to 325°F. Cut dough into squares using a fluted 2¼-inch square cookie cutter. Reroll scraps; continue cutting out squares. Space about 1 inch apart on baking sheets lined with parchment. Lightly brush tops with beaten egg white; sprinkle with remaining ½ cup coconut. Bake until golden, 20 to 25 minutes, rotating sheets halfway through. Let cool on sheets on wire racks. Cookies can be stored in airtight containers at room temperature up to 1 week.

Vanilla Malted Cookies

Malt powder enriches these cookies with a creamy caramel and vanilla flavor that calls to mind a malted milk shake at an old-time soda fountain.

MAKES ABOUT 6 DOZEN

- 2¾ cups all-purpose flour
- ¾ cup plain malted-milk powder
- 1 teaspoon baking powder
- ¾ teaspoon salt
- 1 cup (2 sticks) unsalted butter, room temperature
- 3 ounces cream cheese, room temperature
- 1 cup sugar
- 1 vanilla bean, split, seeds scraped and reserved
- 1 large egg
- ½ teaspoon pure vanilla extract

1. Preheat oven to 350°F. Whisk together flour, malted-milk powder, baking powder, and salt.

2. With an electric mixer on medium speed, beat butter and cream cheese until creamy. Mix in sugar and vanilla seeds (reserve pod for another use). Add egg and vanilla extract, and combine. Reduce speed to low. Add flour mixture and mix to combine.

3. Transfer dough to a pastry bag fitted with a ½-inch star tip (such as Ateco #825). Pipe 2½-inch strips onto parchment-lined baking sheets, spacing them about 1 inch apart.

4. Bake until bottom edges are golden brown, 11 to 15 minutes, rotating sheets halfway through. Transfer to wire racks to cool completely. Cookies can be stored in airtight containers at room temperature up to 1 week.

Vanilla-Bean Spritz Wreaths

The name for these pressed cookies comes from the German word *spritzen* ("to squirt"); they can be quickly formed with a cookie press. Although they have a very fine crumb, the wreaths are sturdy enough for packaging (see page 342 for a gift idea). MAKES ABOUT 5 DOZEN

- 3½ cups all-purpose flour
- 1 teaspoon salt
- 3 teaspoons ground cinnamon
- 2 vanilla beans, halved lengthwise, seeds scraped and reserved
- 1 cup plus 4 teaspoons sugar
- 3 sticks unsalted butter, room temperature
- 2 large egg yolks

1. Preheat oven to 350°F. Whisk together flour, salt, and 1 teaspoon cinnamon.

2. Beat vanilla seeds and 1 cup sugar with a mixer on medium speed until incorporated, about 3 minutes (sugar will clump together slightly). Add butter, and beat until pale and fluffy. Add egg yolks, 1 at time, beating well after each addition. Reduce speed to low. Add flour mixture, and beat just until smooth.

3. Divide dough into 3 portions. Pack 1 portion into a cookie press fitted with wreath disk (cover remaining portions with an inverted bowl or refrigerate in an airtight container for up to 3 days; bring to room temperature before using), and press shapes about 2 inches apart onto baking sheets. Bake until edges are just golden, 9 to 12 minutes.

4. Meanwhile, combine remaining 2 teaspoons cinnamon with remaining 4 teaspoons sugar. Sprinkle over hot cookies. Let cool on sheets on wire racks. Repeat. Cookies can be stored in a single layer in airtight containers at room temperature up to 4 days.

Bourbon Currant Cookies

Stack the deck in your favor by baking these unbeatable treats for your next get-together. Bourbon lends a pleasant bite that counteracts the sweet flavor of the currants. Other whiskeys can be substituted, if desired.

MAKES 6 DOZEN

- 1 cup (2 sticks) unsalted butter, room temperature
- 1 cup sugar
- 2 large eggs
- 3 cups sifted all-purpose flour, plus more for work surface
- ⅓ cup bourbon
- ½ cup dried currants
- ¼ cup heavy cream

1. Preheat oven to 350°F. Put butter and sugar in the bowl of an electric mixer fitted with the paddle attachment; mix on medium speed until smooth. Add 1 egg, the flour, bourbon, and currants; mix until well combined.

2. Roll out dough on a lightly floured work surface to ¼ inch thick. Cut into desired shapes (such as 2-inch card suit shapes). Whisk together remaining egg and the cream in a small bowl, and brush cookies with egg wash. Space 1 inch apart on baking sheets lined with parchment paper.

3. Bake until pale golden brown, 12 to 15 minutes. Let cool on sheets on wire racks. Cookies can be stored in airtight containers at room temperature up to 2 days.

Cocoa Shortbread Diamonds

To decorate, drizzle melted white chocolate over each cookie with a spoon, or use a resealable plastic bag with a snipped corner.

MAKES ABOUT 1 DOZEN

- 1 cup all-purpose flour, plus more for work surface
- ½ cup confectioners' sugar
- ¼ cup unsweetened Dutch-process cocoa powder
- ¼ teaspoon coarse salt
- ½ cup (1 stick) cold unsalted butter, cut into small pieces
- ½ teaspoon pure vanilla extract
- 2 ounces best-quality white chocolate, coarsely chopped

1. Preheat oven to 300°F. Pulse flour, confectioners' sugar, cocoa powder, and salt in a food processor to combine. Add butter and vanilla, and process until mixture comes together. Shape the dough into a ball.

2. Roll out dough on a lightly floured surface to ¼ inch thick; cut out shapes with a 3½ by 2½-inch diamond-shape cookie cutter. Space 1½ inches apart on baking sheets lined with parchment paper. Bake cookies until firm to the touch, 20 to 25 minutes, rotating sheets halfway through. Let cookies cool completely on wire racks.

3. Melt white chocolate, stirring, in a heatproof bowl set over a pan of simmering water. Drizzle chocolate over tops of cookies. Let set before serving, about 30 minutes. Cookies can be stored in a single layer in an airtight container at room temperature up to 3 days.

Cream Cheese–Lemon Bows

To make it easy to form these bow-shaped cookies, fill the pastry bag with dough in small batches; pipe two loops and then two tails rather than trying to pipe one continuous bow. Be sure all parts are touching so they bake together into one big cookie. MAKES ABOUT 1½ DOZEN

- 3 cups sifted all-purpose flour
- 1 teaspoon baking powder
- ¾ teaspoon coarse salt
- 1 cup (2 sticks) unsalted butter, room temperature
- 3 ounces cream cheese, room temperature
- 1 cup granulated sugar
- 1 large egg
- 2 teaspoons finely grated lemon zest
- 2 tablespoons fresh lemon juice
- Confectioners' sugar, for sprinkling

1. Sift together flour, baking powder, and salt into a bowl.

2. Put butter and cream cheese in the bowl of an electric mixer fitted with the paddle attachment; beat on medium speed until creamy. Mix in granulated sugar. Add egg, and lemon zest and juice; mix well. Reduce speed to low and mix in dry ingredients.

3. Preheat oven to 375°F. Transfer a small amount of dough to a pastry bag fitted with a large finely ribbed French tip (such as Ateco #865). Holding tip very close to the surface, pipe 3½-inch bows onto baking sheets lined with parchment paper, spacing 1 inch apart. Refill pastry bag as needed with remaining dough. Bake cookies until golden brown on bottom, about 12 minutes. Let cool completely on sheets on wire racks. Sprinkle with confectioners' sugar. Cookies can be stored in airtight containers at room temperature up to 3 days.

Cream Cheese-Walnut Cookies

At holiday time, package some of these buttery, nut-edged beauties in a pretty glass jar as a gift. The slice-and-bake dough can be shaped into logs and frozen for up to two weeks. MAKES ABOUT 4 DOZEN

- 4 cups all-purpose flour
- 1¼ teaspoons coarse salt
- 2 cups (4 sticks) unsalted butter, room temperature
- 6 ounces cream cheese (not whipped), room temperature
- 1¼ cups sugar
- 2 tablespoons plus ½ teaspoon pure vanilla extract
- 2½ cups walnut halves, 1½ cups toasted (see page 192) and coarsely chopped; 1 cup finely chopped

1. Whisk together flour and salt in a large bowl.

2. Put butter and cream cheese in the bowl of an electric mixer fitted with the paddle attachment. Mix on medium speed until pale and fluffy, about 2 minutes. Mix in sugar and vanilla. Reduce speed to low. Add flour mixture, and mix until just combined (do not overmix). Mix in toasted walnuts.

3. Transfer dough to a work surface. Divide in half; shape each half into an 8½-inch-long log about 2 inches in diameter. Wrap each log in parchment paper; freeze until firm, about 30 minutes or up to 2 weeks.

4. Preheat oven to 350°F with racks in upper and lower thirds. Unwrap one log, and roll in ½ cup chopped walnuts, coating completely. Cut into ¼-inch-thick rounds. Space 1 inch apart on baking sheets lined with parchment paper.

5. Bake cookies, rotating halfway through, until golden around edges, 18 to 20 minutes. Let cool on sheets on wire racks. Repeat with remaining log and remaining ½ cup chopped walnuts. Cookies can be stored in airtight containers at room temperature up to 3 days.

Cranberry-Pistachio Cornmeal Biscotti

Green pistachios and red cranberries combine to make a cookie perfect for Christmas. Cornmeal gives these biscotti an extra crumbly and sandy texture, while the dried cranberries add a chewy element. MAKES ABOUT 2 DOZEN

- 1¼ cups all-purpose flour
- 1¼ cups yellow cornmeal
- ½ teaspoon baking powder
- ½ teaspoon coarse salt
- 6 tablespoons unsalted butter, room temperature
- 1 cup sugar
- 2 large eggs
- 1 tablespoon finely grated lemon zest
- 1 cup dried cranberries
- 1 cup chopped pistachios

1. Preheat oven to 350°F with rack in center. Whisk together flour, cornmeal, baking powder, and salt.

2. Put butter in the bowl of an electric mixer fitted with the paddle attachment; mix on medium speed until smooth. Add sugar and mix until pale and fluffy. Mix in eggs one at a time, until well combined. Reduce speed to low. Add flour mixture all at once; mix until just combined. Add lemon zest, cranberries, and pistachios, and mix until combined.

3. Transfer dough to a baking sheet lined with parchment paper. Pat into a log that is roughly 14 by 3½ inches. Bake until firm, lightly browned, and slightly cracked on top, 30 to 35 minutes. Let cool on sheet on a wire rack, about 15 minutes.

4. Transfer log to a cutting board. Using a serrated knife, cut on the diagonal into ½-inch-thick slices. Arrange slices on a baking sheet lined with parchment. Bake cookies, rotating sheet halfway through, until they begin to brown at edges, 15 to 18 minutes. Let cool on sheet on a wire rack. Cookies can be stored in an airtight container at room temperature up to 2 weeks.

CRANBERRY-PISTACHIO CORNMEAL BISCOTTI, **opposite**

CHERRY ALMOND BISCOTTI, **page 162**

Cherry Almond Biscotti

Unlike many crumbly cookies, these biscotti are sturdy enough to mail. For a holiday gift, send a batch along with a pound of your favorite coffee beans. MAKES ABOUT 3 DOZEN

- 1¾ cups dried cherries
- ½ cup amaretto (almond-flavored liqueur), plus more if needed
- 3 cups all-purpose flour, plus more for work surface
- 2 teaspoons baking powder
- ½ teaspoon coarse salt
- 4 tablespoons (½ stick) unsalted butter, room temperature
- 1 cup granulated sugar
- 4 large eggs (3 whole, 1 lightly beaten)
- 2 teaspoons pure vanilla extract
- ¾ cup whole blanched almonds, chopped
- 3 tablespoons coarse sanding sugar

1. Preheat oven to 325°F. Heat cherries and liqueur in a small saucepan over medium-low heat, stirring occasionally, until cherries have softened, about 8 minutes. Drain, reserving 2 tablespoons liquid. If liquid equals less than 2 tablespoons, add enough liqueur to make 2 tablespoons.

2. Sift together flour, baking powder, and salt into a bowl. Put butter and granulated sugar in the bowl of an electric mixer fitted with the paddle attachment; mix on medium speed until fluffy, about 2 minutes. Mix in 3 whole eggs, one at a time. Mix in reserved cherry liquid and the vanilla. Reduce speed to low, and gradually mix in flour mixture. Stir in cherries and almonds.

3. On a lightly floured surface, halve dough. Shape each half into a 12½ by 2½-inch log. Flatten logs to ½ inch thick. Transfer to a baking sheet lined with parchment paper. Brush logs with beaten egg; sprinkle with the sanding sugar.

4. Bake 35 minutes, rotating sheets halfway through. Transfer to wire racks to cool, about 20 minutes. Reduce oven temperature to 300°F.

5. Cut each log on the diagonal into 16 to 18 pieces. Transfer pieces to racks, laying them on sides. Set racks on baking sheets. Bake 8 minutes; flip. Bake 8 minutes more. Let cool until crisp. Cookies can be stored in an airtight container at room temperature up to 1 week.

Giant Chocolate Sugar Cookies

These oversize sweets don't need any mix-ins or frostings—their bold chocolate flavor says it all. In addition to butter, this recipe calls for melted vegetable shortening, which produces an unbeatable texture. (Melted unsalted butter can be substituted for the shortening, if desired.) MAKES 8

- 1½ cups all-purpose flour
- ½ cup unsweetened Dutch-process cocoa powder
- 1 teaspoon baking powder
- ½ teaspoon salt
- ½ cup (1 stick) unsalted butter, room temperature
- 1½ cups sugar
- ½ cup vegetable shortening (or ½ cup unsalted butter), melted and cooled
- 1 large egg
- 1½ teaspoons pure vanilla extract

1. Preheat oven to 375°F. Whisk together flour, cocoa powder, baking powder, and salt in a bowl.

2. Put butter and sugar into the bowl of an electric mixer fitted with the paddle attachment. Mix on medium-high speed until pale and fluffy. Mix in melted shortening (or butter). Add egg and vanilla; mix until creamy. Reduce speed to low. Gradually add flour mixture, and mix until just combined.

3. Using a 2½-inch ice cream scoop, drop dough onto baking sheets lined with parchment paper, spacing about 4 inches apart. Bake until edges are firm, 18 to 20 minutes. Let cool on sheets on wire racks. Cookies can be stored in an airtight container at room temperature up to 2 days.

chunky *and* nutty

The recipes in this section are for people who love desserts with limitless possibilities. The simple combination of butter, flour, eggs, and sugar is usually what gives a cookie character, but here that quartet forms a delicious base for other ingredients. The resulting goodies can be as wholesome or decadent as desired. Top an almond-rich dough with blueberry jam and homemade granola, for example, and you have a lunch-box treat you can feel good about. Or try a batch of Rocky Ledge Bars, featuring two kinds of chocolate morsels, miniature marshmallows, butterscotch chips, and melted caramel candies. Feel free to experiment with other types of chocolate, chopped nuts, or dried fruits. After all, these are the cookies to bake when you just can't choose between favorites.

ROCKY LEDGE BARS, **page 166**

Rocky Ledge Bars

It's no wonder kids adore these bar cookies. A gooey topping spills over a base filled with butterscotch chips, miniature marshmallows, chocolate chunks, and—as if that weren't enough—melted caramels. MAKES ABOUT 16

- 2¼ cups all-purpose flour
- 2¼ teaspoons baking powder
- 1 teaspoon coarse salt
- ½ cup (1 stick) unsalted butter, room temperature, plus more for pan
- 1½ cups packed dark brown sugar
- 3 large eggs
- 1 teaspoon pure vanilla extract
- 1 cup miniature marshmallows
- 1 cup semisweet chocolate, coarsely chopped
- 1 cup white chocolate, coarsely chopped
- 1 cup butterscotch chips
- 18 soft caramel-candy cubes, coarsely chopped

1. Preheat oven to 350°F. Lightly butter a 9 by 13-inch baking pan. Line with parchment, allowing a 2-inch overhang on the longer sides. Brush parchment with butter (not overhang).

2. Whisk together flour, baking powder, and salt in a bowl. Using a wooden spoon, mix butter and brown sugar in a medium bowl until fluffy, about 2 minutes. Add eggs and vanilla; mix until well combined. Mix in flour mixture until combined. Fold in half of each of the marshmallows, chocolates, butterscotch chips, and caramels.

3. Spread batter in prepared pan. Scatter remaining marshmallows, chocolates, butterscotch chips, and caramels on top. Bake until top is golden brown and a cake tester inserted into center comes out clean, about 35 minutes. Let cool on a wire rack. Lift out of pan, and transfer to a baking sheet. Refrigerate until set, at least 30 minutes.

4. Remove parchment, and cut into about 16 triangles. Bars can be stored in an airtight container at room temperature up to 1 week.

Chocolate Chip Cookies for Passover

Matzo is an unleavened bread, made with flour and water and traditionally served during Passover; matzo farfel is made from dried noodles that are broken into small pieces. Both can be found in kosher sections of grocery stores. Vegetable oil is used in place of butter, to keep the cookies nondairy. MAKES 2 DOZEN

- 1 cup matzo meal
- 1 cup matzo farfel
- ¾ cup granulated sugar
- ¼ cup packed light brown sugar
- ¼ teaspoon salt
- 2 large eggs
- ½ cup vegetable oil
- 1 teaspoon pure vanilla extract
- 1 cup nondairy semisweet chocolate chips
- ½ cup chopped walnuts, toasted

1. Preheat oven to 350°F. Stir together matzo meal, farfel, sugars, and salt. Whisk together eggs, oil, and vanilla in a small bowl. Stir egg mixture into sugar mixture. Stir in chocolate chips and nuts.

2. Roll dough into 1¾-inch balls; space 2 inches apart on parchment paper–lined baking sheets. Bake until golden, 16 to 18 minutes, rotating sheets halfway through. Let cool on sheets on wire racks. Cookies can be stored in an airtight container at room temperature up to 3 days.

Ne Plus Ultra Cookies

Oversize and dense with chocolate chips, raisins, and pecans, these chunky treats might just be the ultimate cookies. The recipe has been a staff favorite since it first appeared in *Martha Stewart Living* in 1990.

MAKES ABOUT 1 DOZEN

- ½ cup (1 stick) unsalted butter, room temperature
- ⅔ cup packed dark brown sugar
- ¼ cup granulated sugar
- 1 teaspoon pure vanilla extract
- 2 large eggs
- 1¼ cups sifted all-purpose flour
- ½ teaspoon coarse salt
- ½ teaspoon baking soda
- 1 cup semisweet chocolate chips
- 1 cup raisins
- 1 cup pecans, coarsely chopped

1. Preheat oven to 350°F. Put butter and sugars in the bowl of an electric mixer fitted with the paddle attachment; mix on medium speed until pale and fluffy, about 3 minutes. Add vanilla and eggs; mix until well combined.

2. Sift flour, salt, and baking soda into a bowl; add to butter mixture on low speed until just combined. Stir in chocolate chips, raisins, and pecans.

3. Roll dough into 2½-inch balls, then flatten to 1-inch thick. Transfer to baking sheets lined with parchment paper, spacing 2 inches apart. Bake cookies until golden brown, about 20 minutes, rotating sheets halfway through. Let cool on sheets on wire racks. Cookies can be stored in an airtight container at room temperature up to 3 days.

Banana-Walnut Chocolate-Chunk Cookies

In one batch, find the flavors of two bakery classics: chocolate chip cookies and banana bread. Chopped walnuts and rolled oats add texture and more layers of taste. Use a ripe banana, which has more concentrated flavor, and is easier to mash, than an unripe one. MAKES ABOUT 3 DOZEN

- 1 cup all-purpose flour
- ½ cup whole wheat flour
- 1 teaspoon coarse salt
- ½ teaspoon baking soda
- ¾ cup (1½ sticks) unsalted butter, room temperature
- ½ cup granulated sugar
- ½ cup packed light brown sugar
- 1 large egg
- 1½ teaspoons pure vanilla extract
- ½ cup mashed ripe banana (about 1 large)
- 1 cup old-fashioned rolled oats
- 8 ounces semisweet chocolate, coarsely chopped into ¼-inch chunks
- ½ cup coarsely chopped walnuts (about 2 ounces), toasted (see page 192)

1. Preheat oven to 375°F. Whisk together both flours, salt, and baking soda in a bowl.

2. Put butter and both sugars into the bowl of an electric mixer fitted with the paddle attachment; mix on medium speed until pale and fluffy. Reduce speed to low. Add egg and vanilla; mix until combined. Mix in banana. Add flour mixture; mix until just combined. Stir in oats, chocolate chunks, and walnuts.

3. Using a 1½-inch ice cream scoop, drop dough onto baking sheets lined with parchment paper, spacing about 2 inches apart. Bake cookies, rotating sheets halfway through, until golden brown and just set, 12 to 13 minutes. Let cool on sheets on wire racks 5 minutes. Transfer cookies to wire racks; let cool completely. Cookies can be stored in airtight containers at room temperature up to 2 days.

White Chocolate-Chunk Cookies

A glass of milk is the ideal accompaniment to these drop cookies. Besides white chocolate, the cookies are also chockablock with oats, coconut, golden raisins, and walnuts. MAKES ABOUT 4 DOZEN

- 1 cup (2 sticks) unsalted butter, room temperature
- ½ cup granulated sugar
- ½ cup packed light brown sugar
- 2 large eggs
- 1 teaspoon pure vanilla extract
- 2 cups all-purpose flour
- 1 teaspoon baking soda
- ½ teaspoon baking powder
- ½ teaspoon coarse salt
- 2 cups old-fashioned rolled oats
- 2 cups good-quality white chocolate chunks
- 1 cup sweetened flaked coconut
- 1 cup golden raisins
- 1 cup coarsely chopped walnuts (about 4 ounces)

1. Preheat oven to 350°F. Put butter and sugars in the bowl of an electric mixer fitted with the paddle attachment. Mix on medium speed until smooth and creamy, about 2 minutes. Mix in eggs one at a time until combined. Stir in vanilla.

2. Sift flour, baking soda, baking powder, and salt into a medium bowl. Gradually stir into butter mixture until combined. Stir in oats, chocolate, coconut, raisins, and walnuts.

3. Drop batter by heaping tablespoons onto baking sheets lined with parchment paper, spacing about 2 inches apart. Flatten slightly. Bake cookies until golden, 16 to 18 minutes. Let cool on sheets on wire racks for 2 minutes. Transfer cookies to racks to cool completely. Cookies can be stored in airtight containers at room temperature up to 3 days.

Double Chocolate Coconut Cookies

The title refers to the cocoa powder and white chocolate in this recipe; the coconut and pecans lend additional chunky, nutty appeal. You can swap in hazelnuts, almonds, or pecans for some or all of the walnuts.

MAKES ABOUT 5 DOZEN

- 1 cup (2 sticks) unsalted butter, room temperature
- ½ cup granulated sugar
- ¾ cup packed light brown sugar
- 2 large eggs
- 1 teaspoon pure vanilla extract
- 1¾ cups all-purpose flour
- ¼ cup unsweetened Dutch-process cocoa powder
- 1 teaspoon baking soda
- ½ teaspoon baking powder
- ½ teaspoon coarse salt
- 2 cups white chocolate chunks (about 9 ounces)
- 1¾ cups sweetened flaked coconut
- 1¾ cups coarsely chopped walnuts (about 6 ounces)

1. Preheat oven to 350°F. Put butter and sugars in the bowl of an electric mixer fitted with the paddle attachment; mix on medium speed until smooth, about 2 minutes. Mix in eggs one at a time. Stir in vanilla.

2. Sift flour, cocoa powder, baking soda, baking powder, and salt into a bowl. Mix into butter mixture on low speed until well combined. Stir in chocolate, coconut, and walnuts.

3. Using a 1½-inch ice cream scoop, drop batter onto baking sheets lined with parchment paper, spacing 2 inches apart. Flatten slightly. Bake until set, 10 to 12 minutes. Let cool on sheets on wire racks 2 minutes. Transfer cookies on parchment to racks to cool completely. Cookies can be stored in airtight containers at room temperature up to 1 week.

Macadamia-Maple Sticky Bars

Layers of texture—crumbly shortbread and a chewy toffee-like topping—balance these indulgent nut bars. Diced candied ginger adds pleasantly surprising spice. MAKES 16

- ½ cup plus 6 tablespoons (1¾ sticks) unsalted butter, room temperature, plus more for pan
- 1¼ cups all-purpose flour
- ½ teaspoon salt
- ¾ cup coarsely chopped toasted (see note on page 148) macadamia nuts (about 4 ounces)
- ¼ cup plus 3 tablespoons packed light brown sugar
- 2 teaspoons pure maple syrup
- ¼ cup finely chopped candied ginger
- ¼ cup plus 1½ teaspoons maple sugar
- 2 tablespoons light corn syrup
- 3 tablespoons heavy cream

1. Preheat oven to 350°F. Butter an 8-inch square baking pan; line with parchment, allowing a 2-inch overhang on two sides. Butter lining (not overhang).

2. Whisk together flour, ¼ teaspoon salt, and ¼ cup nuts in a bowl.

3. Put ½ cup butter and ¼ cup brown sugar into the bowl of an electric mixer fitted with the paddle attachment; mix on medium speed until pale and fluffy. Mix in flour mixture and 1 teaspoon maple syrup. Press dough evenly into bottom of prepared dish. Refrigerate 30 minutes.

4. Bake until set in center and pale golden, 22 to 25 minutes. Transfer to a wire rack; let cool slightly.

5. Put remaining 6 tablespoons butter and ½ cup nuts into a small saucepan. Cook over medium-high heat, stirring constantly, until butter is very foamy and nuts are fragrant, 2 to 3 minutes. Add remaining ¼ teaspoon salt, 3 tablespoons brown sugar, 1 teaspoon maple syrup, and the ginger, maple sugar, corn syrup, and cream. Boil, stirring constantly, 2 minutes.

6. Spread over crust. Let cool completely. Run a knife around nonparchment sides; lift out of dish using overhang. Cut into sixteen 2-inch squares. Bars can be stored in an airtight container at room temperature up to 3 days.

Pine Nut Cookies

Pignoli, or pine nut, cookies are a specialty of many Italian bakeries and cafés. They make a perfect companion to an after-dinner espresso. The rich dough gets a boost from almond paste. MAKES ABOUT 3 DOZEN

- 2 cups pine nuts
- 1 cup confectioners' sugar
- ¼ cup almond paste
- 1 teaspoon pure vanilla extract
- 1 large egg
- ½ cup all-purpose flour
- ¼ teaspoon baking powder
- ¼ teaspoon coarse salt

1. Preheat oven to 350°F. Process ¾ cup pine nuts, the confectioners' sugar, almond paste, and vanilla in a food processor until fine crumbs form. Add egg; pulse to combine. Add flour, baking powder, and salt; process until dough just comes together.

2. Roll dough into ¾-inch balls. Roll balls in remaining 1¼ cups pine nuts, gently pressing to coat. Space 2 inches apart on baking sheets lined with parchment paper.

3. Bake cookies until golden brown, about 20 minutes, rotating sheets halfway through. Let cool completely on sheets on wire racks. Cookies can be stored in an airtight container at room temperature up to 3 days.

Chunky Peanut, Chocolate, and Cinnamon Cookies

Lucinda Scala Quinn, editorial director of food and entertaining for *Martha Stewart Living,* keeps this cookie dough on hand for casual get-togethers. After forming the dough into 1-inch balls, she flattens them slightly before freezing on cookie sheets until firm; the ready-to-bake pieces are then frozen in resealable plastic bags for up to one month. MAKES ABOUT 5 DOZEN

- 2 cups all-purpose flour
- 1 teaspoon baking soda
- 1 teaspoon salt
- ½ teaspoon ground cinnamon
- ¾ cup (1½ sticks) unsalted butter, room temperature
- ½ cup smooth peanut butter
- 1 cup packed light brown sugar
- ½ cup granulated sugar
- 2 large eggs
- 1½ cups semisweet chocolate chips
- ⅔ cup roasted, salted peanuts, coarsely chopped
- 2 teaspoons pure vanilla extract

1. Preheat oven to 350°F. Whisk together flour, baking soda, salt, and cinnamon in a bowl.

2. Put butter and peanut butter in the bowl of an electric mixer fitted with the paddle attachment; mix on medium speed until combined, about 2 minutes. Add sugars; mix 2 minutes. Mix in eggs. Gradually add flour mixture; mix until just combined. Fold in chocolate chips, peanuts, and vanilla until well distributed. Refrigerate dough until slightly firm, 15 minutes.

3. Roll dough into 1-inch balls. Space balls 2 to 3 inches apart on baking sheets lined with parchment paper. Flatten slightly. Bake until just golden, about 13 minutes, rotating sheets halfway through. Transfer cookies to wire racks to cool. Cookies can be stored in airtight containers at room temperature up to 3 days.

Magic Blondies

These single-serving goodies are kitchen wizardry: Blondie batter is tucked into cupcake liners, topped with a combination of coconut, chocolate chips, walnuts, and dried cherries, and baked until golden. MAKES 1 DOZEN

- 2/3 cup sweetened flaked coconut
- 2/3 cup semisweet chocolate chips
- 2/3 cup chopped walnuts (about 2½ ounces)
- 2/3 cup dried cherries or cranberries
- 1⅔ cups all-purpose flour
- 1 teaspoon baking powder
- ¾ teaspoon coarse salt
- 9 tablespoons (1 stick plus 1 tablespoon) unsalted butter, room temperature
- 1 cup packed light brown sugar
- 2 large eggs
- 1 teaspoon pure vanilla extract

1. Preheat oven to 350°F. Line a standard 12-cup muffin tin with paper liners. Stir together coconut, chocolate, walnuts, and cherries in a bowl. Whisk together flour, baking powder, and salt in another bowl.

2. Put butter and brown sugar in the bowl of an electric mixer fitted with the paddle attachment; mix on medium speed until pale and fluffy, about 3 minutes. Add eggs and vanilla; mix until combined. Reduce speed to low. Add flour mixture, and mix, scraping down sides of bowl, until well combined. Mix in 1 cup coconut mixture.

3. Divide batter among muffin cups, filling each about three-quarters full. Sprinkle remaining coconut mixture over tops. Bake until a cake tester inserted into center comes out with a few crumbs but is not wet, about 25 minutes. Transfer to a wire rack; let cool completely. Blondies can be stored in an airtight container at room temperature up to 2 days.

Fruit and Nut Cookies

Stash a few of these hearty cookies into a backpack on your next hiking trip. They are packed with wholesome dried fruits and nuts. For variety, try other combinations of dried fruit and nuts: Bananas, mangoes, and macadamias lend a tropical note; hazelnuts and pecans go well with figs, pears, and cranberries. MAKES ABOUT 3 DOZEN

- 2¼ cups all-purpose flour
- 1 teaspoon baking soda
- 1 teaspoon coarse salt
- 1 cup (2 sticks) unsalted butter, room temperature
- 1 cup packed light brown sugar
- ½ cup granulated sugar
- 2 large eggs
- 1 teaspoon pure vanilla extract
- 1½ cups sweetened shredded coconut
- 1½ cups chopped dried apricots
- 1½ cups chopped dates
- 1½ cups chopped macadamia nuts
- 1½ cups chopped pistachios

1. Preheat oven to 350°F. Whisk together flour, baking soda, and salt in a bowl.

2. Put butter in the bowl of an electric mixer fitted with the paddle attachment; mix on medium speed until smooth. Add sugars, and mix until pale and fluffy, about 3 minutes. Mix in eggs one at a time until combined; mix in vanilla.

3. Reduce mixer speed to low. Add flour mixture and mix until just combined. Stir in coconut, apricots, dates, macadamias, and pistachios.

4. Drop batter, 2 heaping tablespoons at a time, onto baking sheets lined with parchment paper, spacing 2 inches apart. Flatten slightly. Bake cookies until golden brown, 12 to 15 minutes, rotating sheets halfway through. Transfer on parchment to a wire rack to cool. Cookies can be stored in airtight containers at room temperature up to 3 days.

Peanut Butter Cookies

Recipes for peanut butter cookies abound, but this one packs a particularly powerful punch. The dough is studded with whole salted peanuts for extra crunch. Sandwich a few with jelly for an afternoon snack. Or embellish them instead by piping melted semisweet chocolate into the lines of the cross-hatch pattern. MAKES 2½ DOZEN

- 1¼ cups all-purpose flour, plus more for flattening cookies
- ¾ teaspoon baking soda
- 1 cup (2 sticks) unsalted butter, room temperature
- ½ cup granulated sugar
- ½ cup packed light brown sugar
- 1 large egg
- ½ teaspoon pure vanilla extract
- 1 cup smooth peanut butter
- ½ cup salted peanuts

1. Preheat oven to 350°F. Sift flour and baking soda into a bowl.

2. Put butter and both sugars in the bowl of an electric mixer fitted with the paddle attachment; mix on medium speed until pale and fluffy, about 3 minutes. Add egg; mix until well combined. Mix in vanilla and then peanut butter. Reduce speed to low. Add flour mixture; mix until just combined. Stir in peanuts.

3. Drop batter by heaping tablespoons onto baking sheets lined with parchment paper, spacing 1½ inches apart. Dip the bottom of a glass in flour, tapping off excess, and use it to flatten balls slightly. Firmly press fork tines into each dough ball to make a cross-hatch pattern.

4. Bake cookies, rotating sheets halfway through, until centers are firm and edges are lightly browned, about 25 minutes. Transfer cookies on parchment to a wire rack to cool completely. Cookies can be stored in airtight containers at room temperature up to 3 days.

PEANUT BUTTER COOKIES, **opposite**

BLUEBERRY BONANZA BARS, **page 186**

Blueberry Bonanza Bars

This chunky bar cookie recipe presents a perfect opportunity for improvisation, as you can use whatever flavors of jam and granola you have on hand. MAKES 2 DOZEN

- ½ cup slivered almonds, toasted (see page 192)
- 2 cups all-purpose flour
- ¾ cup confectioners' sugar
- 1½ teaspoons baking powder
- ½ teaspoon coarse salt
- ¾ cup (1½ sticks) unsalted butter, cold, cut into pieces
- 1 large egg plus 1 large egg yolk
- ¾ teaspoon pure vanilla extract
- 1½ cups blueberry jam
- Almond-Coconut Granola (recipe follows)
- Vegetable oil cooking spray

1. Line a 9 by 13-inch baking pan with foil, allowing a 2-inch overhang. Coat with cooking spray.

2. Process almonds in a food processor until finely ground. Add flour, confectioners' sugar, baking powder, and salt; pulse to combine. Add butter; process until mixture resembles coarse meal.

3. Lightly beat egg, egg yolk, and vanilla in a small bowl. With processor running, add egg mixture; process just until clumps form. Pat dough into bottom of dish; refrigerate until firm and cold, about 30 minutes.

4. Preheat oven to 350°F. Prick dough all over with a fork. Bake until edges are golden, about 25 minutes. Let cool on a wire rack.

5. Spread jam over crust; top with granola. Bake until jam is bubbling and granola topping is browned, about 30 minutes. Let cool on wire rack. Lift out, and cut into 2-inch squares. Bars can be stored in airtight containers at room temperature up to 1 day or frozen up to 1 week.

ALMOND-COCONUT GRANOLA

MAKES ABOUT 5 CUPS

- 4 tablespoons unsalted butter
- ¼ cup honey
- ½ cup packed light brown sugar
- 2 tablespoons water
- 3 cups old-fashioned rolled oats
- ⅔ cup slivered almonds
- ½ cup sweetened shredded coconut

Preheat oven to 325°F. Melt butter with honey in a small saucepan over low heat. Add brown sugar; stir until dissolved, about 2 minutes. Remove from heat, and stir in the water. Stir together oats, almonds, and coconut in a large bowl. Pour butter mixture over oat mixture; stir until combined. Evenly spread out granola on a large rimmed baking sheet. Bake, stirring frequently, until golden brown, 25 to 30 minutes. Let cool completely on sheet on a wire rack. Granola can be stored in an airtight container at room temperature up to 2 weeks.

Turtle Brownies

A moist, chocolaty brownie topped with caramel and nuts brings together the classic components of turtle candies. MAKES 16

for the batter:

- 4 tablespoons (½ stick) unsalted butter, plus more for the pan
- 3 ounces good-quality unsweetened chocolate, coarsely chopped
- ½ cup all-purpose flour
- ¼ teaspoon baking powder
- ½ teaspoon coarse salt
- 1 cup sugar
- 2 large eggs
- ¼ cup whole milk
- 1 teaspoon pure vanilla extract

for the topping:

- 1 cup sugar
- ⅓ cup water
- ⅓ cup heavy cream
- 1 teaspoon pure vanilla extract
- ½ teaspoon coarse salt
- 1 cup coarsely chopped toasted (see page 192) pecans (about 4 ounces)

1. Preheat oven to 325°F. Line a buttered 8-inch square baking pan with parchment, allowing a 2-inch overhang. Butter lining (not overhang).

2. Make batter: Put chocolate and butter in a heatproof bowl set over a pan of simmering water; stir until melted. Let cool slightly. Whisk together flour, baking powder, and salt in another bowl.

3. Put sugar and eggs in the bowl of an electric mixer fitted with the whisk attachment, and beat on medium speed until pale and fluffy, about 4 minutes. Add chocolate mixture, milk, and vanilla, and mix until combined. Reduce speed to low. Add flour mixture; mix, scraping down sides of bowl as needed, until well combined.

4. Pour batter into prepared dish. Bake until a cake tester inserted into center of brownies comes out with a few crumbs but is not wet, 27 to 30 minutes. Let cool on a wire rack.

5. Make topping: Bring sugar and the water to a boil in a medium saucepan over medium-high heat, stirring, until sugar has dissolved. When mixture comes to a boil, stop stirring, and wash down sides of pan with a wet pastry brush to prevent crystals from forming. Continue to cook, swirling pan occasionally, until medium amber, 5 to 7 minutes.

6. Remove from heat and immediately add cream, vanilla, and salt. Gently stir with a wooden spoon or heatproof spatula until smooth. Add pecans; stir until caramel begins to cool and thickens slightly, about 1 minute.

7. Pour caramel over cool brownies; spread with an offset spatula. Refrigerate until cold, 30 minutes to 1 hour.

8. Let brownies stand at room temperature at least 15 minutes before serving. Lift out, and cut into 16 squares, wiping knife with a hot, damp cloth between each cut. Brownies can be refrigerated in an airtight container up to 2 days.

cakey *and* tender

The word *cookie* comes from the Dutch *koekje,* which means "little cake," and the tender selections in this category live up to their name. Like most full-size cakes, these are usually best enjoyed the same day you bake them. The springy texture is partially achieved by blending wet and dry ingredients separately, then mixing them together until just combined. A madeleine is the best example of this method; its airy quality is gained by beating melted butter, sugar, eggs, and liquid together, then gently folding in flour and leavening. These mini-cakes are wonderful on their own, but if you wish, you can decorate them just as you would a large one: Layer them, top them with swirls of creamy frosting, or leave them unadorned but for a simple dusting of powdered sugar.

LEMON MADELEINES, **page 190**

Lemon Madeleines

Like little cakes with a citrus perfume, these shell-shape treats are equally delightful as a light dessert with fresh fruit or as an accompaniment to a cup of tea. Madeleines are most often associated with the French author Marcel Proust, who immortalized them in the opening scene of the novel *Remembrance of Things Past*. MAKES 2 DOZEN

- 1½ cups sifted cake flour (not self-rising)
- ½ teaspoon baking powder
- ¼ teaspoon coarse salt
- 3 large eggs plus 2 large egg yolks
- ¾ cup granulated sugar
- 1 teaspoon pure vanilla extract
- 2 tablespoons finely grated lemon zest
- 2 tablespoons fresh lemon juice
- ¾ cup (1½ sticks) unsalted butter, melted, plus more for pans
- Confectioners' sugar, for dusting (optional)

1. Sift together flour, baking powder, and salt into a bowl.

2. Put eggs, egg yolks, granulated sugar, vanilla, and lemon zest and juice in the bowl of an electric mixer fitted with the paddle attachment. Mix on medium-high speed until pale and thickened, about 5 minutes. Mix in butter. Using a spatula, fold flour mixture into egg mixture. Let batter rest 30 minutes.

3. Preheat oven to 350°F. Butter two madeleine pans.

4. Pour batter into prepared pans, filling the molds three-quarters full. Bake cookies, rotating pans halfway through, until edges are crisp and golden, 7 to 8 minutes. Let cookies cool slightly in pans on wire racks. Invert, and unmold. Dust with confectioners' sugar, if desired. Cookies can be stored between layers of parchment in airtight containers at room temperature up to 1 day.

Gingerbread-White Chocolate Blondies

These moist, relatively thin blondies burst with gingerbread spices and white chocolate chunks. MAKES 4 DOZEN

- 2¾ cups plus 1 tablespoon all-purpose flour
- 1¼ teaspoons baking soda
- 1¼ teaspoons salt
- 1¼ teaspoons ground cinnamon
- 1 teaspoon ground ginger
- ¼ teaspoon ground cloves
- 1¼ cups (2½ sticks) unsalted butter, room temperature
- 1¼ cups packed light brown sugar
- ½ cup plus 2 tablespoons granulated sugar
- 2 large eggs plus 1 egg yolk
- 1¼ teaspoons pure vanilla extract
- ⅓ cup unsulfured molasses
- 1¾ cups coarsely chopped best-quality white chocolate (10 ounces)
- Nonstick vegetable oil spray

1. Preheat oven to 350°F. Coat a 12 by 17-inch rimmed baking sheet with nonstick spray and line the bottom with parchment paper. Spray the parchment and set aside.

2. Whisk together flour, soda, salt, and spices in a bowl.

3. In the bowl of an electric mixer fitted with the paddle attachment, beat butter and sugars on medium-high speed until creamy and pale, about 3 minutes. Add eggs and yolk one at a time, scraping down sides of bowl as needed. Add vanilla and molasses and mix on medium speed until combined. Add flour mixture on low speed until combined. Stir in white chocolate.

4. Spread batter evenly into prepared pan and bake until golden on edges, about 25 minutes. Let cool completely in pan; cut into 2-inch squares. Blondies can be stored in airtight containers at room temperature up to 1 week.

Lebkuchen

Lebkuchen are traditional German Christmas cookies, spiced with the flavors of gingerbread, studded with candied citrus peel, and topped with a sweet sugar-and-milk glaze. To toast nuts, spread them in a single layer on a rimmed baking sheet, and bake in a 350°F oven for about ten minutes. MAKES ABOUT 1½ DOZEN

for the cookies:

- ¾ cup all-purpose flour
- ½ teaspoon baking powder
- ¼ teaspoon salt
- ½ teaspoon ground cinnamon
- ½ teaspoon ground ginger
- ¼ teaspoon ground cloves
- ½ teaspoon mace
- 1¾ ounces blanched whole almonds, toasted (⅓ cup), plus more untoasted for decorating
- 1½ ounces blanched hazelnuts, toasted (¼ cup)
- ⅓ cup diced good-quality candied orange peel
- ⅓ cup diced good-quality candied lemon peel
- 4 Medjool dates, pitted and finely chopped
- 3 ounces almond paste, broken into small pieces
- ⅓ cup apricot jam
- 3 large eggs
- ¾ cup packed light brown sugar

for the glaze:

- ½ cup plus 3 tablespoons confectioners' sugar
- 2 tablespoons whole milk

1. Make cookies: Whisk together flour, baking powder, salt, cinnamon, ginger, cloves, and mace in a bowl. Place almonds and hazelnuts in the bowl of a food processor. Pulse until very finely chopped. Add peels and dates and pulse until finely chopped. Add almond paste and pulse to combine. Add jam and pulse to combine. Add eggs and brown sugar and pulse to combine. Add dry ingredients; pulse to combine. Cover mixture and refrigerate overnight or up to 3 days.

2. Preheat oven to 325°F. Using a 2-inch ice cream scoop, scoop mounds onto baking sheets lined with a nonstick baking mat (such as Silpat). Place 3 almonds close together on top of each cookie (they will spread while baking). Bake until golden brown, about 14 minutes, rotating sheets halfway through. Let cool completely on sheets on a wire rack.

3. Make glaze: Mix confectioners' sugar and milk in a small bowl. Brush all over tops of cookies and let set. Cookies can be stored in an airtight container at room temperature up to 3 days.

Surprise Cookies

Some of the same ingredients used for hot chocolate go right into these crowd pleasers. Cocoa powder gives them their chocolate flavor, while marshmallows are the squishy centers. Slathered on top is a chocolate frosting that hides the marshmallow—creating a delightful surprise for the lucky person who takes a bite. MAKES 2½ DOZEN

for the cookies:

- 1¾ cups all-purpose flour
- ¾ cup unsweetened cocoa powder (not Dutch-process)
- ½ teaspoon baking soda
- ½ teaspoon coarse salt
- ½ cup (1 stick) unsalted butter, room temperature
- 1 cup granulated sugar
- 1 large egg
- ½ cup whole milk
- 1 teaspoon pure vanilla extract
- About 15 marshmallows, halved crosswise

for the frosting:

- 3 cups confectioners' sugar
- 6 tablespoons unsalted butter, room temperature
- ¼ cup plus 1½ teaspoons unsweetened cocoa powder (not Dutch-process)
- ¼ cup plus 2 tablespoons whole milk
- ¾ teaspoon pure vanilla extract

1. Preheat the oven to 375°F. Make cookies: Sift together flour, cocoa powder, baking soda, and salt into a bowl.

2. Put butter and sugar into the bowl of an electric mixer fitted with the paddle attachment. Mix on medium-high speed until pale and fluffy, about 2 minutes. Reduce speed to medium-low; mix in egg, milk, and vanilla. Mix in flour mixture, ½ cup at a time, until combined.

3. Using a 1¾-inch ice cream scoop, drop dough onto baking sheets lined with parchment paper, spacing 2 inches apart. Bake cookies, rotating sheets halfway through, until firm, 8 to 10 minutes. Immediately press a marshmallow half on top of each cookie. Bake until marshmallows begin to melt, 2 minutes more. Let cool completely on sheets on wire racks.

4. Make frosting: Put confectioners' sugar in a medium bowl. Melt butter with the cocoa powder in a saucepan over medium-low heat, stirring occasionally. Add butter mixture to the confectioners' sugar. Whisk in milk and vanilla.

5. Spread about 1 tablespoon of frosting on top of each cookie to cover marshmallow. Let stand until set, about 10 minutes. Cookies can be stored in single layers in airtight containers at room temperature up to 2 days.

PUMPKIN COOKIES WITH BROWN-BUTTER ICING, **opposite**

CAKEY CHOCOLATE CHIP COOKIES, **page 198**

Pumpkin Cookies with Brown-Butter Icing

You're guaranteed to get a bit of brown butter–flecked icing in every bite of these pillowy spice cookies. Offer them at a Halloween party or as part of a Thanksgiving dessert buffet. MAKES ABOUT 6 DOZEN

for the cookies:

- 2¾ cups all-purpose flour
- 1 teaspoon baking powder
- 1 teaspoon baking soda
- 1¼ teaspoons coarse salt
- 1½ teaspoons ground cinnamon
- 1¼ teaspoons ground ginger
- ¾ teaspoon freshly grated nutmeg
- ¾ cup (1½ sticks) unsalted butter, room temperature
- 2¼ cups packed light brown sugar
- 2 large eggs
- 1½ cups canned solid-pack pumpkin (14 ounces)
- ¾ cup evaporated milk
- 1 teaspoon pure vanilla extract

for the icing:

- 4 cups confectioners' sugar, sifted
- 10 tablespoons (1¼ sticks) unsalted butter
- ¼ cup plus 1 tablespoon evaporated milk, plus more if needed
- 2 teaspoons pure vanilla extract

1. Preheat the oven to 375°F. Make cookies: Whisk together flour, baking powder, baking soda, salt, cinnamon, ginger, and nutmeg in a bowl.

2. Put butter and brown sugar in the bowl of an electric mixer fitted with the paddle attachment. Beat on medium speed until pale and fluffy, about 3 minutes. Mix in eggs. Reduce speed to low. Add pumpkin, evaporated milk, and vanilla; mix until well blended, about 2 minutes. Add flour mixture; mix until combined.

3. Transfer 1½ cups batter to a pastry bag fitted with a ½-inch plain tip (such as Ateco #806). Pipe 1½-inch rounds onto parchment paper–lined baking sheets, spacing 1 inch apart. Bake cookies, rotating sheets halfway through, until tops spring back, about 12 minutes. Cool on sheets on wire racks 5 minutes. Transfer cookies to wire racks; let cool completely.

4. Make icing: Put confectioners' sugar in a bowl. Melt butter in a small saucepan over medium heat. Cook, swirling pan occasionally, until golden brown, about 3 minutes. Immediately add butter to confectioners' sugar, scraping any browned bits from sides and bottom of pan. Add evaporated milk and vanilla; stir until smooth.

5. Spread about 1 teaspoon icing onto each cookie. If icing stiffens, stir in more evaporated milk, a little at a time. Cookies can be stored in single layers in airtight containers at room temperature up to 3 days.

Cakey Chocolate Chip Cookies

Incorporating less butter and brown sugar into the batter yields cookies that are thicker and fluffier than other chocolate chip cookies, with just as many chips—and just as much appeal. MAKES 3 DOZEN

- 2¼ cups all-purpose flour
- ½ teaspoon baking soda
- 14 tablespoons (1¾ sticks) unsalted butter, room temperature
- ¾ cup granulated sugar
- ¼ cup packed light brown sugar
- 1 teaspoon coarse salt
- 2 teaspoons pure vanilla extract
- 2 large eggs
- 2 cups semisweet or milk chocolate chips, or a combination of both (12 ounces)

1. Preheat oven to 350°F. Whisk together flour and baking soda in a bowl.

2. Put butter and both sugars in the bowl of an electric mixer fitted with the paddle attachment. Beat on medium speed until pale and fluffy, about 2 minutes. Reduce speed to low. Add salt, vanilla, and eggs; mix until combined, about 1 minute. Add flour mixture; mix until just combined. Stir in chocolate chips.

3. Drop heaping tablespoons of dough onto baking sheets lined with parchment paper, spacing 2 inches apart. Bake cookies until centers are set and edges are golden, 10 to 12 minutes, rotating sheets halfway through. Let cool on baking sheets 2 minutes. Transfer cookies to wire racks; let cool completely. Cookies can be stored in airtight containers at room temperature up to 1 week.

Raspberry Almond Blondies

A generous topping of fresh berries and toasted almond slices embellishes these basic blondies. MAKES 16

- 9 tablespoons (1 stick plus 1 tablespoon) unsalted butter, room temperature, plus more for pan
- 1⅔ cups all-purpose flour
- 1 teaspoon baking powder
- ¾ teaspoon coarse salt
- 1 cup packed light brown sugar
- 2 large eggs
- 1 teaspoon pure vanilla extract
- 1 cup sliced almonds (about 3 ounces), toasted
- 2⅔ cups raspberries

1. Preheat oven to 325°F. Butter an 8-inch square baking pan. Line with parchment paper, allowing 2 inches to hang over two sides. Butter parchment.

2. Whisk together flour, baking powder, and salt in a bowl.

3. Put butter and brown sugar in the bowl of an electric mixer fitted with the paddle attachment. Mix on medium speed until pale and fluffy, about 3 minutes. Add eggs and vanilla; mix until combined. Reduce speed to low. Add flour mixture; mix until combined. Mix in ¾ cup almonds.

4. Pour batter into prepared dish; smooth top. Scatter berries and remaining ¼ cup almonds over batter. Bake, rotating dish halfway through, until a cake tester inserted into center comes out with moist crumbs, 55 to 60 minutes.

5. Let blondies cool 15 minutes. Transfer blondies to a wire rack, and let cool completely. Cut into 2-inch squares. Blondies can be stored in single layers in airtight containers at room temperature up to 3 days.

Pear, Pistachio, and Ginger Blondies

Blondies are usually baked in a square or rectangular pan and cut into bars. Here we've used a springform pan to bake a round that's then cut into wedges. The familiar flavor is made even more irresistible with the spice of candied ginger, the sweetness of dried pears, and the crunch of pistachios. MAKES ABOUT 1 DOZEN

- 9 tablespoons (1 stick plus 1 tablespoon) unsalted butter, room temperature, plus more for pan
- 1⅔ cups all-purpose flour
- 1 teaspoon baking powder
- ¾ teaspoon coarse salt
- 1 cup packed light brown sugar
- 2 large eggs
- 1 teaspoon pure vanilla extract
- ¾ cup coarsely chopped dried pears (4 ounces)
- ¾ cup shelled pistachios, coarsely chopped (3¼ ounces)
- ¼ cup coarsely chopped candied ginger (1¼ ounces)

1. Preheat oven to 325°F. Butter a 9-inch springform or round cake pan. Line bottom with parchment paper; butter parchment.

2. Whisk together flour, baking powder, and salt in a bowl. Put butter and brown sugar in the bowl of an electric mixer fitted with the paddle attachment. Mix on medium speed until pale and fluffy, about 3 minutes. Add eggs and vanilla; mix until combined. Reduce speed to low; mix in flour mixture until combined. Mix in pears, pistachios, and candied ginger.

3. Pour batter into prepared pan; smooth top. Bake, rotating pan halfway through, until a cake tester inserted into center comes out clean, about 50 minutes. Let cool on a wire rack 15 minutes. Remove side of springform (or invert pan if using a cake pan). Transfer to a wire rack and let cool completely. Cut into wedges. Blondies can be stored between layers of parchment in airtight containers at room temperature up to 3 days.

Carrot Cake Cookies

These are like tiny inside-out carrot cakes, with the signature cream cheese frosting on the inside and spiced "cake" on the outside.

MAKES ABOUT 3 DOZEN

- 1 cup (2 sticks) unsalted butter, room temperature
- 1 cup packed light brown sugar
- 1 cup granulated sugar
- 2 large eggs, room temperature
- 1 teaspoon pure vanilla extract
- 2 cups all-purpose flour, plus more for flattening cookies
- 1 teaspoon baking soda
- 1 teaspoon baking powder
- ¼ teaspoon salt
- 1 teaspoon ground cinnamon
- ½ teaspoon freshly grated nutmeg
- ½ teaspoon ground ginger
- 2 cups old-fashioned rolled oats
- 1½ cups finely grated carrots (about 3 large carrots)
- 1 cup raisins
- Cream Cheese Frosting (recipe follows)

1. Line two baking sheets with parchment paper. In an electric mixer fitted with the paddle attachment, beat butter and both sugars on medium speed until light and fluffy, 3 to 4 minutes. Add eggs and vanilla, and beat on medium speed until well combined.

2. Sift together flour, baking soda, baking powder, salt, cinnamon, nutmeg, and ginger; stir to combine. Gradually add flour mixture to butter mixture; mix on low speed until just blended. Mix in oats, carrots, and raisins. Chill until firm, at least 1 hour.

3. Preheat oven to 350°F. Shape tablespoons of dough into balls, and place on prepared baking sheets, spacing 2 inches apart.

4. Bake until browned and crisp, 12 to 15 minutes, rotating halfway through. Transfer to a wire rack to cool completely. Using an offset spatula, spread about 2 teaspoons of frosting onto flat sides of half the cookies. Sandwich together with remaining cookies. Cookies can be refrigerated in airtight containers up to 3 days.

CREAM CHEESE FROSTING

- 8 ounces cream cheese, room temperature
- ½ cup (1 stick) unsalted butter, room temperature
- 1 cup confectioners' sugar
- 1 teaspoon pure vanilla extract

Place cream cheese in a mixing bowl. Using a rubber spatula, beat cream cheese until smooth. Gradually add butter and continue beating until smooth and well blended. Sift in confectioners' sugar and continue beating until smooth. Add vanilla and stir to combine.

Raspberry Honey Financiers

For a twist on the traditional French petit fours known as *financiers,* we baked these cookie "cakes" in mini-muffin tins instead of small rectangular pans. They have a nutty, buttery flavor with floral hints of honey. Tiny raspberry heart decorations make them an appropriate gift for Valentine's Day. MAKES ABOUT 4 DOZEN

- ½ cup unsalted butter (1 stick), cut into small pieces
- ⅓ cup mild honey
- 2 cups blanched sliced almonds, lightly toasted and finely ground
- ½ cup granulated sugar
- ¼ cup confectioners' sugar, sifted
- ¾ cup cake flour (not self-rising), sifted
- ½ teaspoon salt
- 5 large egg whites
- 1 cup fresh raspberries (or thawed frozen raspberries), pureed and strained
- Nonstick cooking spray, for tins

1. Preheat oven to 350°F. Coat nonstick mini-muffin tins (each cup should have a 1-ounce capacity) with cooking spray.

2. In a small saucepan, melt the butter over medium-low heat, whisking frequently, until it is golden brown, 6 to 7 minutes. Carefully pour in the honey, whisking to combine completely, then remove from the heat; keep warm.

3. Put the ground almonds, both sugars, cake flour, and salt in the bowl of an electric mixer fitted with the whisk attachment. Mix on low speed until combined. Add the egg whites one at a time on medium-high speed, beating well after each addition and scraping down the sides of the bowl as necessary. On low speed, add the warm honey mixture in a thin stream; mix on high speed until blended, about 45 seconds.

4. Spoon batter into the prepared muffin tins, filling them about half full (you will need about 1 tablespoon batter for each). Spoon a small dollop of raspberry puree along one side of the batter. Using the tip of a wooden skewer or the sharp point of a paring knife, draw through the middle of the puree from the top of the dollop to the other side of the batter to make a heart shape.

5. Bake until the edges are golden brown, 15 to 20 minutes, rotating pan halfway through. Transfer muffin pans to a wire rack to cool for 5 minutes. Using a small offset spatula, loosen financiers around the edges and transfer to a wire rack to cool slightly. These are best served warm from the oven, or at least the same day baked. However, they can be stored in an airtight container at room temperature up to 3 days.

Peanut Butter Whoopie Pies

The origins of the whoopie pie remain a mystery, but many believe that the cookie, a specialty of Pennsylvania Dutch country and parts of New England, was created when leftover cake batter was baked, iced, and sandwiched as a treat for children. We used a peanut butter filling, but substitute Seven-Minute Frosting (recipe below) if you prefer. MAKES ABOUT 3 DOZEN

for the cookies:

- 3½ cups all-purpose flour
- 1½ cups unsweetened cocoa powder
- 1 tablespoon baking soda
- 1 teaspoon baking powder
- 1 teaspoon salt
- 2 sticks (1 cup) unsalted butter, room temperature
- 2 cups sugar
- 2 large eggs
- 2 cups buttermilk, room temperature
- 2 teaspoons pure vanilla extract

for the filling:

- 1⅓ cup natural, creamy peanut butter
- 1 cup (2 sticks) unsalted butter, room temperature
- 1½ cups confectioners' sugar
- Coarse salt (optional)

1. Preheat oven to 400°F. Make cookies: Line two rimmed baking sheets with nonstick baking mats (such as Silpats), or with parchment. Sift together flour, cocoa powder, baking soda, baking powder, and salt. With an electric mixer, beat butter and sugar on medium speed until light and fluffy. Add eggs, buttermilk, and vanilla. Beat until well combined. On low speed, slowly add dry ingredients; mix until combined.

2. Drop 1½ tablespoons of batter onto prepared baking sheets, spacing 2 inches apart. Bake until set, about 8 minutes, rotating halfway through. (When the top of a cookie is gently touched, it should feel soft but not wet.) Cool completely on a wire rack.

3. Make filling: With an electric mixer, beat peanut butter and butter on high speed until smooth. Reduce speed to low. Add confectioners' sugar; mix until combined. Raise speed to high, and mix until fluffy and smooth, about 3 minutes. Season with salt, if desired.

4. Assemble cookies: Spread 1 heaping tablespoon filling on the flat side of 1 cookie. Sandwich with another cookie. Repeat with remaining cookies and filling. Cookies can be refrigerated in single layers in airtight containers up to 3 days. Bring to room temperature before serving.

SEVEN-MINUTE FROSTING

Timing is key, so have everything you need ready, and start whisking egg whites once the syrup is at a full boil.

- 1 cup plus 1 tablespoon sugar
- 1 teaspoon light corn syrup
- ½ cup water
- 4 large egg whites
- ½ teaspoon pure vanilla extract

In a small, heavy saucepan over medium heat, combine 1 cup sugar, the corn syrup, and the water; bring to a boil, washing down sides of the pan with a pastry brush dipped in water. Raise heat to medium-high. Cook without stirring until a candy thermometer reaches 230°F. Meanwhile, with an electric mixer, beat egg whites on medium speed until soft peaks form. Gradually add remaining tablespoon sugar, and beat until peaks are very fluffy but still soft. When the syrup reaches 230°F, reduce mixer speed to medium-low; pour syrup in a steady stream down the sides of the bowl. Increase speed to medium-high, and beat until cool, about 7 minutes. Add vanilla, and beat until fully incorporated. The frosting should be shiny and fluffy and hold stiff peaks. Use immediately.

Brown-Butter Toffee Blondies

Brown butter is simply butter that has been cooked until it takes on a delicious, subtle nutty flavor and aroma—which explains its French name, *beurre noisette,* or "hazelnut butter." Be sure to keep an eye on it as it cooks, to avoid burning. MAKES ABOUT 1 DOZEN

- 1¼ cups (2½ sticks) unsalted butter, plus more for pan
- 2¼ cups all-purpose flour, plus more for pan
- 1½ teaspoons baking powder
- 1½ teaspoons salt
- 2 cups packed light brown sugar
- ½ cup granulated sugar
- 3 large eggs
- 2½ teaspoons pure vanilla extract
- 1 cup chopped walnuts (about 4 ounces)
- 1 cup toffee bits

1. Preheat oven to 350°F. Butter a 9 by 13-inch baking pan. Line bottom of pan with parchment; butter and flour parchment.

2. In a saucepan over medium heat, cook the butter until it turns golden brown; remove from heat, and let cool. Whisk together flour, baking powder, and salt.

3. In the bowl of an electric mixer, combine browned butter and both sugars; stir with a wooden spoon until combined. Attach bowl to mixer; add eggs. Using the paddle attachment, beat on medium-high speed until light and fluffy, about 3 minutes. Add the vanilla, and beat to combine. Add the flour mixture, walnuts, and toffee bits. Mix until thoroughly combined, and pour into prepared pan.

4. Bake until a cake tester inserted in the center comes out clean, 35 to 40 minutes (do not overbake). Transfer to a wire rack to cool completely before turning out of pan onto a cutting board. Peel off parchment paper; cut blondies into shapes with 3- to 3½-inch cookie cutters. Blondies can be stored in airtight containers at room temperature up to 3 days.

Orange-Cardamom Madeleines

Buttery madeleine batter is sweetened with honey and spiced with ground cardamom. Once baked, the mini cakes are glazed with a simple citrus icing. MAKES 2 DOZEN

for the batter:

- 4 tablespoons unsalted butter, plus more for pan
- 1 tablespoon good-quality honey
- 1 teaspoon pure vanilla extract
- ¾ cup all-purpose flour
- 1 teaspoon baking powder
- ¾ teaspoon ground cardamom
- ¼ teaspoon salt
- ¼ cup granulated sugar
- 2 large eggs

for the glaze:

- ¾ cup confectioners' sugar
- 1 teaspoon finely grated orange zest
- 2 tablespoons strained fresh orange juice

1. Brush molds of a madeleine pan with butter. Make batter: Melt butter in a small saucepan over low heat. Remove from heat, and stir in honey and vanilla. Let cool 10 minutes.

2. Whisk together flour, baking powder, cardamom, and salt in a bowl. Stir together sugar and eggs in a bowl. Gently fold in flour mixture until combined. Add butter mixture, and fold until combined. Cover with plastic wrap, and refrigerate 30 minutes.

3. Preheat oven to 325°F, with rack in center. Spoon batter into prepared pan, filling each mold halfway. Tap pan on work surface to eliminate air bubbles. Bake until cookies are puffed and edges are golden, 7 to 8 minutes. Transfer pan to a wire rack; let cool slightly. Unmold cookies onto a wire rack, and let cool completely.

4. Make glaze: Stir together sugar and orange zest and juice in a bowl until glaze is smooth, thick, and opaque. Using a small pastry brush, coat ridged side of each cookie with glaze. Let set 15 minutes. Cookies can be stored in a single layer in airtight containers at room temperature up to 3 days.

Mini Black-and-White Cookies

Jumbo versions of these iced cookies are a New York City specialty. Deciding where to begin presents the sweetest of dilemmas: chocolate first, or vanilla? Don't worry if you can't choose—these petite versions are just the right size to eat in one bite. MAKES ABOUT 4 DOZEN

for the cookies:

- 1¼ cups all-purpose flour
- ½ teaspoon baking soda
- ½ teaspoon coarse salt
- 6 tablespoons unsalted butter, room temperature
- ½ cup granulated sugar
- 1 large egg
- ½ teaspoon pure vanilla extract
- ⅓ cup low-fat buttermilk

for the icing:

- 2 cups confectioners' sugar
- 1 tablespoon plus 1 teaspoon light corn syrup
- 2½ teaspoons fresh lemon juice
- ¼ teaspoon pure vanilla extract
- 1 tablespoon water, plus more if needed
- 1 tablespoon unsweetened Dutch-process cocoa powder

1. Preheat the oven to 350°F. Make cookies: Sift together flour, baking soda, and salt into a bowl.

2. Put butter in the bowl of an electric mixer fitted with the paddle attachment. Mix until creamy, about 2 minutes. Add granulated sugar; mix until fluffy, about 3 minutes. Mix in egg and vanilla. Mix in flour mixture in three batches, alternating with buttermilk.

3. Roll tablespoons of dough into balls; drop onto baking sheets lined with parchment paper, spacing 2 inches apart. Bake cookies, rotating sheets halfway through, until bottoms turn golden, about 10 minutes. Let cool completely on sheets on wire racks.

4. Make icing: Whisk confectioners' sugar, corn syrup, lemon juice, vanilla, and the water in a small bowl until smooth. Add more water, if needed, to achieve a consistency slightly thicker than honey. Transfer half the icing to a small bowl. Stir in cocoa powder; thin with water if needed.

5. Spread white icing on half of each cookie's flat side and cocoa icing on other half. Let stand until set, 30 minutes. Cookies can be stored between layers of parchment in airtight containers at room temperature up to 3 days.

Chocolate Waffles

A morning treat gains all-day appeal with these cakey chocolate cookies. Like breakfast waffles, the cookies are prepared on a waffle iron. For best results, make sure the surface is nice and hot before you pour the batter.

MAKES ABOUT 4 DOZEN

- 3 ounces unsweetened chocolate, coarsely chopped
- 18 tablespoons (2¼ sticks) unsalted butter
- 4 large eggs
- 1 teaspoon pure vanilla extract
- 1½ cups granulated sugar
- ½ teaspoon coarse salt
- 1½ teaspoons ground cinnamon
- ½ cup plus 2 tablespoons unsweetened Dutch-process cocoa powder
- 1½ cups all-purpose flour
- ¼ cup confectioners' sugar, plus more for dusting
- 1½ tablespoons whole milk
- Vegetable oil cooking spray

1. Melt chocolate with 1 cup butter (2 sticks) in a saucepan over medium-high heat, stirring constantly. Let cool slightly.

2. Put eggs, vanilla, and granulated sugar in the bowl of an electric mixer fitted with the paddle attachment. Mix on medium speed until pale, 4 to 5 minutes. Mix in chocolate mixture, salt, cinnamon, ½ cup cocoa powder, and the flour.

3. Heat a waffle iron until hot. Lightly coat grids with cooking spray. Spoon about 1 tablespoon batter onto center of each waffle-iron square to make 1½-inch rounds. Close cover; cook until set, about 1½ minutes. Transfer to a wire rack, bottom sides up. Let cool completely. Repeat with remaining batter, coating grids with cooking spray after each batch.

4. Melt remaining 2 tablespoons butter in a small saucepan over low heat. Add confectioners' sugar and remaining 2 tablespoons cocoa powder; stir until smooth. Stir in milk.

5. Gently dip one surface of each cookie in icing so that just the waffle lines (not gaps) are coated. Repeat with remaining cookies and icing. Transfer to wire racks; let stand until set, about 10 minutes. Dust iced surfaces of cookies with confectioners' sugar. Cookies can be stored in single layers in airtight containers at room temperature up to 2 days.

CHOCOLATE WAFFLES, **opposite**

OATMEAL BARS WITH DATES AND WALNUTS, **page 216**

Oatmeal Bars with Dates and Walnuts

These fruit-and-nut-rich cookies are like soft granola bars; they make a hearty and delicious after-school snack. MAKES ABOUT 2 DOZEN

- 2¾ cups old-fashioned rolled oats
- ¾ cup whole wheat flour
- 1½ teaspoons baking powder
- 1½ teaspoons coarse salt
- ½ teaspoon ground cinnamon
- ¼ teaspoon allspice
- ¾ cup (1½ sticks) unsalted butter, room temperature
- 2 cups packed light brown sugar
- 3 large eggs
- 2½ teaspoons pure vanilla extract
- 1½ cups walnuts (about 5½ ounces), toasted and chopped
- 1 cup dates (5 ounces), pitted and coarsely chopped
- Vegetable oil cooking spray

1. Preheat oven to 350°F. Finely grind 1¼ cups oats in a food processor. Stir together ground oats, 1 cup whole oats, the whole wheat flour, baking powder, salt, cinnamon, and allspice in a large bowl.

2. With an electric mixer beat butter and brown sugar on medium speed until pale and fluffy, about 5 minutes. Mix in eggs and vanilla. Reduce speed to low; mix in oat mixture until just combined. Mix in walnuts and dates.

3. Coat a 9 by 13-inch baking dish with cooking spray. Using an offset spatula, spread batter evenly in dish. Scatter remaining ½ cup whole oats over top. Bake, rotating dish halfway through, until golden and a cake tester inserted into center comes out clean, about 35 minutes. Let cool completely in dish on a wire rack. Cut into bars. Cookies can be stored between layers of parchment in airtight containers at room temperature up to 3 days.

Fresh-Peach Drop Cookies

Moist, cakey, and flecked with fresh fruit in every bite, these cookies are just the thing to pack into a picnic basket on a late-summer day.

MAKES ABOUT 4 DOZEN

- 2 cups plus 2 tablespoons all-purpose flour
- ¾ teaspoon salt
- ½ teaspoon baking soda
- ½ cup (1 stick) unsalted butter, room temperature
- 1 cup granulated sugar
- 1 large egg
- ½ teaspoon pure vanilla extract
- 2 large ripe peaches (about 8 ounces each) peeled, pitted, and chopped into ¼-inch pieces (1¾ cups)
- ⅓ cup peach jam or preserves
- 2 tablespoons fine sanding sugar
- ⅛ teaspoon ground cinnamon

1. Preheat oven to 375°F. Whisk together flour, salt, and baking soda.

2. Put butter and granulated sugar into the bowl of an electric mixer fitted with the paddle attachment. Mix on medium-high speed until pale and fluffy, about 4 minutes. Reduce speed to low. Add egg and vanilla; mix until well blended, about 1 minute. Add flour mixture and mix until combined. Add diced peaches and peach jam; mix until just combined.

3. Using a 1½-inch ice cream scoop or a tablespoon, drop dough onto baking sheets lined with parchment paper, spacing 2 inches apart. (Chill remaining dough between batches.)

4. Combine sanding sugar and cinnamon in a small bowl. Sprinkle each cookie with ⅛ teaspoon cinnamon-sugar mixture. Bake cookies until golden brown and just set, 11 to 13 minutes, rotating sheets halfway through. Let cool on sheets on wire racks 5 minutes. Transfer cookies to wire racks to cool completely. Cookies are best eaten the day they are made, but they can be stored in an airtight container at room temperature up to 2 days.

crisp *and* crunchy

The cookies in this category are distinguished by the sounds they make when broken in half: They crack. They crunch. They snap. Most use a large proportion of granulated sugar, which tends to give a crisper texture than brown sugar or molasses, but are formed using a variety of techniques: Chocolate–Black Pepper Cookies and Earl Grey Tea Cookies are slice-and-bake; Stained Glass Trees and Gingerbread Snowflakes are rolled and cut; Butter Twists and Chocolate Pretzels are shaped by hand. Refrigerating the dough ensures that the butter in these recipes will not melt too fast, so the cookies spread minimally in the oven. This is particularly important for cutouts, which should be chilled once again before baking in order to retain their clean-lined shapes.

CHOCOLATE-ORANGE-ESPRESSO THINS, **page 220**

Chocolate-Orange-Espresso Thins

These very thin, very crisp cookies have a strong mocha flavor with just a hint of orange. It's important to use Dutch-process cocoa, which is richer and darker than plain cocoa. Dutch-process powder is treated with alkali to help neutralize the cocoa's natural acidity. MAKES ABOUT 4 DOZEN

- 1½ cups all-purpose flour
- ½ cup unsweetened Dutch-process cocoa powder
- 1½ teaspoons good-quality instant espresso powder
- ½ teaspoon coarse salt
- 1 cup (2 sticks) unsalted butter, room temperature
- 1 cup confectioners' sugar
- 1 teaspoon finely grated orange zest
- 1 teaspoon pure vanilla extract
- Coarse sanding sugar, for sprinkling

1. Sift together flour, cocoa powder, espresso powder, and salt into a medium bowl.

2. Put butter, confectioners' sugar, orange zest, and vanilla in the bowl of an electric mixer fitted with the paddle attachment. Mix on medium speed until pale and fluffy, about 3 minutes. Reduce speed to medium-low, and gradually add flour mixture until just combined.

3. Transfer dough to a 12 by 16-inch piece of parchment paper; shape into a log. Roll in parchment to 1½ inches in diameter, pressing a ruler along edge of paper at each turn to narrow the log and force out air. Transfer in parchment to a paper towel tube; chill at least 2 hours or overnight.

4. Preheat oven to 350°F. Cut log into ¼-inch-thick slices; transfer to baking sheets lined with parchment paper. Brush tops with water; sprinkle with sanding sugar. Bake until set, 15 to 17 minutes. Cool on sheets on wire racks. Cookies can be stored in airtight containers at room temperature up to 1 week.

Almond Spice Wafers

These are a variation on the Moravian spice cookie, which is traditionally made with molasses. Although this version is sweetened with brown sugar, it retains the characteristic thinness of the original variety. MAKES 6 DOZEN

- 3 cups all-purpose flour
- 1 teaspoon baking soda
- ¼ teaspoon salt
- 1 cup (2 sticks) unsalted butter, room temperature
- 1½ cups packed dark brown sugar
- 2 large eggs
- 2 teaspoons ground cinnamon
- ½ teaspoon freshly grated nutmeg
- 1½ teaspoons ground ginger
- ¼ teaspoon ground cloves
- ¼ cup blanched sliced almonds

1. Line two mini loaf pans (each 6 by 3¼ by 2 inches) with plastic wrap, allowing a 2-inch overhang. Whisk together flour, baking soda, and salt. With an electric mixer, cream butter and sugar on medium speed until fluffy, 3 to 5 minutes. Reduce mixer speed to low. Add eggs and spices, and mix well to combine.

2. Add flour mixture in three parts, mixing well after each addition. Remove dough from mixer, and divide between prepared pans. Cover dough with plastic overhang, and freeze until firm, about 1½ hours or overnight.

3. Preheat oven to 400°F. Remove plastic wrap from one piece of dough; slice dough as thinly as possible with a very sharp knife. (Keep remaining dough chilled between batches.) Place slices 2 inches apart on baking sheets lined with nonstick baking mats (such as Silpats). Top each slice with 2 to 3 sliced almonds. Bake until dark golden brown, 9 to 10 minutes. Transfer to wire racks to cool completely. Cookies can be stored in airtight containers at room temperature up to 1 week.

Chocolate Pretzels

A generous sprinkle of coarse sanding sugar is the only embellishment on these sweet versions of the salty snack. MAKES 2 DOZEN

- ¼ cup unsweetened Dutch-process cocoa powder
- 1 teaspoon good-quality instant espresso powder
- 3 tablespoons boiling water
- ½ cup (1 stick) unsalted butter, room temperature
- ¼ cup granulated sugar
- 1 teaspoon pure vanilla extract
- ½ teaspoon coarse salt
- 1 large egg
- 2 cups all-purpose flour
- 1 large egg yolk
- 1 teaspoon water
- Coarse sanding sugar, for sprinkling

1. Stir cocoa and espresso powders into the boiling water in a small bowl until dissolved.

2. Put butter and granulated sugar in the bowl of an electric mixer fitted with the paddle attachment; mix on medium speed until creamy. Mix in vanilla and salt. Reduce speed to medium-low. Mix in egg, then cocoa mixture. Gradually add flour, and mix until a smooth dough forms. Turn out onto a piece of plastic; pat into a square. Wrap dough, and refrigerate until cold, about 30 minutes.

3. Preheat oven to 325°F. Divide dough into 24 equal pieces. Roll into balls. Shape balls into 12-inch-long ropes. Form each rope into a pretzel shape. Space 1 inch apart on baking sheets lined with parchment paper.

4. Whisk egg yolk with water in a small bowl. Brush cookies with egg wash; sprinkle with sanding sugar. Bake cookies, rotating sheets halfway through, until dry, about 35 minutes. Let cool on sheets on wire racks. Pretzels can be stored in airtight containers at room temperature up to 1 week.

Umbrella Sugar Cookies

These crisp, lemony sugar cookies will lend a touch of whimsy to a spring bridal or baby shower, but you can enjoy them anytime—rain or shine.

MAKES ABOUT 2½ DOZEN

- 1½ cups all-purpose flour, plus more for dusting
- ½ teaspoon baking powder
- ¼ teaspoon salt
- 6 tablespoons (¾ stick) unsalted butter, room temperature
- ½ cup plus 2 tablespoons granulated sugar
- 2 tablespoons confectioners' sugar
- 1 vanilla bean, split, seeds scraped and reserved
- Finely grated zest of ½ lemon
- 1 large egg
- Small-Batch Royal Icing (recipe below)
- Fine sanding sugar, for sprinkling

1. Whisk together flour, baking powder, and salt in a bowl.

2. Put butter, granulated and confectioners' sugars, vanilla seeds, and zest into the bowl of an electric mixer fitted with the paddle attachment; mix on medium speed until pale and fluffy. Mix in egg. Reduce speed to low. Add flour mixture in 3 batches; mix until combined.

3. Roll out dough between 2 pieces of lightly floured parchment paper to ⅛ inch thick. Refrigerate until firm, about 45 minutes.

4. Remove parchment. Using a 3-inch umbrella cutter, cut out shapes. Chill in freezer until dough is very firm, about 15 minutes. Reroll scraps, cut out, and chill in same manner.

5. Preheat oven to 375°F. Space cookies 2 inches apart on parchment paper–lined baking sheets. Bake until pale golden, 5 to 6 minutes. Transfer cookies to wire racks to cool.

6. Transfer icing to a pastry bag fitted with a small plain round tip, such as Ateco #2. Decorate each cookie with icing, and then immediately sprinkle with sanding sugar. Let set, about 2 hours. Cookies can be stored in an airtight container at room temperature up to 1 week.

SMALL-BATCH ROYAL ICING

- 2¼ cups confectioners' sugar
- 7 ½ teaspoons meringue powder
- ¼ cup water

Put confectioners' sugar, meringue powder, and water into the bowl of an electric mixer fitted with the whisk attachment; beat on low speed 10 minutes. Use immediately, or store in an airtight container up to 2 days (icing hardens quickly when exposed to air). Beat well with a rubber spatula before using.

STRIPED ICEBOX COOKIES, **opposite**

PEANUT BUTTER-CHOCOLATE CHIP OATMEAL COOKIES, **page 228**

Striped Icebox Cookies

Three layers of cornmeal shortbread are separated by a chunky cherry-almond filling. Because the flavor of almond extract is so intense, only a tiny amount is needed to flavor the jam for all of the cookies. MAKES ABOUT 3 DOZEN

for the filling:

- ¾ cup dried cherries
- ⅓ cup cherry jam or other red fruit jam
- 1 tablespoon sugar
- ⅛ teaspoon pure almond extract

for the dough:

- 1¼ cups all-purpose flour
- ½ cup yellow cornmeal
- 1 teaspoon baking powder
- ¼ teaspoon coarse salt
- ½ cup (1 stick) unsalted butter, room temperature
- 1 cup sugar
- 1 large egg
- 1 teaspoon pure vanilla extract

1. Make filling: Process cherries, jam, and sugar in a food processor until coarsely pureed. Transfer to a small saucepan. Bring to a boil over medium heat, stirring occasionally. Remove from heat, and stir in almond extract. Let cool completely.

2. Make dough: Whisk together flour, cornmeal, baking powder, and salt in a bowl. Put butter and sugar in the bowl of an electric mixer fitted with the paddle attachment; mix on medium speed until pale and fluffy, 2 to 4 minutes. Mix in egg and vanilla. Reduce speed to low. Add flour mixture; mix until just combined.

3. Transfer dough to a work surface. Divide into four equal pieces. Roll one piece of dough between two sheets of parchment paper to a 3½ by 9-inch rectangle about ¼ inch thick. Repeat with the remaining dough pieces. Transfer with parchment to a baking sheet, and freeze 30 minutes.

4. Assemble cookies: Remove top pieces of parchment. Spread one-third of the filling evenly over one rectangle. Top with another rectangle; remove parchment. Repeat with remaining filling and rectangles, leaving the top rectangle uncoated. Wrap in plastic, and freeze 1 hour.

5. Preheat oven to 350°F. Trim dough to a 3¼ by 8½-inch brick. Cut into ¼-inch-thick slices. Space 2½ inches apart on baking sheets lined with nonstick baking mats (such as Silpats). Bake cookies, rotating sheets halfway through, until edges are pale golden brown, 12 to 15 minutes. Let cool on sheets on wire racks. Cookies can be stored in airtight containers at room temperature up to 2 weeks.

Peanut Butter-Chocolate Chip Oatmeal Cookies

This recipe calls for natural peanut butter, which gives the cookies a richer peanut flavor. Old-fashioned rolled oats produce a heartier texture than the smaller-cut quick-cooking variety, while whole peanuts deliver added crunch. MAKES ABOUT 6 DOZEN

- 3 cups old-fashioned rolled oats
- ⅓ cup whole wheat flour
- 1 teaspoon baking soda
- 1 teaspoon baking powder
- ½ teaspoon coarse salt
- 1 cup packed light brown sugar
- 1 cup granulated sugar
- 1 cup (2 sticks) unsalted butter, room temperature
- ½ cup natural peanut butter
- 2 large eggs
- 1 teaspoon pure vanilla extract
- 2 cups salted whole peanuts
- 2 cups (12 ounces) semisweet chocolate chips

1. Preheat oven to 350°F. Stir together oats, flour, baking soda, baking powder, and salt in a bowl.

2. Put sugars, butter, and peanut butter in the bowl of an electric mixer fitted with the paddle attachment. Mix on medium speed until pale and fluffy, about 5 minutes. Mix in eggs and vanilla.

3. Reduce speed to low. Add oat mixture, and mix until just combined. Mix in peanuts and chocolate chips.

4. Using a 1½-inch ice cream scoop, drop balls of dough 2 inches apart on baking sheets lined with parchment paper.

5. Bake cookies, rotating sheets halfway through, until golden brown and just set, 13 to 15 minutes. Let cool on sheets on wire racks 5 minutes. Transfer cookies to wire racks to cool completely. Cookies can be stored in airtight containers at room temperature up to 2 days.

Biscuit Sandwich Cookies

The biscuits for these sandwich cookies are ultrathin, crisp, and downright chic. And since they're not terribly sweet, they marry well with the milk chocolate filling. In a pinch, use store-bought chocolate-hazelnut spread—it's also divine. MAKES 1½ DOZEN

- 1 cup all-purpose flour
- ¼ cup sugar
- ½ teaspoon coarse salt
- 4 tablespoons cold unsalted butter, cut into small pieces
- ¼ cup plus 1 tablespoon heavy cream
- ½ teaspoon pure vanilla extract
- 1 egg yolk
- 8 ounces finely chopped milk chocolate, melted, or ¾ cup chocolate-hazelnut spread

1. Put flour, sugar, and salt in the bowl of a food processor and pulse to combine. Add butter and pulse to form coarse crumbs. With machine running, pour in ¼ cup cream and the vanilla and process until dough almost comes together.

2. Remove dough from processor and bring together on a work surface. Roll dough between two floured sheets of parchment paper until 1/16 inch thick. Using a 2½-inch fluted round cookie cutter, cut 36 circles, rerolling scraps as necessary. Place rounds on parchment-lined baking sheets and transfer to freezer to chill until firm, about 15 minutes.

3. Preheat oven to 325°F. Combine egg yolk and remaining tablespoon heavy cream in a small bowl. Brush tops of cookies with yolk mixture and bake until golden brown, 15 to 20 minutes. Let cool on sheets on wire racks.

4. Spread 1 heaping teaspoon melted chocolate on undersides of half of cookies. Sandwich with remaining cookies. Refrigerate until set, about 15 minutes. Cookies can be stored between layers of parchment in airtight containers at a cool room temperature up to 3 days.

Earl Grey Tea Cookies

The addition of Earl Gray tea in this recipe gives the cookies the slightest hint of bergamot orange flavoring. Grind the tea leaves in a small food processor or a spice grinder. MAKES ABOUT 8 DOZEN

- 2 cups all-purpose flour
- 2 tablespoons finely ground Earl Grey tea leaves (from about 4 bags)
- ½ teaspoon coarse salt
- 1 cup (2 sticks) unsalted butter, room temperature
- ½ cup confectioners' sugar
- 1 tablespoon finely grated orange zest

1. Whisk together flour, tea, and salt in a bowl.

2. Put butter, confectioners' sugar, and orange zest in the bowl of an electric mixer fitted with the paddle attachment. Mix on medium speed until pale and fluffy, about 3 minutes. Reduce speed to low; gradually mix in flour mixture until just combined.

3. Divide dough in half. Transfer each half to a piece of parchment paper; shape into logs. Roll in parchment to 1¼ inches in diameter, pressing a ruler along edge of parchment at each turn to narrow the log and force out air. Transfer in parchment to paper towel tubes; freeze until firm, 1 hour.

4. Preheat oven to 350°F. Cut logs into ¼-inch-thick slices. Space 1 inch apart on baking sheets lined with parchment.

5. Bake cookies, rotating sheets halfway through, until edges are golden, 13 to 15 minutes. Let cool on sheets on wire racks. Cookies can be stored in airtight containers at room temperature up to 5 days.

Chocolate-Ginger Leaves and Acorns

Crisp, sugar-dusted leaves and acorns celebrate the autumn months, but these cookies can be made any time of year. Cut them into other shapes and sizes if you wish. Score them with a paring knife to add stylized details and adjust the baking time if the size of the cutter is different. MAKES 4 DOZEN

- 2½ cups all-purpose flour, plus more for work surface
- ½ cup unsweetened Dutch-process cocoa powder
- ½ teaspoon ground ginger
- 1 teaspoon ground cinnamon
- ½ teaspoon freshly grated nutmeg
- ¼ teaspoon ground cloves
- ½ teaspoon coarse salt
- ½ teaspoon baking powder
- ½ teaspoon baking soda
- ¾ cup (1½ sticks) unsalted butter, room temperature
- ¾ cup packed dark brown sugar
- 1 large egg
- ½ cup unsulfured molasses
- 1 tablespoon peeled grated fresh ginger
- Fine sanding sugar, for sprinkling

1. Whisk together flour, cocoa, ground ginger, cinnamon, nutmeg, cloves, salt, baking powder, and baking soda in a bowl.

2. Put butter and brown sugar in the bowl of an electric mixer fitted with the paddle attachment; mix on medium speed until pale and fluffy, about 4 minutes. Add egg, molasses, and grated ginger; mix until combined. Reduce speed to low. Add flour mixture; mix until just combined.

3. Halve dough; shape into disks. Wrap each disk in plastic; refrigerate until cold, about 1 hour.

4. Preheat oven to 325°F. Working with one disk at a time, roll out dough on a lightly floured surface to ¼ inch thick. (If dough becomes too soft at any time, freeze until firm.) Cut out shapes with 3-inch acorn- or leaf-shape cookie cutters; space 1 inch apart on baking sheets lined with parchment paper. Refrigerate until firm, about 20 minutes.

5. Score designs with a paring knife; sprinkle with sanding sugar. Bake, rotating sheets halfway through, until firm, 11 to 13 minutes. Cool on sheets on wire racks. Cookies can be stored in an airtight container at room temperature up to 5 days.

Chocolate Sandwiches

White chocolate ganache fills these sandwich cookies, which are finished with a drizzle of melted white chocolate. Pipe heart shapes, letters, or other designs on top of each for a personalized gift. MAKES 3 DOZEN

- 1¾ cups all-purpose flour, plus more for work surface
- ¼ cup unsweetened Dutch-process cocoa powder
- ½ teaspoon baking powder
- ¼ teaspoon coarse salt
- ½ cup (1 stick) unsalted butter
- 1 cup sugar
- 1 large egg
- 1 teaspoon pure vanilla extract
- 12 ounces best-quality white chocolate, finely chopped
- ½ cup heavy cream

1. Sift flour, cocoa powder, baking powder, and salt into a large bowl.

2. Put butter and sugar in the bowl of an electric mixer fitted with the paddle attachment; mix on medium speed until creamy. Mix in egg and vanilla. Reduce speed to low. Add flour mixture; mix until just combined. Halve dough, and wrap in plastic. Refrigerate about 1 hour.

3. Roll dough on a lightly floured surface to ⅛ inch thick. Cut into 1½-inch squares. Space 1 inch apart on baking sheets lined with parchment paper. Refrigerate 30 minutes. Wrap scraps in plastic, and refrigerate 30 minutes; reroll and cut.

4. Preheat oven to 325°F. Bake cookies until edges just begin to brown, about 12 minutes, rotating halfway through. Cool on sheets on wire racks.

5. Put 9 ounces chopped white chocolate in a bowl. Bring cream to a boil. Pour over chocolate; let stand 5 minutes. Stir until smooth. Chill until spreadable, about 1 hour, stirring occasionally. Spread onto bottom of half the cookies. Sandwich with remaining cookies.

6. Melt remaining chocolate in a small heatproof bowl set over a pan of simmering water. Fill a parchment paper cone, or a small pastry bag fitted with a round tip (such as Ateco #2), with melted chocolate; decorate cookies. Cookies can be refrigerated in airtight containers up to 1 week.

Chrusciki Leaves

These leaf-shaped chrusciki (khroost-CHEE-kee) are adapted from Martha's mother's classic Polish recipe. The dough is kneaded for a while, to incorporate lots of air into it and keep the finished cookies light and delicate. If you're storing fried cookies, wait until just before serving to dust them with confectioners' sugar. MAKES 9 TO 10 DOZEN

- 1 tablespoon unsalted butter, melted
- 2 large eggs, plus 10 large egg yolks
- 3 tablespoons granulated sugar
- ½ teaspoon coarse salt
- 2 teaspoons pure vanilla extract
- 1 teaspoon finely grated lemon zest
- 1 teaspoon finely grated orange zest
- 3 tablespoons Cognac or brandy
- ½ cup sour cream
- 4½ cups sifted all-purpose flour, plus more for work surface
- 4½ cups vegetable oil, for frying
- Sifted confectioners' sugar, for sprinkling

1. Put butter, whole eggs and yolks, granulated sugar, salt, vanilla, zests, Cognac, and sour cream in the bowl of an electric mixer fitted with the whisk attachment; beat on medium speed until pale and thick, 8 to 10 minutes. Reduce speed to low; gradually add enough flour to form a fairly stiff dough. Turn out dough onto a floured work surface; knead until dough blisters, becomes elastic, and can be handled easily, 6 to 8 minutes, adding flour if needed.

2. Divide dough into four pieces. Keep dough under an inverted bowl to prevent it from drying out. Working with one piece at a time, roll out dough to ⅛ inch thick. If dough becomes too elastic while rolling, cover with plastic and let rest 15 minutes. Cut out leaves with a leaf-shape cookie cutter; transfer to a tray lined with parchment paper. Repeat with remaining dough, layering leaves between sheets of parchment. Collect all scraps, and let rest 20 minutes before rerolling.

3. Heat oil in a medium to heavy saucepan until it registers 375°F on a deep-fry thermometer. Stretch leaves slightly so they will curl while frying. Fry in batches of 12, turning occasionally, until pale golden brown, about 3 minutes. Transfer to baking sheets lined with paper towels to drain and cool. Cookies can be stored in airtight containers at room temperature up to 2 days. Sprinkle with confectioners' sugar before serving.

CHRUSCIKI LEAVES, **opposite**

ANZAC BISCUITS, **page 238**

ANZAC Biscuits

During World War I, families Down Under sent cookies to their loved ones in the Australia and New Zealand Army Corps (ANZAC). ANZAC Biscuits were made from rolled oats, coconut, and golden syrup; the ingredients, and thus the cookies, would survive the long journey to the troops. The dough for these cookies should be mixed just before baking. MAKES ABOUT 2½ DOZEN

- 2 cups all-purpose flour
- 1¾ cups old-fashioned rolled oats
- 1½ cups sugar
- 1 cup unsweetened shredded coconut
- Pinch of salt
- ¾ cup (1½ sticks) unsalted butter
- 2 tablespoons Lyle's Golden Syrup
- ¾ teaspoon baking soda
- 6 tablespoons boiling water

1. Preheat oven to 350°F. Line two baking sheets with parchment paper.

2. In a large bowl, combine flour, oats, sugar, coconut, and salt.

3. In a small saucepan over medium heat, melt butter with syrup. Dissolve baking soda in boiling water, and add to butter mixture. Stir to combine. (Be careful; it will bubble up considerably.)

4. Add butter mixture to dry ingredients and stir to combine. Using a 1½-inch ice-cream scoop or rounded tablespoon, drop balls of dough onto prepared baking sheets, about 2 inches apart. Flatten with the heel of your hand.

5. Bake until golden brown and firm but not hard, about 15 minutes, rotating sheets halfway through. Transfer to wire racks to cool. Cookies can be stored between layers of parchment in an airtight container at room temperature up to 1 week.

Chocolate Cookie Cutouts

These all-purpose cutouts are dark and rich, they keep well, and the dough can be rolled again and again without any compromise in texture or flavor. We decorated ours with nonpareils before baking, but you could decorate them after baking with Royal Icing instead—see the recipe on page 241. MAKES 3 TO 4 DOZEN

- 1½ cups all-purpose flour, plus more for dusting
- ½ cup plus 2 tablespoons unsweetened Dutch-process cocoa powder
- ⅛ teaspoon salt
- ¼ teaspoon ground cinnamon
- ¾ cup (1½ sticks) unsalted butter, room temperature
- 1½ cups sifted confectioners' sugar
- 1 large egg, lightly beaten
- ½ teaspoon pure vanilla extract
- Nonpareils, for sprinkling (optional)

1. Sift flour, cocoa powder, salt, and cinnamon into a bowl.

2. Put butter and confectioners' sugar in the bowl of an electric mixer fitted with the paddle attachment. Mix on medium-high speed until pale and fluffy, about 3 minutes. Mix in egg and vanilla. Reduce speed to low. Gradually mix in flour mixture. Wrap dough in plastic wrap. Refrigerate until firm, 1 hour or overnight.

3. On a lightly floured work surface, roll out dough to ⅛ inch thick. Transfer to a parchment paper–lined baking sheet. Chill in freezer 15 minutes.

4. Preheat oven to 350°F. Using a 3-inch cookie cutter, quickly cut out shapes from dough (if dough begins to soften, chill it in freezer 3 to 5 minutes). Reroll and cut scraps. Transfer shapes to prepared baking sheets, spacing them 2 inches apart. Brush flour from shapes. Sprinkle with nonpareils, if using. Chill in freezer until firm, about 15 minutes.

5. Bake cookies until crisp, about 8 minutes. Let cool completely on sheets on wire racks. Cookies can be stored between layers of parchment in an airtight container at room temperature up to 1 week.

Sugar Cookie Cutouts

Sugar cookies are buttery classics, with a nice crunch. They are delicious on their own, but they also make ideal holiday cookies when festively decorated with Royal Icing. Try customizing the dough to your own taste with an addition such as finely grated lemon zest, a bit of brandy, or a hint of cinnamon. MAKES ABOUT 2 DOZEN 4-INCH COOKIES

- 4 cups sifted all-purpose flour, plus more for dusting
- 1 teaspoon baking powder
- ½ teaspoon salt
- 1 cup (2 sticks) unsalted butter, room temperature
- 2 cups sugar
- 2 large eggs
- 2 teaspoons pure vanilla extract
- Royal Icing (optional; recipe follows)
- Gel-paste food coloring (optional)
- Fine sanding sugar (optional)

1. Sift flour, baking powder, and salt into a bowl.

2. Put butter and sugar in the bowl of an electric mixer fitted with the paddle attachment. Mix on medium speed until pale and fluffy. Mix in eggs and vanilla. Reduce speed to low. Gradually mix in flour mixture. Divide dough in half; flatten each half into a disk. Wrap each in plastic. Refrigerate until firm, at least 1 hour or overnight.

3. Preheat oven to 325°F, with racks in upper and lower thirds. Let one disk of dough stand at room temperature just until soft enough to roll, about 10 minutes. Roll out dough on a lightly floured work surface to just under ¼ inch thick, adding more flour as needed to keep dough from sticking. Cut out cookies with a 4- to 5-inch cookie cutter, transferring shapes to parchment paper–lined baking sheets as you work. Roll out the scraps, and repeat. Repeat with remaining disk of dough. Chill cookies in freezer until very firm, about 15 minutes.

4. Bake, switching positions of sheets and rotating halfway through, until edges turn golden, 15 to 18 minutes. Let cool on sheets on wire racks. To decorate, tint icing with food coloring, if using. Flood tops of cookies with icing (see how-to photos on page 327). While icing is wet, you can pipe polka dots with icing in contrasting colors on top; stretch dots into flourishes with the tip of a wooden skewer for a marbleized look. Flock wet icing with sanding sugar if desired. After icing cookies, let them sit out overnight to set. Cookies can be stored between layers of parchment in an airtight container at room temperature up to 1 week.

ROYAL ICING MAKES 2½ CUPS

- 1 pound confectioners' sugar, sifted
- 5 tablespoons meringue powder
- Scant ½ cup water

Combine all ingredients in the bowl of an electric mixer fitted with the paddle attachment. Mix on low speed until smooth, about 7 minutes. If icing is too thick, add more water; if too thin, beat icing 2 to 3 minutes more or add more confectioners' sugar a tablespoon at a time. Use icing immediately, or store in an airtight container up to 2 days (icing hardens quickly when exposed to air). Beat well with a rubber spatula before using.

Biscochitos

These cookies originated in Spain, but today they are often associated with the American Southwest, particularly New Mexico, where they are the official state cookie. Lard imparts incomparable flavor—it's worth seeking it out, although vegetable shortening can be substituted. MAKES ABOUT 2 DOZEN

- 1 cup sugar, plus ¾ cup for sprinkling
- 1¼ cups lard or vegetable shortening
- 1 large egg
- 1 teaspoon pure vanilla extract
- 2 tablespoons orange-flavored liqueur, such as Grand Marnier, or triple sec
- Finely grated zest of 1 orange
- 3 cups all-purpose flour, plus more for work surface
- ½ teaspoon baking powder
- ¼ teaspoon salt
- 2 teaspoons anise seeds
- 2 tablespoons water
- ½ teaspoon ground cinnamon

1. In the bowl of an electric mixer fitted with the paddle attachment, beat 1 cup sugar and the lard on medium-high speed until light and fluffy, about 3 minutes. Add egg; beat to combine. Add vanilla, liqueur, and zest; beat to combine.

2. Sift together flour, baking powder, and salt into a bowl. Gradually beat flour mixture into sugar mixture on low speed. Beat in anise seeds. On medium, gradually add the water and mix until dough forms a ball (add more water if necessary). Wrap dough in plastic wrap; chill 30 minutes.

3. Preheat oven to 350°F with rack in center. Combine cinnamon and remaining ¾ cup sugar in a small bowl.

4. On a lightly floured surface, roll the dough to ¼-inch thickness. Cut dough into shapes with a 4-inch fleur-de-lis cutter; lightly sift cinnamon-sugar over each shape. Place on parchment paper–lined baking sheets. Chill in freezer until dough is very firm, about 15 minutes. Bake one sheet at a time for 12 to 14 minutes, rotating halfway through; cookies should be set but not brown. Transfer the cookies and parchment to a wire rack to cool. Cookies can be stored between layers of parchment in an airtight container at room temperature up to 1 week.

Chocolate-Black Pepper Cookies

These sparkle-edged treats gain flavor from a hefty dose of instant espresso powder, along with a bit of ground black pepper and cinnamon. Don't be tempted to substitute instant coffee for the espresso powder—the flavor and texture will not be as good. MAKES ABOUT 4 DOZEN

- 1½ cups all-purpose flour
- ¾ cup unsweetened Dutch-process cocoa powder
- ¼ teaspoon coarse salt
- ¼ teaspoon finely ground pepper, plus more for sprinkling
- 1 tablespoon plus 1 teaspoon instant espresso powder
- ½ teaspoon ground cinnamon
- ¾ cup (1½ sticks) unsalted butter, room temperature
- 1 cup granulated sugar
- 1 large egg
- 1½ teaspoons pure vanilla extract
- Coarse sanding sugar, for rolling

1. Sift together flour, cocoa powder, salt, pepper, espresso powder, and cinnamon into a large bowl.

2. Put butter and granulated sugar in the bowl of an electric mixer fitted with the paddle attachment; mix on medium speed until pale and fluffy, about 3 minutes. Mix in egg and vanilla. Reduce speed to low. Add flour mixture; mix until just combined.

3. Turn out dough onto a piece of parchment paper, and roll into a 2-inch-diameter log. Roll log in the parchment. Refrigerate at least 1 hour or overnight.

4. Preheat oven to 350°F. Remove log from parchment. Let soften slightly at room temperature, about 5 minutes. Roll log in sanding sugar, gently pressing down to adhere sugar to dough. Transfer log to a cutting board, and slice into ¼-inch-thick rounds. Place rounds on baking sheets lined with parchment paper, spacing 1 inch apart. Sprinkle each round with freshly ground pepper.

5. Bake cookies until there is slight resistance when you lightly touch centers, about 10 minutes, rotating halfway through. Transfer cookies to wire racks to cool completely. Cookies can be stored in airtight containers at room temperature up to 3 days.

Chocolate Pistachio Biscotti

Cocoa powder and chocolate lend rich, fudgy flavor to these twice-baked treats. They are thicker than most biscotti, and perfect for dunking in milk or coffee. MAKES ABOUT 1 DOZEN

- 2 cups all-purpose flour, plus more for baking sheet
- ½ cup unsweetened cocoa powder
- 1 teaspoon baking soda
- ¼ teaspoon salt
- 6 tablespoons unsalted butter, room temperature
- 1 cup sugar
- 2 large eggs
- 1 cup shelled pistachios (4½ ounces)
- ½ cup semisweet chocolate chips

1. Preheat oven to 350°F. Line a baking sheet with parchment paper.

2. Whisk together flour, cocoa powder, baking soda, and salt into a bowl. In bowl of electric mixer fitted with paddle attachment, beat butter and sugar on medium until light and fluffy. Add eggs; beat on low speed until well combined, scraping down sides of bowl if necessary. Add flour mixture; beat to form stiff dough. Beat in pistachios and chocolate chips until just combined.

3. Transfer dough to prepared baking sheet; form into a slightly flattened log, about 12 by 4 inches. Bake until slightly firm, about 25 minutes. Cool about 5 minutes. Reduce oven to 300°F.

4. On a cutting board, using a sharp, serrated knife, cut biscotti diagonally into 1-inch-thick slices. Arrange cut sides down on baking sheet; bake until crisp but still slightly soft in center, about 8 minutes. Transfer to a wire rack to cool completely. Cookies can be stored in an airtight container at room temperature up to 1 week.

Butter Twists

To make these buttery treats, we fashioned 6-inch lengths of dough into twisted rope shapes. You could also form the lengths into pretzel shapes and sprinkle them with coarse sanding sugar before baking.

MAKES ABOUT 3 DOZEN

- ½ cup (1 stick) unsalted butter, room temperature
- ½ cup sugar
- 1 teaspoon pure vanilla extract
- 1 large egg white
- 1½ cups plus 2 tablespoons all-purpose flour
- ½ teaspoon coarse salt

1. Preheat oven to 350°F. Put butter and sugar in the bowl of an electric mixer fitted with the paddle attachment; mix on medium speed until creamy. Mix in vanilla and egg white. Reduce speed to low. Add flour and salt; mix until combined.

2. Roll dough into ¾-inch balls. Roll each ball into a 6-inch log. Bend log in half, then twist. Space 1 inch apart on baking sheets lined with parchment paper.

3. Bake, rotating halfway through, until cookies just begin to turn golden, 13 to 15 minutes. Let cool on parchment on wire racks. Cookies can be stored in airtight containers at room temperature up to 3 days.

Coconut Biscuits

Crunchy coconut biscuits are a Jamaican specialty and are crispest the day they're baked. To toast coconut, preheat the oven to 325°F. Spread the coconut in a single layer on a rimmed baking sheet and toast, stirring occasionally, until light golden and fragrant, about 10 minutes. MAKES ABOUT 3 DOZEN

- 1 cup all-purpose flour, plus more for work surface
- 1 cup granulated sugar
- 1 cup unsweetened shredded coconut, lightly toasted
- ½ teaspoon freshly grated nutmeg
- ¼ teaspoon baking soda
- ¼ teaspoon coarse salt
- Sanding sugar, for sprinkling

1. Stir together all the ingredients except the sanding sugar in a medium bowl. Stir in enough water (about 5 tablespoons) to form a stiff dough that holds together. Shape dough into a rectangle, and wrap in plastic. Refrigerate until cold, 15 minutes.

2. Preheat oven to 375°F. Roll out dough on a lightly floured surface to ⅛ inch thick. Transfer to baking sheets lined with parchment paper; refrigerate until cold, about 15 minutes.

3. Using a 2-inch round cutter, cut out dough. Space rounds 2 inches apart on baking sheets lined with parchment paper. Brush tops with water; sprinkle with sanding sugar. Bake until pale golden brown, about 11 minutes, rotating sheets halfway through. Let cool completely on sheets on wire racks before serving. Cookies can be stored in airtight containers at room temperature up to 1 day.

Lime Flowers

Sugar cookies become tangy treats when the batter is enhanced with lime juice and zest. Cut the dough into big daisy-like shapes, and finish the baked cookies with a dusting of confectioners' sugar. MAKES ABOUT 2 DOZEN

- 2 cups all-purpose flour, plus more for work surface
- ½ teaspoon baking powder
- ¼ teaspoon coarse salt
- 1 cup granulated sugar
- 2 tablespoons finely grated lime zest
- ¾ cup (1½ sticks) unsalted butter, room temperature
- 1 teaspoon pure vanilla extract
- ¼ cup fresh lime juice
- Confectioners' sugar, for dusting

1. Sift together flour, baking powder, and salt into a bowl.

2. Put granulated sugar and lime zest in the bowl of an electric mixer fitted with the paddle attachment. Mix on medium speed 1 minute. Add butter, and mix until fluffy, about 2 minutes. Mix in vanilla and lime juice. Reduce speed to low, and gradually mix in flour mixture.

3. On a lightly floured work surface, halve the dough. Flatten each half into a 10-inch disk, and wrap each in plastic. Freeze until firm, about 30 minutes.

4. Working with one half at a time, roll out dough on parchment paper to ⅛ inch thick. Cut shapes with a 3-inch flower-shape cookie cutter. Space 1 inch apart on baking sheets lined with parchment paper. Cut a hole in center of each with a 1-inch round cutter. Repeat with remaining disk. Wrap scraps in plastic. Freeze 30 minutes; reroll, and cut.

5. Preheat oven to 325°F. Bake until cookies are set, 12 to 13 minutes, rotating sheets halfway through. Let cool on a wire rack. Before serving, sift confectioners' sugar over cookies. Cookies can be stored in airtight containers at room temperature up to 3 days.

Hazelnut Jam Thumbprints

Various flavors of jams or preserves can be used to fill these cookies—strawberry, raspberry, and apricot all make lovely accompaniments to hazelnuts. To toast hazelnuts, see note on page 37. Coarsely grind hazelnuts by pulsing them in a food processor; be careful not to overprocess them or you will end up with nut butter. MAKES ABOUT 2 DOZEN

- ½ cup (1 stick) unsalted butter, room temperature
- ½ cup plus 2 tablespoons sugar
- 1 large egg, separated, each part lightly beaten
- 1 teaspoon pure vanilla extract
- 1¼ cups all-purpose flour, plus more for flattening cookies
- ⅛ teaspoon coarse salt
- ½ cup toasted skinned hazelnuts, ground
- Strawberry, raspberry, or apricot jam, for filling

1. Put butter and ½ cup sugar in the bowl of an electric mixer fitted with the paddle attachment; mix on medium speed until pale and fluffy, about 3 minutes. Add egg yolk and vanilla, and mix well. Reduce speed to low. Add flour and salt, and mix until just combined. Refrigerate dough for 2 hours.

2. Preheat oven to 325°F. Stir together hazelnuts and remaining 2 tablespoons sugar in a small bowl. Roll dough into 1-inch balls; dip balls in beaten egg white, then in hazelnut mixture. Space 1 inch apart on baking sheets lined with parchment paper. Press down center of each ball with your thumb. Bake for 10 minutes. Remove from oven; press down centers again with the lightly floured end of a wooden spoon. Return to oven. Bake cookies until golden brown, 8 to 10 minutes more. Let cool slightly on sheets on wire racks. Fill each center with jam. Cookies can be stored in a single layer in airtight containers at room temperature up to 2 days.

Cassis Crisps

Crème de cassis is a black currant–flavored liqueur. Chambord, a raspberry-flavored liqueur, makes a fine substitute. MAKES ABOUT 2½ DOZEN

- 2¾ cups sifted all-purpose flour, plus more for work surface
- 2 teaspoons baking powder
- ½ teaspoon coarse salt
- ½ cup (1 stick) unsalted butter, room temperature
- 1 cup granulated sugar
- 2 large eggs
- ¼ cup crème de cassis
- Coarse sanding sugar, for sprinkling

1. Sift together flour, baking powder, and salt into a bowl. Put butter and granulated sugar in the bowl of an electric mixer fitted with the paddle attachment; mix on medium speed until pale and fluffy, about 4 minutes.

2. Add eggs and crème de cassis, and mix until combined. Add flour mixture, and mix on low until smooth. Divide dough in half, and wrap each in plastic; refrigerate until cold, about 1 hour.

3. Preheat oven to 350°F. Working with one half at a time, roll out dough on a lightly floured surface to ¼ inch thick, and cut into 3-inch squares. Space 2 inches apart on baking sheets lined with parchment paper, and sprinkle with sanding sugar. Reroll scraps; repeat with remaining dough.

4. Bake cookies until golden brown all over, 12 to 15 minutes, rotating sheets halfway through. Let cool on sheets on wire racks. Cookies can be stored in an airtight container at room temperature up to 3 days.

Homemade Graham Crackers

Once you taste one of these sweet whole wheat crackers, you may never go back to the store-bought variety again. Use them as the base for homemade s'mores, sandwich them with peanut butter, or simply enjoy them on their own. MAKES 4 DOZEN

- 1½ cups all-purpose flour, plus more for work surface
- 1 cup whole wheat flour
- ½ cup untoasted wheat germ
- ½ teaspoon salt
- 1 teaspoon baking soda
- 1 teaspoon ground cinnamon
- 1 cup (2 sticks) unsalted butter, room temperature
- ¾ cup packed light brown sugar
- 2 tablespoons honey

1. Whisk together both flours, wheat germ, salt, baking soda, and cinnamon in a bowl.

2. Put butter, brown sugar, and honey in the bowl of an electric mixer fitted with the paddle attachment; mix on medium speed until pale and fluffy, 2 to 3 minutes, scraping down sides of bowl as needed. Reduce speed to low. Add the flour mixture, and mix until combined.

3. Turn out dough onto a floured surface and divide into quarters. Roll out each piece between two sheets of floured parchment paper into rectangles a bit larger than 9 by 6 inches, about ⅛ inch thick.

4. Using a fluted pastry wheel, trim the outermost edges of each rectangle, and divide into three 6 by 3-inch rectangles. Pressing lightly, so as not to cut all the way through, score each piece in half lengthwise and crosswise, to form four 3 by 1½-inch crackers. Stack parchment and dough on a baking sheet and chill in freezer until firm, about 20 minutes.

5. Remove two sheets of dough from freezer. Pierce crackers using the tines of a fork. Transfer to large baking sheets lined with parchment paper. Bake, rotating halfway through, until dark golden brown, 8 to 9 minutes. Repeat with remaining dough. Let cool on sheet 5 minutes; transfer crackers to wire racks to cool completely. Cookies can be stored in an airtight container at room temperature up to 3 days.

Stained Glass Trees

These luminescent sugar cookies have "windows" that begin as bits of hard candy. To make a template, draw a tree or other simple shape onto card stock or a thin plastic sheet, and cut it out. Place the cutout on rolled-out cookie dough, and cut around it with a paring knife. Alternatively, use cookie cutters (wide shapes work best). MAKES ABOUT 3 DOZEN

- 2 cups sifted all-purpose flour, plus more for work surface
- ¼ teaspoon coarse salt
- ½ teaspoon baking powder
- ½ cup (1 stick) unsalted butter, room temperature
- 1 cup sugar
- 1 large egg
- 1 teaspoon pure vanilla extract
- 7 ounces (about 30) assorted colored hard candies, such as Jolly Rancher, colors separated, and finely chopped with a chef's knife

1. Sift together flour, salt, and baking powder into a bowl.

2. Put butter and sugar in the bowl of an electric mixer fitted with the paddle attachment; mix on medium speed until pale and fluffy, about 3 minutes. Add egg; mix until smooth, 1 minute. Reduce speed to low. Add flour mixture, and mix until combined. Stir in vanilla. Wrap dough in plastic, and refrigerate until cold, about 45 minutes.

3. Preheat oven to 325°F with racks in upper and lower thirds. Roll out chilled dough on a well-floured surface to a little more than ⅛ inch thick. Cut out shapes using a 5-inch tree-shape cookie cutter. Using a metal spatula, transfer shapes to baking sheets lined with parchment paper, spacing 2 inches apart. Using the tip of a paring knife, make a triangular cutout in center of each cookie for candy filling. Reroll scraps, and cut.

4. Sprinkle candy in a single layer in hole of each cookie, avoiding edges of triangle. Refrigerate until dough is firm, about 15 minutes.

5. Bake cookies until candy has melted and completely filled cutout and cookie edges are just starting to turn pale golden brown, 11 to 12 minutes. Do not let the cookies brown, or the candy centers may become bubbly. Let cool completely on sheets on wire racks. Use a metal spatula to remove cookies from parchment. Cookies can be stored in airtight containers at room temperature up to 5 days.

HOW TO MAKE STAINED GLASS TREES Use a paring knife to cut out a triangular center from each tree; fill each triangle with a single layer of chopped candies. Keep the pieces a slight distance from the edge of the triangle, as the heat of the oven will melt the candy, and it will spread. Midway through baking, quickly open the oven door and check for any little holes in the "glass"; use a toothpick to fill them in.

Gingerbread Snowflakes

This snowflake gets its icy sheen from piped Royal Icing dusted with sanding sugar. You can use this basic recipe to make gingerbread men or other cutout shapes; just alter the baking time if the size of the cutter is different. Decorate each with Royal Icing, candies, sprinkles, and other embellishments, as desired. MAKES ABOUT 2 DOZEN

- 5½ cups all-purpose flour, plus more for work surface
- 1 teaspoon baking soda
- 1½ teaspoons salt
- 4 teaspoons ground ginger
- 4 teaspoons ground cinnamon
- 1½ teaspoons ground cloves
- 1 teaspoon freshly grated nutmeg
- 1 cup (2 sticks) unsalted butter, room temperature
- 1 cup packed dark brown sugar
- 2 large eggs
- 1½ cups unsulfured molasses
- Royal Icing (page 241)
- Fine sanding sugar, for sprinkling

1. Whisk together flour, baking soda, salt, and spices in a large bowl. Set aside.

2. Put butter and brown sugar in the bowl of a standing electric mixer fitted with the paddle attachment. Mix on medium speed until fluffy. Add eggs and molasses and mix until combined. Add flour mixture; mix on low until combined. Divide dough into thirds; wrap each in plastic. Chill 1 hour.

3. Preheat oven to 350°F. Line two large baking sheets with parchment paper.

4. On a generously floured piece of parchment, roll dough just under ¼ inch thick. Brush off excess flour and freeze until firm, about 15 minutes.

5. Cut dough into snowflake shapes with a 7-inch cookie cutter. Transfer to prepared baking sheets, and freeze until firm, 15 minutes.

6. Bake cookies for 12 to 14 minutes, or until crisp but not darkened, rotating sheets halfway through once and firmly tapping down pan. Transfer cookies to wire racks to cool completely.

7. Place icing in a pastry bag fitted with a small plain tip (Ateco #7). Pipe designs on snowflakes; immediately sprinkle with sanding sugar. Tap off excess sugar and allow icing to set completely at room temperature, about 1 hour. Cookies can be stored between layers of parchment in an airtight container at room temperature up to 1 week.

HOW TO DECORATE GINGERBREAD SNOWFLAKES To create these lacy designs, fill a piping bag fitted with a small plain tip (Ateco #7) with Royal Icing. Pipe a line along each axis, applying a little extra pressure to create a dot. Pipe several dots around center axis. While icing is wet, sprinkle it with fine sanding sugar. Let stand 5 minutes; shake off excess. To package cookies, dry for several hours; remove excess granules with a dry pastry brush.

THIN AND CRISP
CHOCOLATE CHIP COOKIES, **opposite**

LEMON-POPPY SEED CRISPS, **page 262**

Thin and Crisp Chocolate Chip Cookies

This variation on the classic chocolate chip cookie will snap and crumble with every bite. Adding more butter and granulated sugar contributes to the crunch. MAKES ABOUT 3 DOZEN

- 2¼ cups all-purpose flour
- ½ teaspoon baking soda
- 1¼ cups (2½ sticks) unsalted butter, room temperature
- 1¼ cups granulated sugar
- ¾ cup packed light brown sugar
- 1 teaspoon coarse salt
- 2 teaspoons pure vanilla extract
- 2 large eggs
- ¼ cup water
- 2 cups semisweet chocolate chips (about 12 ounces)

1. Preheat oven to 350°F. Whisk flour and baking soda in a bowl.

2. Put butter and both sugars in the bowl of an electric mixer fitted with the paddle attachment; mix on medium speed until pale and fluffy, about 3 minutes. Reduce speed to low. Add salt, vanilla, eggs, and water; mix until combined, about 1 minute. Add flour mixture; mix until just combined. Stir in chocolate chips.

3. Drop heaping tablespoon-size balls of dough about 2 inches apart on baking sheets lined with parchment paper. Bake cookies, rotating sheets halfway through, until golden brown, 20 to 25 minutes. Let cool on baking sheets on wire racks 1 to 2 minutes. Transfer cookies to the rack to cool completely. Cookies can be stored in airtight containers at room temperature up to 1 week.

Lemon-Poppy Seed Crisps

These delicate cookies are made with lots of juice and zest for a delightful tang; poppy seeds add crunch. (Poppy seeds can turn rancid quickly, so purchase them from a store with a high turnover and keep them in the freezer.) MAKES 2½ DOZEN

- ¼ cup fresh lemon juice
- 1 cup (2 sticks) unsalted butter
- 2 cups all-purpose flour
- 1 teaspoon baking powder
- ½ teaspoon coarse salt
- 1½ cups sugar
- 1 large egg
- 2 teaspoons pure vanilla extract
- 3½ teaspoons finely grated lemon zest
- 1 tablespoon poppy seeds, plus more for sprinkling

1. Preheat oven to 350°F. Bring lemon juice to a simmer in a small saucepan over medium heat; cook until reduced by half. Add ½ cup (1 stick) butter, and stir until melted.

2. Whisk together flour, baking powder, and salt in a bowl. Put remaining ½ cup butter and 1 cup sugar in the bowl of an electric mixer fitted with the paddle attachment; mix on medium speed until creamy. Add egg and reserved lemon butter; mix until pale, about 3 minutes. Mix in vanilla and 2 teaspoons lemon zest. Reduce speed to low. Mix in flour mixture and poppy seeds.

3. Stir together remaining ½ cup sugar and 1½ teaspoons lemon zest in a small bowl. Roll dough into 1¼-inch balls; roll balls in lemon-sugar mixture. Space 2 inches apart on baking sheets lined with parchment paper. Press each with the bottom of a glass dipped in sugar mixture until ¼ inch thick. Sprinkle with poppy seeds.

4. Bake until just browned around edges, 12 to 13 minutes, rotating sheets halfway through. Let cool completely on sheets on wire racks. Cookies can be stored in an airtight container at room temperature up to 1 week.

Sweet Cardamom Crackers

Cardamom-flavored cookies are a traditional specialty of the Scandinavian countries. This crisp cracker-like variety is made more crunchy with a topping of finely chopped pistachios and shredded coconut. MAKES 2 DOZEN

- ½ cup sugar
- 1 tablespoon finely chopped pistachios
- 1 tablespoon unsweetened shredded coconut
- ½ cup (1 stick) unsalted butter, room temperature
- 1 large egg, separated, white lightly beaten
- ½ teaspoon pure vanilla extract
- 1 cup all-purpose flour, plus more for rolling
- ¾ teaspoon ground cardamom
- ¼ teaspoon salt

1. Stir together 1 tablespoon sugar, the pistachios, and coconut in a small bowl.

2. Put butter and remaining sugar into the bowl of an electric mixer fitted with paddle attachment. Mix on medium speed until combined. Add egg yolk and vanilla; beat until pale and fluffy, about 2 minutes. Reduce speed to low. Add flour, cardamom, and salt; mix until smooth. Wrap dough in plastic, and refrigerate until firm, about 2 hours.

3. Preheat oven to 350°F. Transfer dough to a nonstick baking mat (such as Silpat), or parchment paper. With a floured rolling pin, roll out a 12 by 8-inch rectangle about ¼ inch thick. Use a pizza wheel to create straight sides, discarding scraps. Carefully transfer mat or paper to a baking sheet. Cut into twenty-four 2-inch squares. Brush with egg white and sprinkle with pistachio mixture.

4. Bake until firm and edges are pale golden brown, 10 to 12 minutes. Remove from oven and run pizza wheel over original cuts. Gently break into individual crackers. Transfer to a wire rack to cool. Cookies can be stored in an airtight container at room temperature up to 3 days.

rich and dense

Sometimes nothing will do but the most decadent of sweets. That's when we seek out brownies, blondies, lemon bars, and similar luxuriously rich and dense desserts. The truffle-like texture of many of these cookies comes from using a free hand with butter, heavy cream, and in many cases, a generous dose of dark chocolate. The butter in these recipes carries the flavors of the other ingredients, delivering powerful taste in every bite. Tangy cream cheese frequently plays a supporting role: Here you'll find it swirled through a thick batter for blondies, whipped into a ginger-rich filling for cheesecake bars, and mixed into a flaky pastry dough to make rugelach. Because they are so rich, most of these cookies are best enjoyed cut into small pieces and shared in batches.

LEMON SQUARES, **page 266**

Lemon Squares

Pucker up: This version of the bake-sale favorite is the most intensely lemony one we've tried. A generous crown of powdered sugar not only adds to the flavor of these sweet squares, but also makes them easier to stack for storage. MAKES ABOUT 2 DOZEN

for the crust:

- 3/4 cup (1 1/2 sticks) unsalted butter, frozen, plus more for dish
- 1 3/4 cups all-purpose flour
- 3/4 cup confectioners' sugar
- 3/4 teaspoon coarse salt

for the filling:

- 4 large eggs, lightly beaten
- 1 1/3 cups granulated sugar
- 3 tablespoons all-purpose flour
- 1/4 teaspoon coarse salt
- 3/4 cup fresh lemon juice
- 1/4 cup whole milk
- Confectioners' sugar, for dusting

1. Preheat oven to 350°F. Butter a 9 by 13-inch glass baking dish, and line with parchment.

2. Make crust: Grate butter on a cheese grater with large holes; set aside. Whisk together flour, confectioners' sugar, and salt in a large bowl. Add butter; stir with a wooden spoon until combined and mixture looks crumbly.

3. Transfer mixture to prepared dish; press evenly onto bottom with your hands. Freeze crust 15 minutes. Bake until slightly golden, 16 to 18 minutes. Leave oven on.

4. Meanwhile, make filling: Whisk together eggs, granulated sugar, flour, and salt in a bowl until smooth. Stir in lemon juice and milk. Pour over hot crust.

5. Reduce oven temperature to 325°F, and bake until filling is set and edges are slightly golden brown, about 18 minutes. Let cool slightly on a wire rack. Lift out; let cool completely on a wire rack before cutting into 2-inch squares. Dust with confectioners' sugar. Lemon squares can be refrigerated in airtight containers up to 2 days.

Baci di Dama

Baci di dama, or "lady's kisses" in Italian, are bite-size chocolate-and-nut cookies with a melted chocolate filling. This flourless variation substitutes almonds for the more common hazelnuts. MAKES ABOUT 1½ DOZEN

for the cookies:

- 2 large egg whites
- 1 cup sugar
- ¼ cup plus 2 tablespoons unsweetened Dutch-process cocoa powder, sifted
- 6¼ ounces (1½ cups) medium-finely ground blanched almonds

for the filling:

- ½ teaspoon solid vegetable shortening
- 4 ounces semisweet chocolate, melted

1. Preheat oven to 325°F. Line a baking sheet with parchment.

2. Make cookies: Place egg whites in the bowl of an electric mixer fitted with the whisk attachment. Beat on high speed until egg whites form stiff peaks. Add the sugar slowly; continue beating until egg whites are very thick, 2 to 3 minutes. Beat in cocoa until combined. Stir in almonds; mix until completely blended. Batter should be quite thick and sticky.

3. Transfer to a pastry bag fitted with a ½-inch round tip (such as Ateco #806). Pipe teaspoon-size, peaked mounds onto baking sheets lined with parchment paper, spacing about 2 inches apart.

4. Bake until slightly cracked, 15 to 17 minutes, rotating sheets halfway through. Let cool on sheets several minutes, then transfer to a rack to cool completely.

5. Make filling: In a small bowl, combine shortening and melted chocolate. Spoon about ½ teaspoon of chocolate onto flat side of a cookie; place another cookie on top. Press together gently so chocolate oozes out slightly. Return cookie to a wire rack to set; repeat with remaining cookies. Cookies can be stored between layers of parchment in airtight containers at room temperature up to 3 days.

Peanut Butter Swirl Brownies

Dollops of peanut butter filling are spooned onto brownie batter; pulling a knife back and forth through both results in a marbleized look.

MAKES 9 LARGE OR 16 SMALL

for the batter:

- ½ cup (1 stick) unsalted butter, cut into small pieces, plus more for pan
- 2 ounces unsweetened chocolate, coarsely chopped
- 4 ounces semisweet chocolate, coarsely chopped
- ⅔ cup all-purpose flour
- ½ teaspoon baking powder
- ¼ teaspoon coarse salt
- ¾ cup granulated sugar
- 3 large eggs
- 2 teaspoons pure vanilla extract

for the filling:

- 4 tablespoons (½ stick) unsalted butter, melted
- ½ cup confectioners' sugar
- ¾ cup smooth peanut butter
- ¼ teaspoon coarse salt
- ½ teaspoon pure vanilla extract

1. Preheat oven to 325°F. Butter an 8-inch square baking pan and line with parchment, allowing a 2-inch overhang. Butter lining (not overhang).

2. Make batter: Put butter and chocolates in a heatproof medium bowl set over a pan of simmering water; stir until melted. Let cool slightly. Whisk together flour, baking powder, and salt in a bowl.

3. Whisk granulated sugar into chocolate mixture. Add eggs, and whisk until mixture is smooth. Stir in vanilla. Add flour mixture; stir until well combined.

4. Make filling: Stir together butter, confectioners' sugar, peanut butter, salt, and vanilla in a bowl until smooth.

5. Pour one-third of batter into prepared pan; spread evenly with a rubber spatula. Drop dollops of peanut butter filling (about 1 tablespoon each) on top of batter, spacing about 1 inch apart. Drizzle remaining batter on top, and gently spread to fill pan. Drop dollops of remaining peanut butter mixture on top. Gently swirl peanut butter filling into batter with a butter knife, running the knife lengthwise and crosswise through layers.

6. Bake until a cake tester inserted into brownies (avoid center and edges) comes out with a few crumbs but is not wet, about 45 minutes. Let cool slightly in pan, about 15 minutes. Lift out; let cool completely on a wire rack before cutting into squares. Brownies can be stored in an airtight container at room temperature up to 3 days.

HOW TO MARBLEIZE BROWNIES Use two large spoons to drop dollops of filling over a base of chocolate batter. Add more batter on top, then more dollops of filling. Drag a butter knife back and forth with the tip touching the bottom of the pan.

Rum Balls

To make these holiday party standbys, you have to first bake a batch of brownies, then break them into bits, flavor them with rum, and roll them into balls. A generous coat of sanding sugar provides a sparkly finish.

MAKES 4 DOZEN

- ¾ cup (1½ sticks) unsalted butter, cut into pieces
- 6 ounces semisweet chocolate, finely chopped
- 3 large eggs
- ½ cup packed light brown sugar
- 1 teaspoon pure vanilla extract
- ½ teaspoon coarse salt
- ¾ cup all-purpose flour
- ¼ cup plus 2 tablespoons dark rum
- Coarse sanding sugar, for rolling
- Vegetable oil cooking spray

1. Preheat oven to 350°F. Coat a 12 by 17-inch rimmed baking sheet with cooking spray.

2. Melt butter and chocolate in a small heatproof bowl set over a pan of simmering water, stirring occasionally.

3. Whisk together eggs, brown sugar, vanilla, and salt in a large bowl. Stir in chocolate mixture, then fold in flour. Pour batter into prepared baking sheet. Spread evenly with a rubber spatula. Bake until top is shiny and a cake tester inserted into center comes out with some crumbs attached, about 10 minutes. Let cool completely on a wire rack.

4. Break up brownie into small pieces; transfer to the bowl of an electric mixer fitted with the paddle attachment. With machine on low, pour in rum, and mix until crumbs start to come together to form a ball.

5. Shape into 1-inch balls and roll in sanding sugar to coat. Transfer to a baking sheet; refrigerate, uncovered, until cold, about 2 hours. Serve chilled or at room temperature. Rum balls can be refrigerated in an airtight container up to 1 week.

Ginger Cheesecake Bars

A double dose of spice flavors these creamy bar cookies: Chopped candied ginger is mixed into the filling, and crushed gingersnaps compose the crust. MAKES ABOUT 4 DOZEN

- 12 ounces store-bought gingersnaps (about 45 cookies)
- 4 tablespoons (1/2 stick) unsalted butter, melted
- 12 ounces cream cheese, room temperature
- 3/4 cup sugar
- 1 large egg
- 1 large egg yolk
- 3 tablespoons sour cream
- 3/4 teaspoon pure vanilla extract
- 2 tablespoons finely chopped candied ginger
- Vegetable oil cooking spray

1. Preheat oven to 350°F. Coat a 9 by 13-inch rimmed baking pan with cooking spray.

2. Place gingersnaps in a food processor; pulse to a powder. Transfer to a small bowl, and stir in butter until well combined. Press gingersnap mixture evenly into bottom of prepared baking pan. Bake crust until firm, about 12 minutes. Let cool completely.

3. Meanwhile, put cream cheese in the bowl of an electric mixer fitted with the paddle attachment; beat on medium speed until smooth and softened. Mix in sugar, egg, egg yolk, sour cream, and vanilla until well combined. Mix in candied ginger.

4. Pour the cream cheese mixture onto crust, and spread evenly with a rubber spatula. Bake, rotating pan halfway through, until filling has puffed and feels slightly firm to the touch (do not let brown), 20 to 25 minutes. Let cool completely on a wire rack. Refrigerate, covered with plastic wrap, until set, about 1 hour. Cut into bars. Bars can be refrigerated in single layers in airtight containers up to 2 days.

GINGER CHEESECAKE BARS, **opposite**

COCONUT SWIRL BROWNIES, **page 274**
CREAM CHEESE SWIRL BLONDIES, **page 275**

Coconut Swirl Brownies

Sweetened condensed milk adds an unmistakable richness to the coconut batter for these swirly treats. When marbleizing the coconut and brownie batters, make sure the butter knife reaches the bottom of the pan.

MAKES 9 LARGE OR 16 SMALL

- ½ cup (1 stick) unsalted butter, cut into small pieces, plus more for pan
- ¾ cup plus 1 tablespoon sugar
- ⅓ cup sweetened condensed milk
- ⅔ cup unsweetened shredded coconut
- 1 large egg white
- 2¼ teaspoons pure vanilla extract
- 2 ounces unsweetened chocolate, coarsely chopped
- 4 ounces semisweet chocolate, coarsely chopped
- ⅔ cup all-purpose flour
- ½ teaspoon baking powder
- ¼ teaspoon coarse salt
- 3 large eggs

1. Preheat oven to 350°F. Line a buttered 8-inch square baking pan with parchment, allowing a 2-inch overhang. Butter lining (not overhang).

2. Stir together 1 tablespoon of sugar, the condensed milk, coconut, egg white, and ¼ teaspoon of the vanilla in a bowl.

3. Put butter and both chocolates in a heatproof bowl set over a pan of simmering water; stir until melted. Let cool slightly.

4. Whisk together flour, baking powder, and salt in a bowl.

5. Whisk remaining ¾ cup sugar into chocolate mixture. Add eggs; whisk until mixture is smooth. Stir in remaining 2 teaspoons vanilla. Add flour mixture; stir until well combined.

6. Pour one-third of chocolate batter into prepared pan. Spread evenly with an offset spatula. Drop dollops of coconut mixture (about 1 tablespoon each) on top of batter, spacing about 1 inch apart. Drizzle remaining batter on top, and gently spread to fill pan. Drop dollops of remaining coconut mixture on top.

7. Gently swirl coconut mixture into batter with a butter knife, running the knife lengthwise and crosswise through layers. Bake until a cake tester inserted into brownies (avoid center and edges) comes out with a few crumbs but is not wet, 35 to 40 minutes. Let cool slightly in pan, about 15 minutes. Lift out; let cool completely on a wire rack before cutting into squares. Brownies can be stored between layers of parchment in an airtight container at room temperature up to 2 days.

Cream Cheese Swirl Blondies

Velvety, delicately tart cream cheese blends well with the more cakey, sugary blondie batter. The resulting bar cookies are remarkably rich and highly habit-forming. MAKES 9 LARGE OR 16 SMALL

- 11 tablespoons (1 stick plus 3 tablespoons) unsalted butter, room temperature, plus more for pan
- 1⅔ cups plus 2 tablespoons all-purpose flour
- 1 teaspoon baking powder
- ¾ teaspoon coarse salt
- 1 cup packed light brown sugar
- 3 large eggs
- 1½ teaspoons pure vanilla extract
- 6 ounces cream cheese, room temperature
- ¼ cup granulated sugar

1. Preheat oven to 325°F. Line a buttered 8-inch square baking pan with parchment, allowing a 2-inch overhang. Butter lining (not overhang).

2. Whisk together 1⅔ cups flour, the baking powder, and salt in a bowl.

3. Put 9 tablespoons butter and the brown sugar in the bowl of an electric mixer fitted with the paddle attachment; mix on medium speed until pale and fluffy, about 3 minutes. Add 2 eggs and 1 teaspoon vanilla; mix until combined. Reduce speed to low. Add flour mixture; mix, scraping down sides of bowl, until well combined. Transfer to a large bowl.

4. Put cream cheese, granulated sugar, remaining 2 tablespoons butter, 2 tablespoons flour, 1 egg, and ½ teaspoon vanilla into the clean bowl of an electric mixer fitted with the clean paddle attachment; mix on medium speed until smooth.

5. Pour half of the blondie batter into prepared pan, and spread evenly with an offset spatula. Spoon two-thirds of cream cheese mixture on top, and spread evenly. Drop dollops of remaining batter on top (spacing about 1 inch apart), and spread. Top with dollops of remaining cream cheese mixture, about 1 inch apart.

6. Gently swirl cream cheese mixture into batter with a butter knife, running the knife lengthwise and crosswise through layers. Bake until golden brown and a cake tester inserted into center comes out with a few crumbs but is not wet, 45 to 47 minutes. Let cool slightly in pan, about 15 minutes. Lift out; let cool completely on a wire rack before cutting into squares. Blondies can be stored between layers of parchment in an airtight container at room temperature up to 2 days.

Chocolate-Ginger Brownies

To make the batter for these super-quick brownies, melt butter and chocolate in a saucepan, then stir the other ingredients right in. Set a batch out on a serving platter, and watch it disappear just as quickly. MAKES 16

- ½ cup (1 stick) unsalted butter, plus more for baking dish
- 3 ounces bittersweet chocolate, coarsely chopped
- 1 cup sugar
- ⅔ cup all-purpose flour
- ¼ cup unsweetened Dutch-process cocoa powder
- 2 large eggs
- 1 teaspoon grated peeled fresh ginger
- ½ teaspoon pure vanilla extract
- ½ teaspoon freshly grated nutmeg
- ½ teaspoon ground ginger
- ¼ teaspoon coarse salt
- ⅛ teaspoon ground cloves

1. Preheat oven to 325°F. Butter an 8-inch square baking dish. Line bottom with parchment, allowing 2 inches to hang over two sides. Butter lining (not overhang).

2. Melt butter and chocolate together in a medium saucepan over medium-low heat, stirring until smooth. Remove from heat, and stir in remaining ingredients.

3. Pour batter into prepared dish. Spread evenly with a rubber spatula. Bake until a cake tester inserted into center comes out with moist crumbs, 30 to 35 minutes. Let cool in pan on a wire rack 15 minutes. Lift out, and let cool completely on rack. Cut into sixteen 2-inch squares. Brownies can be stored in an airtight container at room temperature up to 4 days.

Butterscotch-Cashew Blondies

These scrumptious bar cookies are dense with plenty of cashew chunks, toffee bits, and butterscotch chips. MAKES 9 LARGE OR 16 SMALL

- 9 tablespoons (1 stick plus 1 tablespoon) unsalted butter, room temperature, plus more for pan
- 1⅔ cups all-purpose flour
- 1 teaspoon baking powder
- ¾ teaspoon coarse salt
- 1 cup packed light brown sugar
- 2 large eggs
- 1 teaspoon pure vanilla extract
- ⅓ cup butterscotch chips
- ½ cup unsalted cashews, coarsely chopped (about 3 ounces)
- ¼ cup toffee bits

1. Preheat oven to 350°F. Butter an 8-inch square baking pan and line with parchment, allowing a 2-inch overhang. Butter lining (not overhang).

2. Whisk together flour, baking powder, and salt in a bowl.

3. Put butter and brown sugar in the bowl of an electric mixer fitted with the paddle attachment; mix on medium speed until pale and fluffy, about 3 minutes. Add eggs and vanilla; mix until combined. Reduce speed to low. Add flour mixture, and mix, scraping down sides of bowl, until well combined. Mix in butterscotch chips, cashews, and toffee.

4. Pour batter into prepared pan; spread evenly with a rubber spatula. Bake until golden brown and a cake tester inserted into blondies (avoid center and edges) comes out with a few crumbs but is not wet, 42 to 45 minutes. Let cool slightly in pan, about 15 minutes. Lift out; let cool completely on a wire rack before cutting into squares. Blondies can be stored in an airtight container at room temperature up to 3 days.

Chocolate Thumbprints

Children love these two-bite treats. When you prepare them, have a bowl of ice water ready. If reshaping the thumbprint is necessary during baking, dip your finger in the water for several seconds and allow to dry before reshaping. This will keep your finger cool. MAKES 4½ DOZEN

- 1 cup (2 sticks) plus 6 tablespoons unsalted butter, room temperature
- 1 cup confectioners' sugar
- ¼ teaspoon salt
- 2 teaspoons pure vanilla extract
- 2½ cups all-purpose flour
- 6 ounces semisweet chocolate, chopped
- 2 teaspoons corn syrup

1. Preheat oven to 350°F. Line two baking sheets with parchment paper.

2. In the bowl of an electric mixer fitted with the paddle attachment, beat together 1 cup (2 sticks) butter, the confectioners' sugar, salt, and vanilla on medium speed until smooth, about 2 minutes. Beat in flour, beginning on low speed and increasing to medium until combined.

3. Form balls using 2 teaspoons of dough for each; place balls 1 inch apart on prepared baking sheets. Bake 10 minutes, remove from oven, and press thumb into cookies to make deep, wide indentations. Rotate pan, and return to oven; bake until light brown on the edges, 7 to 9 minutes more. (If the indentations begin to lose definition, remove cookies from oven and press again.) Transfer to a wire rack to cool completely.

4. Combine chocolate, the remaining 6 tablespoons butter, and the corn syrup in a small heatproof bowl set over a pot of simmering water; stir occasionally until melted and smooth. Allow to cool a bit until slightly thickened. Fill thumbprints with the chocolate mixture, and set aside to firm up. Cookies can be stored in single layers in airtight containers at room temperature up to 3 days.

Pecan Bars

John Barricelli, a longtime friend of *Martha Stewart Living* and a very accomplished baker, created the recipe for these irresistible cookies. We've tried lots of pecan bars over the years, but John's are the absolute best.

MAKES ABOUT 3 DOZEN

for the crust:

- 1 cup plus 2 tablespoons (2¼ sticks) unsalted butter, room temperature
- ¾ cup packed light brown sugar
- ½ teaspoon salt
- 3 cups all-purpose flour

for the filling:

- ½ cup (1 stick) unsalted butter
- ½ cup packed light brown sugar
- ¼ cup plus 2 tablespoons honey
- 2 tablespoons granulated sugar
- 2 tablespoons heavy cream
- ¼ teaspoon salt
- 2 cups (8 ounces) pecan halves
- ½ teaspoon pure vanilla extract

1. Preheat oven to 375°F. Make crust: Put butter and brown sugar into the bowl of an electric mixer fitted with the paddle attachment; mix on medium speed until light and fluffy, about 2 minutes. Mix in salt. Add flour, 1 cup at a time, mixing until fully incorporated after each addition. Continue mixing until dough begins to come together in large clumps.

2. Press dough about ¼ inch thick into a 9 by 13-inch baking pan. Pierce the dough with a fork. Chill until firm, about 20 minutes. Bake until golden brown, 18 to 20 minutes. Transfer to a wire rack to cool completely. Reduce oven to 325°F.

3. Make filling: Place butter, brown sugar, honey, granulated sugar, and heavy cream in a saucepan over high heat. Bring to a boil, stirring constantly until mixture coats the back of a spoon, about 1 minute. Remove pan from heat; stir in salt, nuts, and vanilla. Pour filling into the cooled crust.

4. Bake until filling bubbles, 15 to 20 minutes. Carefully transfer to a wire rack to cool completely. Run a paring knife around edges of the pan and invert onto cooling rack. Invert again onto a cutting board. Use a sharp knife to cut into 1 by 3-inch bars. Bars can be stored in an airtight container at room temperature up to 1 week.

Sarah Bernhardt Cookies

Sarah Bernhardt cookies are as multilayered as their namesake—the famed French actress who once starred in the title role of *Hamlet*. An almond macaroon base is topped with silken chocolate filling and then covered in melted chocolate, resulting in a truffle-like cookie with a bit of crunch.

MAKES ABOUT 2½ DOZEN

for the filling:

- 6 ounces semisweet chocolate, coarsely chopped
- ½ cup sugar
- ½ cup water
- 4 large egg yolks, lightly beaten

for the cookies:

- ¼ pound almond paste
- ¼ cup sugar
- 1 large egg white
- ⅛ teaspoon pure almond extract
- Pinch of salt

for the coating:

- 12 ounces semisweet chocolate, coarsely chopped
- 2 tablespoons solid vegetable shortening

1. Make filling: In a heatproof bowl set over a pan of simmering water, melt the chocolate. Remove from heat and allow to cool. Combine the sugar and the water in a small saucepan, and simmer until clear, about 5 minutes. Place egg yolks in the heatproof bowl of an electric mixer set over a pan of simmering water, and whisk until warm to the touch, about 2 minutes.

2. Transfer bowl to the mixer stand fitted with the whisk attachment; with machine on medium, beat in hot sugar syrup. Raise speed to high, and continue beating until cool and fluffy, about 3 minutes. Reduce speed to medium; gradually beat in chocolate until fully combined, scraping down sides of bowl as necessary. Refrigerate until firm and cold, about 1 hour (or up to 1 week).

3. Preheat oven to 350°F. Line a baking sheet with a nonstick baking mat (such as Silpat).

4. Make cookies: In the bowl of an electric mixer fitted with the paddle attachment, beat almond paste and sugar on medium speed until smooth. Add egg white, almond extract, and salt, and beat to combine.

5. Transfer to a pastry bag fitted with a ¼-inch tip (such as Ateco #12). Pipe 1-inch cookies onto prepared baking sheet, leaving about 1 inch between cookies. Bake until firm and golden around edges, about 12 minutes, rotating halfway through. Transfer cookies to a wire rack to cool completely. (Cookies can be stored in an airtight container up to 1 week.)

6. Place cookies flat side down on a cooling rack. Transfer filling to a pastry bag fitted with a ¼-inch tip (such as Ateco #11), and pipe a peaked mound on top of each cookie. Transfer to freezer until very firm, about 1 hour.

7. Make coating: In a heatproof bowl set over a pan of simmering water, melt the chocolate. Stir in the shortening. Cool until barely warm.

8. Remove cookies from freezer. Working quickly so the filling doesn't melt, use a chocolate fork to hold cookie above bowl of chocolate, and spoon melted chocolate over cookie. Place, filling side up, on cooling rack set over a baking sheet. Cookies can be refrigerated in airtight containers up to 4 days.

SARAH BERNHARDT COOKIES, **opposite**

CHOCOLATE MINT SANDWICHES, **page 284**

Chocolate Mint Sandwiches

A mint ganache filling and a shiny chocolate glaze push these cookies over the top, but feel free to omit the glaze—they're delectable without it, too.

MAKES 3 DOZEN

for the cookies:

- 1 cup unsweetened Dutch-process cocoa powder
- ½ cup plus 2 tablespoons all-purpose flour
- ½ cup (1 stick) unsalted butter, room temperature
- ½ cup granulated sugar
- 1 large egg, room temperature
- Confectioners' sugar, for work surface

for the ganache:

- ¼ cup heavy cream
- 6 ounces semisweet chocolate, very finely chopped
- ¾ teaspoon pure peppermint extract

for the glaze:

- 6 ounces semisweet chocolate, very finely chopped

1. Make cookies: Whisk together cocoa powder and flour in a bowl. Put butter and granulated sugar in the bowl of an electric mixer fitted with the paddle attachment. Mix on medium-high speed until pale and fluffy, about 3 minutes. Mix in egg until well blended. Reduce speed to low. Add flour mixture; mix until just combined. Divide dough in half, and shape each half into a disk; wrap in plastic. Refrigerate until firm, about 1 hour (or overnight).

2. Preheat oven to 350°F. Transfer dough to a work surface lightly dusted with confectioners' sugar. Roll out dough to ⅛ inch thick. Cut out cookies using a 2-inch round cookie cutter; space ½ inch apart on baking sheets lined with parchment paper. Repeat with remaining scraps of dough. Bake cookies until firm, rotating sheets halfway through, 10 to 12 minutes. Let cool completely on sheets on wire racks.

3. Meanwhile, make ganache: Bring cream to a boil in a small saucepan over medium-high heat. Add chocolate. Cook, stirring constantly, until chocolate is smooth. Stir in peppermint extract. Let cool slightly, 10 to 15 minutes.

4. Spoon 1 teaspoon ganache onto the bottom of one cookie; sandwich with another cookie. Repeat with remaining cookies and ganache. Refrigerate until firm, about 10 minutes.

5. Make glaze: Melt chocolate in a heatproof bowl set over a pan of simmering water, stirring constantly. Let cool slightly. Dip one flat side of each sandwich into melted chocolate to coat; gently shake off excess. Place sandwiches, chocolate sides up, on wire racks set over baking sheets. Refrigerate until set, about 15 minutes. Cookies can be refrigerated in a single layer in airtight containers up to 2 days.

Truffle Brownies

A thick layer of poured chocolate ganache frosts the top of these wedge-shaped brownies. Sprinkle with tiny heart-shaped candies for your Valentine, change the garnish to suit other occasions, or simply present them unadorned. MAKES ABOUT 1 DOZEN

for the batter:

- 4 tablespoons (½ stick) unsalted butter, plus more for pan
- 3 ounces unsweetened chocolate, coarsely chopped
- ½ cup all-purpose flour
- ¼ teaspoon baking powder
- ½ teaspoon coarse salt
- 1 cup sugar
- 2 large eggs
- ¼ cup whole milk
- 1 teaspoon pure vanilla extract

for the ganache:

- 4 ounces quality semisweet chocolate, coarsely chopped
- ⅔ cup heavy cream

for the garnish:

- Candy sprinkles (optional)

1. Preheat oven to 325°F. Butter a 9-inch springform pan.

2. Make batter: Put butter and chocolate in a heatproof bowl set over a pan of simmering water; stir until melted. Let cool slightly.

3. Whisk together flour, baking powder, and salt in a bowl.

4. Put sugar and eggs in the bowl of an electric mixer fitted with the whisk attachment, and mix on medium speed until pale and fluffy, about 4 minutes. Add chocolate mixture, the milk, and vanilla, and mix until combined. Reduce speed to low. Add flour mixture; mix, scraping down sides of bowl, until well combined.

5. Pour batter into prepared pan. Bake until a cake tester inserted into brownies (avoid center and edges) comes out with a few crumbs but is not wet, 27 to 30 minutes. Let cool completely in pan on a wire rack.

6. Make ganache: Put chocolate in a bowl. Heat cream in a small saucepan over medium-high heat until just simmering. Pour over chocolate; let stand 5 minutes. Gently stir until smooth. Let ganache cool, stirring every 10 minutes, until slightly thickened, 25 to 30 minutes.

7. Pour ganache over cooled brownies in pan; let set, about 20 minutes. Refrigerate until cold, 30 minutes to 1 hour.

8. Let brownies stand at room temperature at least 15 minutes before serving. Release springform, and remove brownies; cut into wedges, wiping knife with a hot damp cloth between each cut. Scatter sprinkles on top, if desired. Brownies can be refrigerated in a single layer in an airtight container up to 2 days. Bring to room temperature before serving.

Double Chocolate Brownies

Fans of fudgy brownies say this is the recipe of their dreams. In fact, it's one of our all-time reader favorites. The brownies are versatile, too—they're equally welcome packed into a picnic basket or stacked atop a cake stand and presented at the end of a dinner party. MAKES 9 LARGE OR 16 SMALL

- 6 tablespoons unsalted butter, plus more for pan
- 6 ounces semisweet chocolate, coarsely chopped
- 1/4 cup unsweetened Dutch-process cocoa powder
- 3/4 cup all-purpose flour
- 1/4 teaspoon baking powder
- 1/4 teaspoon coarse salt
- 1 cup sugar
- 2 large eggs
- 2 teaspoons pure vanilla extract

1. Preheat oven to 350°F. Line a buttered 8-inch square baking pan with parchment, allowing a 2-inch overhang. Butter lining (not overhang).

2. Put butter, chocolate, and cocoa powder in a heatproof bowl set over a pan of simmering water; stir until butter and chocolate have melted. Let cool slightly.

3. Whisk together flour, baking powder, and salt in a bowl. Put sugar, eggs, and vanilla in the bowl of an electric mixer fitted with the whisk attachment, and mix on medium speed until pale, about 4 minutes. Add chocolate mixture; mix until combined. Reduce speed to low. Add flour mixture; mix, scraping down sides of bowl, until well combined.

4. Pour batter into prepared pan; spread evenly with a spatula. Bake until a cake tester inserted into brownies (avoid center and edges) comes out with a few crumbs but is not wet, about 35 minutes. Let cool slightly in pan, about 15 minutes. Lift out; let cool completely on a wire rack before cutting into squares. Brownies can be stored in an airtight container at room temperature up to 3 days.

Rugelach Fingers

Rugelach are traditionally hand formed into crescent shapes; here we've used the same ingredients to create easy-to-prepare bar cookies. The filling—a combination of chopped chocolate and dried fruit—is more traditional than the prune filling used for the rugelach on page 298.

MAKES ABOUT 5 DOZEN

for the dough:

- ¾ cup (1½ sticks) cold unsalted butter, cut into ½-inch pieces
- 8 ounces cream cheese
- 2 cups all-purpose flour
- ½ teaspoon salt

for the filling:

- 6 ounces coarsely chopped semisweet chocolate
- 1 cup walnuts (about 3 ounces), toasted and cooled
- ½ cup granulated sugar
- 1 tablespoon ground cinnamon
- ¾ cup currants
- Finely grated zest of 1 orange
- 3 tablespoons light corn syrup
- 3 tablespoons unsalted butter, melted

for the egg wash:

- 1 large egg yolk
- 1 tablespoon water
- 3 tablespoons sanding sugar, or granulated sugar

1. Make dough: Place butter and cream cheese in the bowl of an electric mixer fitted with the paddle attachment. Mix on low speed until the cream cheese is broken down but butter is still chunky. On low speed, add flour and salt, and mix until crumbly and just beginning to come together, about 20 seconds. There should still be some small pieces of butter visible. Divide dough into two equal parts. Form each part into a flattened rectangle, and wrap well in plastic. Refrigerate 5 hours or up to overnight.

2. Preheat oven to 350°F. Line a 9 by 13-inch baking pan with parchment paper.

3. Make filling: Place the chocolate in the bowl of a food processor. Pulse until the chocolate is very finely chopped, about 7 seconds. Transfer to a large bowl. Finely chop toasted walnuts by hand, and add to bowl. Add granulated sugar, cinnamon, currants, zest, corn syrup, and melted butter, and stir to combine.

4. Place one rectangle of dough between two large pieces of waxed paper; roll dough into a 9 by 13-inch rectangle. Line prepared baking pan with dough. Spread dough evenly with walnut mixture. Roll remaining rectangle of dough into another 9 by 13-inch rectangle; place on top. Trim the edges of the dough so they are even.

5. Make egg wash: Beat egg yolk with the water in a small bowl. Brush the top of dough with egg wash; sprinkle with sanding sugar. Bake until golden, about 35 minutes, rotating halfway through. Cool completely on a wire rack. Cut into fifty to sixty 2½ by ¾-inch rectangles. Cookies can be stored in single layers in airtight containers at room temperature up to 3 days.

ALFAJORES DE DULCE DE LECHE, **opposite**

LEMON TASSIES, **page 292**

Alfajores de Dulce de Leche

Dulce de leche is a popular sweet in Argentina and throughout the rest of South America, where it is also called *manjar* and *leche quemada* ("burnt milk"). Store-bought versions are increasingly available in North American supermarkets and specialty foods stores; use it in place of the homemade variety, if desired. MAKES 3½ DOZEN

- 4 cups all-purpose flour, plus more for work surface
- ¼ cup plus 2 tablespoons confectioners' sugar
- 1½ cups (3 sticks) chilled unsalted butter, cut into pieces
- ½ cup water
- Sanding sugar, for sprinkling
- Dulce de Leche (recipe follows), chilled

1. Line a baking sheet with parchment paper or a nonstick baking mat (such as Silpat).

2. Sift together flour and confectioners' sugar. In a food processor, pulse together flour mixture, sugar, and butter until the mixture resembles coarse meal, about 20 seconds. With machine running, pour in the water in a slow stream, and process just until the dough comes together, about 20 seconds. Form the dough into two flattened disks and wrap well in plastic. Refrigerate for 1 hour.

3. Preheat oven to 350°F. On a well-floured work surface, roll out one disk of dough to a scant ¼-inch thickness. Using a 1¾-inch round cookie cutter, cut out rounds from the dough and transfer to the prepared baking sheet. Repeat with the other disk of dough. Gather up the scraps from both batches, and reroll and cut. Sprinkle half the rounds with sanding sugar. Bake until golden brown, about 15 minutes, rotating sheets halfway through. Transfer to a wire rack to cool completely.

4. About 30 minutes before serving, spread 1 teaspoon of the cold dulce de leche on the bottom of the unsugared cookies. Place the sugared cookies on top to make sandwiches. Serve immediately. Unfilled cookies can be stored in an airtight container at room temperature up to 3 days.

DULCE DE LECHE MAKES 1¾ CUPS

- 2 (14-ounce) cans sweetened condensed milk

Empty milk into the top of a double boiler or a heatproof bowl over a pan of simmering water. Cover with a tight-fitting lid. Cook, stirring every 10 to 15 minutes, until the milk is thick and amber in color, about 5 hours. Remove from heat, and beat with a wooden spoon to smooth out. Transfer to a clean bowl, and refrigerate several hours or up to 3 days.

Lemon Tassies

These bite-size cookies resemble little lemon pies, with a sweet, short crust and a tart cheesecake filling. MAKES 4 DOZEN

for the crusts:

- 2 cups all-purpose flour
- 10 tablespoons (1¼ sticks) cold unsalted butter, cut into chunks
- ¼ cup plus 2 tablespoons sugar
- 2 large egg yolks
- 1 teaspoon pure vanilla extract
- 2 teaspoons finely grated lemon zest
- ¼ teaspoon coarse salt
- Vegetable oil cooking spray

for the filling:

- 8 ounces cream cheese, room temperature
- ⅓ cup sugar
- 1 large egg
- 3 tablespoons finely grated lemon zest
- 1 tablespoon fresh lemon juice
- ½ teaspoon pure vanilla extract

1. Preheat oven to 350°F with rack in upper third. Coat two 24-cup mini-muffin tins with cooking spray.

2. Make crusts: Process flour and butter in a food processor until mixture is the consistency of fine crumbs. Add sugar, egg yolks, vanilla, lemon zest, and salt. Process just until combined and sandy in texture; do not overprocess.

3. Divide dough into quarters. Divide each quarter into 12 equal pieces, and shape into balls. Place each ball in a muffin cup; press into cup, stretching dough up the sides. Set each muffin tin on a baking sheet.

4. Bake crusts, rotating halfway through, until lightly browned all over and slightly darker at the edges, 18 to 20 minutes. Tap down any puffed centers of the shells with the end of a wooden spoon or your finger. Transfer sheets with muffin tins to wire racks to cool.

5. Make filling: With an electric mixer, beat cream cheese, sugar, egg, lemon zest and juice, and vanilla on medium speed until smooth. Using a 1-inch ice cream scoop, fill the cooled crusts with filling.

6. Bake cookies, rotating sheets halfway through, until filling is set and just beginning to color at the edges, 10 to 12 minutes. Transfer to wire racks to cool completely. Tassies can be refrigerated in single layers in airtight containers up to 3 days.

Chocolate-Strawberry Thumbprints

Any sun-kissed berries will work atop the cream cheese filling in these mini chocolate cheesecake cookies. MAKES ABOUT 3 DOZEN

- ¾ cup all-purpose flour
- ¼ cup unsweetened Dutch-process cocoa powder
- ¼ teaspoon salt
- 2 ounces semisweet chocolate, chopped
- ½ cup (1 stick) unsalted butter, room temperature
- ¼ cup plus 6½ teaspoons granulated sugar
- 1 large egg yolk
- ½ teaspoon pure vanilla extract
- 4 ounces cream cheese, room temperature
- 2 tablespoons confectioners' sugar
- 4 ounces strawberries (about 6 medium), stemmed and finely diced

1. Sift together flour, cocoa, and salt into a bowl. Melt chocolate in a heatproof bowl set over a pan of simmering water, stirring until smooth; set aside to cool.

2. Put butter and ¼ cup granulated sugar into the bowl of a mixer fitted with the paddle attachment; mix on medium speed until pale and fluffy. Mix in yolk, vanilla, and chocolate. Reduce speed to low. Mix in flour mixture until just combined. Refrigerate, covered, 1 hour.

3. Preheat oven to 350°F. Put 6 teaspoons granulated sugar into a small bowl. Form dough into ¾-inch balls; roll in sugar to coat. Space 1 inch apart on baking sheets lined with parchment. Press center of each ball with your thumb. Bake 10 minutes. Press centers again with end of a wooden spoon, making ¾-inch indentations. Bake until slightly cracked and set, about 5 minutes more. Cool completely on racks. (Unfilled cookies can be stored in airtight containers at room temperature up to 3 days.)

4. Stir cream cheese and confectioners' sugar in a bowl. Toss berries with remaining ½ teaspoon granulated sugar in another bowl. Spoon cream cheese mixture into centers of cookies; top with berries, dividing evenly.

Chocolate Pistachio Cookies

Bite-size pistachio cookies, sandwiched around a soft, chocolate filling, are dipped in bittersweet chocolate and garnished with a sprinkle of bright-green, slivered pistachios. They are extravagant enough for a special dinner party. MAKES 15

for the filling:

- ¼ cup sugar
- ¼ cup water
- 2 large egg yolks, lightly beaten
- 3 ounces semisweet chocolate, melted and cooled

for the cookies:

- 4 ounces salted shelled pistachios (about 1 cup), ground to a paste in a food processor
- ¼ cup sugar
- 1 large egg white
- ⅛ teaspoon pure vanilla extract
- Pinch of coarse salt

for the glaze:

- 6 ounces bittersweet chocolate, chopped
- 1 tablespoon vegetable shortening

for the garnish:

- Slivered unsalted shelled pistachios (optional)

1. Make filling: Bring sugar and the water to a simmer in a saucepan over medium heat, stirring until sugar has dissolved.

2. Put egg yolks in the heatproof bowl of an electric mixer set over a pan of simmering water. Whisk by hand until yolks are warm to the touch, about 2 minutes. Fit mixer with the whisk attachment. Mix yolks on medium speed; pour in sugar syrup. Raise speed to high; mix until mixture is cool and fluffy, about 3 minutes. Reduce speed to medium; drizzle in melted chocolate. Refrigerate until firm, about 45 minutes.

3. Make cookies: Put pistachio paste and sugar in the clean bowl of an electric mixer fitted with the paddle attachment. Mix on medium speed until smooth. Mix in the egg white, vanilla, and salt.

4. Preheat oven to 350°F. Transfer dough to a pastry bag fitted with a small (about ¼ inch) plain round tip (such as Ateco #10). Pipe 1-inch rounds onto a baking sheet lined with parchment paper, spacing about 1 inch apart. Bake cookies until firm and golden around edges, about 10 minutes. Transfer on parchment to a wire rack, and let cool completely.

5. Place cookies, bottom sides up, on a wire rack set over a baking sheet. Spread 1 to 1½ teaspoons chocolate filling on bottom of half of the cookies. Sandwich with remaining cookies. Freeze 1 hour.

6. Make glaze: Melt chocolate in a heatproof bowl set over a pan of simmering water, stirring occasionally. Remove from heat. Add shortening; stir until combined. Let cool, stirring, until mixture is lukewarm.

7. Using a chocolate fork or regular fork, hold one cookie at a time above bowl of chocolate glaze. Spoon glaze over cookie, letting excess drip back into bowl. Transfer to a wire rack set over a baking sheet. Garnish with slivered pistachios. Refrigerate until set, 5 minutes. Cookies can be refrigerated in single layers in airtight containers up to 3 days.

NOTE: The yolks in the filling are not fully cooked; it should not be prepared for pregnant women, babies, young children, the elderly, or anyone whose health is compromised.

Dulce de Leche Bat Cookies

These creature-of-the-night creations sandwich a rich dulche de leche filling between chocolate cookies. You will need an aspic cutter to form the bat shapes. MAKES 1½ DOZEN

- ¾ cup all-purpose flour, plus more for dusting
- ¼ cup unsweetened Dutch-process cocoa
- ¾ teaspoon coarse salt
- ¼ teaspoon baking powder
- ¼ cup granulated sugar
- ¼ cup packed light-brown sugar
- 2 tablespoons unsalted butter, room temperature
- 1 large egg plus 1 large egg yolk
- 4 ounces semisweet chocolate, melted and cooled
- ½ teaspoon pure vanilla extract
- ¼ cup plus 2 tablespoons dulce de leche (page 291, or store-bought)

1. Whisk together flour, cocoa, salt, and baking powder. Beat butter and sugars with a mixer on medium speed until pale and fluffy, about 3 minutes. Beat in egg, yolk, chocolate, and vanilla. Reduce speed to low. Add flour mixture, and beat until just combined. Shape into a disk, wrap in plastic, and refrigerate 1 hour.

2. On a lightly floured surface, roll out dough to ⅛ inch thick. Cut out 36 rounds with a 2-inch cutter, and space 1 inch apart on parchment-lined baking sheets. Using an aspic cutter set, cut a triangle, point side up, in the center of half the cookies, and then use the half-moon cutter to make one "wing" on each side of the triangle. Refrigerate 30 minutes.

3. Preheat oven to 375°F. Bake until set, 7 to 9 minutes. Let cool. Top each uncut cookie with 1 teaspoon dulce de leche and a cutout cookie. Cookies can be stored in an airtight container between layers of parchment at room temperature up to 3 days.

Prune Rugelach

Flaky cream cheese dough is filled with a rich dried-fruit filling, sprinkled with cinnamon sugar, and baked until golden brown to form these crescents. The prunes are soaked in brandy overnight for the filling, so plan ahead if you're making them. MAKES ABOUT 2½ DOZEN

- 1 cup (2 sticks) cold unsalted butter, cut into 1-inch pieces
- 8 ounces cream cheese, room temperature
- ½ teaspoon coarse salt
- 2 cups all-purpose flour, plus more for work surface
- 1 cup fresh bread crumbs from soft white bread
- ½ cup plus 3 tablespoons sugar
- ½ teaspoon ground cinnamon
- 1 large egg, beaten
- Prune Filling (recipe follows)

1. Mix butter, cream cheese, and salt in a bowl with hands until crumbly. Add flour; mix until just combined. Turn out onto a lightly floured work surface, and divide in half. Shape each half into a disk; wrap in plastic. Refrigerate until cold, 4 hours or up to overnight.

2. Stir together bread crumbs and ½ cup sugar in a bowl. Stir together remaining 3 tablespoons sugar and the cinnamon in another small bowl.

3. Roll one disk to ⅛ inch thick. Cut out a 12-inch circle. Brush beaten egg in a 1-inch border around circle. Put half the prune filling in center, and spread out to beaten egg border. Sprinkle ½ cup bread crumb mixture over filling. With a pizza wheel, cut circle into 16 wedges. Starting at outside edge of each wedge, roll up into a crescent shape. Space 1 inch apart on a baking sheet lined with parchment paper. Brush with beaten egg, and sprinkle with cinnamon-sugar mixture. Repeat with remaining disk and filling. Refrigerate rugelach until cold, about 2 hours.

4. Preheat oven to 325°F. Bake rugelach until golden brown and cooked through, about 40 minutes. Let cool completely on wire racks. Cookies can be stored in airtight containers at room temperature up to 3 days.

PRUNE FILLING MAKES 1⅓ CUPS

- 1 cup prunes
- ½ cup brandy
- ½ cup fresh bread crumbs from soft white bread
- ½ cup sugar

Soak prunes and brandy in a small airtight container at room temperature overnight. Drain prunes. Puree in a food processor until smooth. Transfer to a small bowl. Stir in bread crumbs and sugar. Refrigerate until ready to use, up to 1 day ahead.

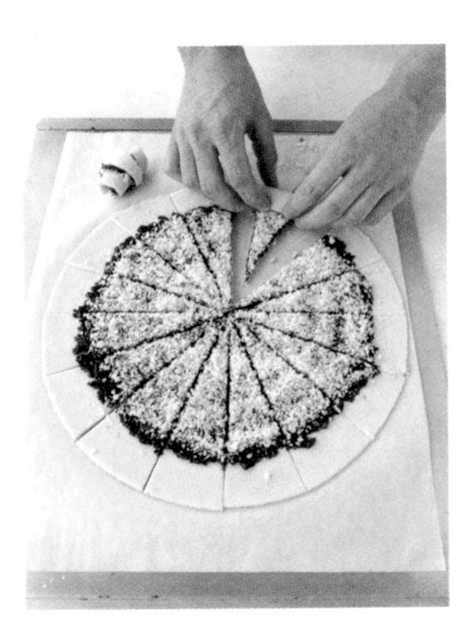

HOW TO FORM RUGELACH Spread the center of a round of dough with pureed fruit filling, then top with bread crumb mixture. With a pizza wheel, cut round into wedges. Tightly roll triangles inward, tucking tails underneath.

Butter Cookie Sandwiches with Chestnut Cream

After they are sandwiched with rich chestnut filling, these cookies are partially dipped into melted chocolate. Crème de marron is chestnut puree sweetened with brown sugar and vanilla. It is available at large supermarkets.

MAKES ABOUT 1½ DOZEN

for the cookies:

- 1½ cups all-purpose flour, plus more for work surface
- ½ teaspoon coarse salt
- ¾ cup (1½ sticks) unsalted butter, room temperature
- ¾ cup sifted confectioners' sugar
- 1 large egg

for the filling:

- 4 tablespoons (½ stick) unsalted butter, room temperature
- ⅔ cup sifted confectioners' sugar
- Pinch of coarse salt
- 2 tablespoons chestnut cream (crème de marron)

for the glaze:

- 6 ounces semisweet chocolate, coarsely chopped

1. Make cookies: Sift together flour and salt into a bowl. Put butter in the bowl of an electric mixer fitted with the paddle attachment. Mix on medium-high speed until fluffy, about 2 minutes. Add confectioners' sugar; mix until smooth. Mix in egg. Reduce speed to low. Add flour mixture; mix until just combined. Wrap dough in plastic, and refrigerate until firm, about 2 hours.

2. Preheat oven to 350°F. Roll out dough on a lightly floured work surface to ⅛ inch thick. Cut into 1½-inch rounds. Using a spatula, transfer rounds to baking sheets lined with parchment paper, spacing 1 inch apart. Bake cookies, rotating sheets halfway through, until edges are golden, about 12 minutes. Transfer to wire racks and let cool completely.

3. Make filling: Put butter in the bowl of an electric mixer fitted with the paddle attachment. Mix on medium speed until smooth, about 3 minutes. Add confectioners' sugar, salt, and chestnut cream; mix until smooth.

4. Make glaze: Melt chocolate in a saucepan over low heat, stirring constantly.

5. Assemble cookies: Spread filling on bottom of half the cookies. Sandwich with remaining cookies. Dip sandwiches a third of the way into the warm glaze; transfer to wire racks set over baking sheets. Refrigerate until set, about 15 minutes. Cookies can be refrigerated in a single layer in airtight containers up to 2 days.

KEY LIME BARS, **opposite**

PECAN TASSIES, **page 304**

Key Lime Bars

This recipe is based on the famous Key lime pie from Joe's Stone Crab restaurant in Miami Beach. If you can't find Key limes, use fresh juice from regular limes. The bars are best garnished with whipped cream and lime immediately before serving. MAKES ABOUT 1½ DOZEN

for the crust:

- 1 cup plus 2½ tablespoons finely ground graham cracker crumbs
- ⅓ cup sugar
- 5 tablespoons unsalted butter, melted

for the filling:

- 3 large egg yolks
- 1½ teaspoons finely grated lime zest
- 1 (14-ounce) can sweetened condensed milk
- ⅔ cup fresh Key lime juice (about 23 Key limes total)

for the garnish:

- ¼ cup heavy cream
- 2 Key limes, thinly sliced into half-moons

1. Preheat oven to 350°F. Make crust: Stir together graham cracker crumbs, sugar, and butter in a small bowl. Press evenly onto bottom of an 8-inch square glass baking dish. Bake until dry and golden brown, about 10 minutes. Let cool completely on a wire rack.

2. Make filling: Put egg yolks and lime zest in the bowl of an electric mixer fitted with the whisk attachment. Mix on high speed until very thick, about 5 minutes. Reduce speed to medium. Add condensed milk in a slow, steady stream, mixing constantly. Raise speed to high; mix until thick, about 3 minutes. Reduce speed to low. Add lime juice; mix until just combined.

3. Spread filling evenly over crust using a spatula. Bake, rotating halfway through, until filling is just set, about 10 minutes. Let cool completely on a wire rack. Refrigerate at least 4 hours or overnight.

4. Make garnish: Cut into 2-inch squares. Put cream in the clean bowl of an electric mixer fitted with the clean whisk attachment. Mix on medium-high speed until stiff peaks form. Garnish bars with whipped cream and a slice of lime. Ungarnished bars can be refrigerated in an airtight container up to 3 days.

Pecan Tassies

These petite pastries feature the flavors and textures of pecan pie—tender, buttery crust, crunchy pecans, and brown sugar filling—all in one bite. Mascarpone, an Italian cream cheese, lends richness to the dough; look for it in the dairy section of large supe rmarkets, or at Italian specialty stores.

MAKES ABOUT 1½ DOZEN

for the dough:

- ½ cup pecans
- ½ cup mascarpone cheese (4 ounces)
- 4 tablespoons (½ stick) unsalted butter, room temperature
- ¾ cup all-purpose flour
- Pinch of salt

for the filling:

- 1 large egg
- ¼ cup packed light brown sugar
- 2 tablespoons pure maple syrup
- 2 teaspoons pure vanilla extract
- 1 tablespoon unsalted butter, room temperature
- ¼ teaspoon salt
- ¾ cup pecans, toasted and coarsely chopped

1. Preheat oven to 350°F. Make dough: Process pecans in a food processor until finely ground (you should have about ½ cup). Put mascarpone and butter into the bowl of an electric mixer fitted with the paddle attachment. Mix on medium-high speed until well blended. Add flour, ground pecans, and salt; mix just until dough comes together. Alternatively, stir together ingredients with a wooden spoon in a large bowl.

2. Roll dough into sixteen 1-inch balls; press into bottoms and up sides of cups of mini-muffin tins.

3. Make filling: Whisk the egg, brown sugar, maple syrup, vanilla, butter, and salt in a bowl. Stir in pecans. Spoon about 1½ teaspoons filling into each muffin cup.

4. Bake until crust begins to turn golden, about 15 minutes. Let cool completely in tins on wire rack. Unmold. Tassies can be stored in single layers in airtight containers at room temperature up to 3 days.

Chocolate Cherry Crumb Bars

The flavor of these dense bars is reminiscent of Black Forest cake, a classic German dessert that originated in the country's southern Black Forest region, renowned for its sour cherries and kirsch (cherry brandy).

MAKES 9 LARGE OR 1 DOZEN SMALL

- 1¼ cups dried cherries, coarsely chopped
- 1¼ cups unsalted butter (2½ sticks), all but 2 tablespoons cut into small pieces
- 1 cup granulated sugar
- ⅔ cup water
- ½ cup unsweetened Dutch-process cocoa powder
- 1 teaspoon coarse salt
- ¾ cup packed light brown sugar
- 1 cup unsweetened shredded coconut (about 3 ounces), lightly toasted
- 2 cups plus 7½ teaspoons all-purpose flour
- 1 large egg
- 2 tablespoons kirsch (optional)
- ½ cup semisweet chocolate chunks
- Vegetable oil cooking spray

1. Preheat oven to 325°F. Coat a 9-inch square baking pan with cooking spray; line with parchment paper, allowing a 2-inch overhang. Coat with cooking spray.

2. Bring cherries, 2 tablespoons butter, ¼ cup granulated sugar, and the water to a simmer in a saucepan over medium heat. Simmer, stirring occasionally, until almost all liquid has been absorbed, about 15 minutes. Remove from heat; stir in ¼ cup granulated sugar. Let cool, stirring occasionally, until sugar has dissolved.

3. Whisk together cocoa powder, salt, brown sugar, toasted coconut, and 2 cups flour in a bowl. Blend in remaining 2¼ sticks butter with a pastry blender or your fingertips until mixture resembles coarse meal; press 3 lightly packed cups cocoa mixture into prepared pan. Bake until just set, about 20 minutes.

4. Put egg, remaining ½ cup granulated sugar, and the kirsch, if using, in the bowl of an electric mixer fitted with the whisk attachment; mix on medium-high speed until pale, about 4 minutes. Fold in cherry mixture and remaining 7½ teaspoons flour; stir in chocolate. Spread mixture evenly over crust; sprinkle with remaining cocoa mixture.

5. Bake until a cake tester inserted into center comes out clean, about 50 minutes. Let cool completely on a wire rack. Run a knife around sides; lift out of pan. Cut into squares. Bars can be stored in an airtight container at room temperature up to 5 days.

tools *and* techniques

Most of us can recall from childhood the excitement of mixing a batch of cookie dough, then carefully dropping it by the spoonful onto a baking sheet. Cookies are usually one of the first things we learn to make, and for many adults the activity remains a favorite kitchen experience. Whether you are an old hand at baking or new to the craft, a few tips and suggestions will make all the difference in your success. If you know how to cream butter and sugar properly, for example, your cookies will turn out better every time. Just as important is choosing the right tools. Buy the best-quality equipment, especially if you plan to bake often. If you find that baking cookies becomes a hobby, invest in cutters in various shapes and sizes; you'll be glad for the opportunity to expand upon your earliest accomplishments.

1
2
4
6
7
3
5

ingredients

1. BUTTER
The most important ingredient in most cookie recipes is butter. We use fresh, unsalted butter sticks for easy measuring; do not substitute whipped butter for sticks, as there is too much air incorporated into these products and they'll throw off your measurements. Before you use it, bring butter to room temperature—soft enough to blend easily—unless the recipe directs otherwise.

2. EGGS
Cookies obtain richness, moisture, tenderness, and volume from eggs. Use fresh large white or brown eggs at room temperature. Cold eggs separate best, but after you separate them, bring them to room temperature so they will blend better with other ingredients. Also, whites beat to their fullest volume when at room temperature.

3. EXTRACTS
Vanilla extract is used in many cookies; almond and lemon extracts are also popular flavorings. Make sure the label reads "pure" on any extract you use and shake well before using.

4. FLOUR
We use unbleached all-purpose flour in most of our cookie recipes; unless the recipe specifies, do not substitute another kind of flour. Use a dry measure to scoop the flour, and level it with a straightedge. You do not need to sift flour if a recipe doesn't call for it; you might want to run a whisk through it beforehand, though, to eliminate any clumps.

5. BAKING SODA AND BAKING POWDER
Baking soda and baking powder are both chemical leaveners. When mixed into batters, they produce carbon dioxide, which makes tiny bubbles that add volume and lighten the texture of baked goods. Baking soda is sometimes used if the recipe has an acidic ingredient such as molasses or cocoa. Baking powder contains baking soda along with a little acid (usually cream of tartar) that reacts with the soda—so you don't need an acidic ingredient in the recipe—and cornstarch, which absorbs moisture. Baking soda and powder are not interchangeable. Measure both with a spoon measure, and level with a straightedge.

6. SALT
To deepen flavors and define the sweetness of cookie dough, a small amount of salt is usually added to the flour with other dry ingredients. Table salt is the default choice for baking; use kosher or other coarse salt only when specified.

7. SUGAR
As well as providing sweetness to cookies, sugar adds texture and color. Most of our recipes call for granulated white sugar; use other kinds of sugar only when specified. Brown sugar—light and dark—is usually firmly packed into measuring cups for accurate measures. Sift confectioners' sugar before measuring, to remove lumps.

TIPS FOR SUCCESS

- Assemble all the ingredients and tools needed before starting.
- Read the recipe through to get a sense of the processes and techniques involved.
- Using an oven thermometer, check your oven's temperature for accuracy.
- Have a baking sheet at room temperature before placing dough on it; a warmer pan will melt the dough, causing cookies to run into one another. Run tepid water over the bottom of the baking sheet to cool it between batches of cookies.

tools for making dough

1. SPOONULA
This tool is helpful when scraping the sides of bowls while mixing cookie dough.

2. SIFTER/SIEVE
A small colander, made of fine-mesh wire and with a long handle, is used to combine dry ingredients and also to aerate flour. This tool can also serve as a sifter; use it to dust confectioners' sugar or cocoa powder on top of cookies after they are baked.

3. GRADUATED MEASURING SPOONS
These are used for measuring both liquid and dry ingredients. Be sure to measure ingredients carefully and accurately: Pour a liquid ingredient, such as vanilla extract, to the brim of the spoon, and level dry ingredients, like salt, with a straightedge, such as a small offset spatula.

4. SMALL FLEXIBLE SPATULA
This heatproof tool is particularly useful to scrape small amounts of ingredients from measuring cups.

5. LARGE FLAT FLEXIBLE SPATULA
Use the heatproof flat spatula to spread thick batters, such as that used for brownies, evenly in a baking pan. Like the spoonula, a large spatula can also be used to scrape down the side of a mixing bowl.

6. RASP GRATER
This grater, which resembles a small ruler, is made of metal and has small, sharp blades. It is used to grate citrus zests and dried spices, such as whole nutmeg.

7. GRADUATED MEASURING CUPS
For greatest accuracy, use measuring cups, preferably metal, for dry and semisolid (peanut butter, jam, shortening, and such) ingredients. Scoop the ingredient into the cup and then level it with a straightedge. Use the right size cup (never estimate portions).

8. SCALE
A small electronic scale is used to weigh nuts and dried fruit when measuring ingredients. It can also be used for measuring dough balls for uniform cookies and weighing bulk amounts of dough.

9. LIQUID MEASURING CUP
Made of heat-resistant glass or plastic, a liquid measure is essential for accuracy; place the cup on a work surface as you pour, and bend down so the marks are at eye level.

1
2
3
1 CUP
1/2 CUP
1/3 CUP
1/4 CUP
7
THINNER
On
Tare
4
5
6
8
LE CREUSET
9

preparing drop-cookie dough

Though recipes and flavorings vary, the method for making any simple drop cookie—chocolate chip, oatmeal, or countless others—is virtually the same.

1. Preheat the oven at least 15 minutes before baking the first batch. When measuring flour or other dry ingredients, scoop and level the top of the measuring cup with a straightedge to ensure accuracy.

2. To evenly distribute dry ingredients such as flour, sugar, and leaveners, sift them together into a mixing bowl. (Or use a whisk instead.)

3. Beat room-temperature butter in a large bowl by hand or with an electric mixer before adding (brown or granulated) sugar. The mixture should be lightened in both color and texture. (This is known as creaming.)

4. Beat the eggs (one at a time if there are several) into the butter mixture until well blended. Add extracts, if using, after the last egg has been incorporated.

5. Combine the dry ingredients with the butter mixture. Stir just until all traces of the flour mixture disappear—overworking the dough sometimes results in a tougher cookie.

6. Fold in the remaining ingredients, such as nuts, dried fruit, candy bits, or chocolate chips, until incorporated. Like other ingredients, chocolate chips (shown above) are best when used at room temperature.

7. Drop rounded spoonfuls of dough at equal distances on a baking sheet lined with parchment or a nonstick baking mat (such as Silpat); amounts and spacing vary from recipe to recipe. Bake until golden brown, rotating the sheet halfway through baking for even coloring. Remove the cookies and parchment from the baking sheet, and transfer to wire racks to cool.

TIPS FOR SUCCESS

- Before dropping dough, make sure it's slightly firm. If it's too soft and sticky to drop easily from a spoon, chill it briefly.
- As an alternative to two tablespoons, use an ice cream scoop for quick work and even results. Be sure to use the scoop size the recipe calls for—if it's specified by volume, measure its capacity with water.
- To ensure cookies remain separate and nicely shaped, follow the guidelines given in a recipe for spacing mounds of dough on the baking sheet. Two inches usually will keep them apart; butter-heavy doughs and those with little leavener sometimes need more space.
- Cool drop cookies on sheets for a minute or two to set, then space apart slightly on wire racks. This prevents the cookies from sticking to one another.
- You can freeze unbaked mounds of cookie dough on baking sheets, then transfer the mounds to resealable freezer bags or airtight containers and return to the freezer for up to one month. Bake according to recipe instructions.

tools for shaping dough

1. RULER
Use a clean wooden or plastic 12-inch ruler for accurate measurements of cookies and to check spacing between dough on sheets.

2. ROLLING PIN
To roll out cookie dough evenly before cutting or shaping, choose a pin that is made of smooth wood and is slightly heavy, with or without a handle.

3. BENCH SCRAPER
A metal or plastic scraper is helpful for loosening and cleaning scraps of dough from work surfaces and scoring certain cookies, such as shortbread. It's also helpful for transferring chopped nuts, fruit, or chocolate from a cutting board into a bowl.

4. SHAPED COOKIE CUTTER
Cookie cutters come in almost every imaginable shape and size, and part of the fun of making cookies is finding ones that appeal to you. Dip cutters lightly in flour to prevent dough from sticking.

5. ICE CREAM SCOOP
Available in graduated sizes, ice cream scoops are used to accurately measure out small amounts of dense dough, such as that used for drop cookies. Choose one with a release mechanism, for convenience.

6. BRUSHES
Use a dry bristle brush to clean excess flour from rolled-out dough and from work surfaces. A 1- to 1½-inch brush is used for brushing liquids on cookie surfaces and buttering pans. Always store brushes separately—dry, liquid, and butter—and label them according to their use.

7. NESTING CUTTERS
Nesting cutters work particularly well when you need to cut out the center from a larger cookie of the same shape or want to create a motif.

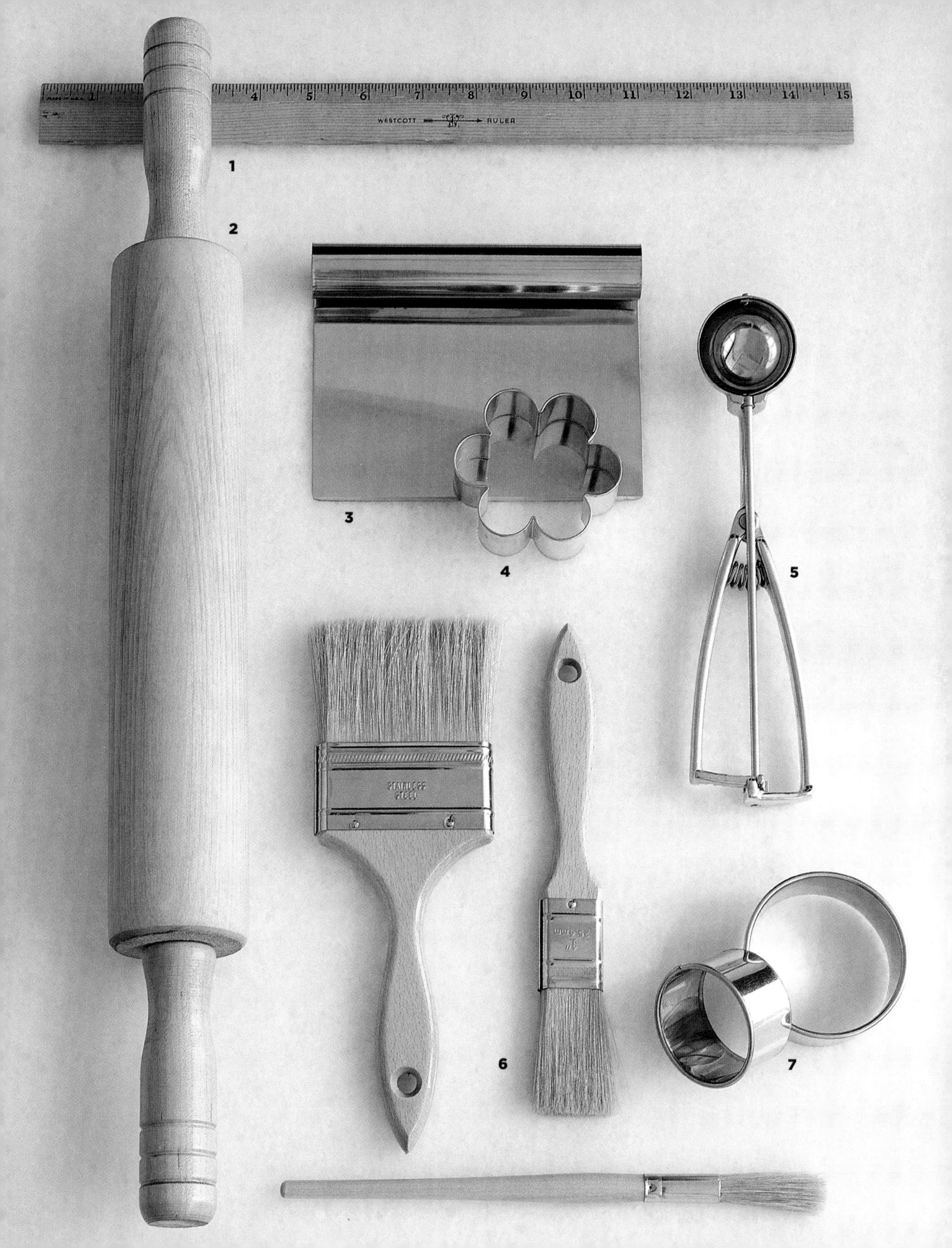
1
2
3
4
5
6
7
WESTCOTT RULER

shaping cookies by hand

Transforming dough into festive shapes only looks like magic. Master the art of scooping and smoothing, and your cookies will be as pretty as they are delicious. Forming the various shapes presents a delightful quandary: which one to make first? In any case, start by making a basic round ball.

1. It is easiest to shape the first balls of dough with a small ice cream scoop. Cookies bake more evenly when they are the same size, and this method ensures uniformity.

2. To create smooth spheres, lightly roll the dough between your palms. Then the almost perfectly rounded dough will be ready for more-detailed shaping.

3. For thumbprints, use the lightly floured handle of a wooden spoon to make same-size indentations—your thumbs will work equally well.

4. For crescent shapes, roll the dough into logs with your hands. Pinch corners with your thumb and index finger; gently bring the ends of the logs into a half circle to make the curved shapes.

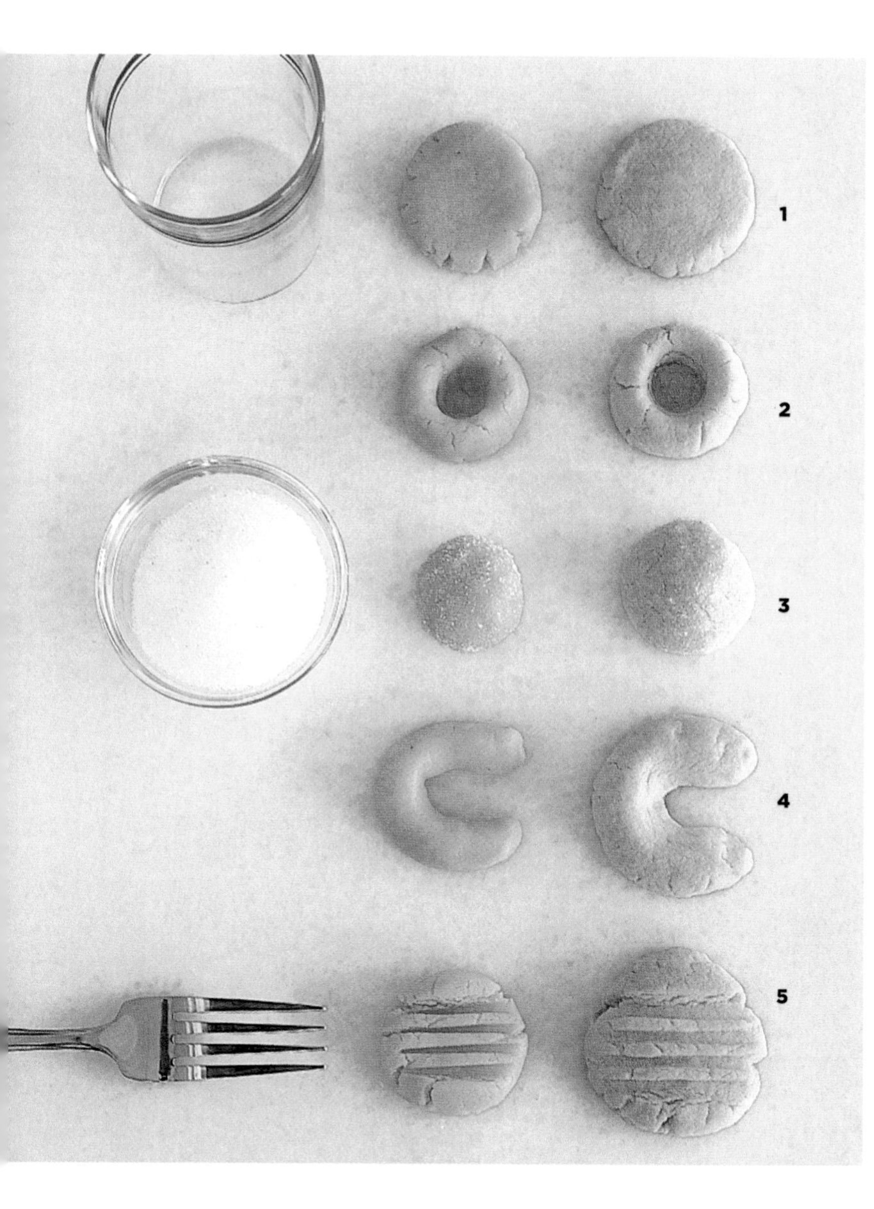

TIPS FOR SUCCESS

- Warm palms can cause butter-rich dough to melt. Keep a bowl of ice water nearby. If dough gets too soft, dip hands in the cold liquid, dry them, and continue shaping.
- To store dough balls, place them on a baking sheet in the freezer until frozen; then transfer to a resealable bag. Thaw, shape, and bake later according to recipe instructions.

First shaped and then baked, these five different forms add variety to any box of cookies.

1. Press the rim of a glass down on dough to make a disk.

2. A thumbprint creates a dimple that can be filled with melted chocolate or jam.

3. For sparkle, roll the ball in sugar before placing on baking sheets.

4. For a crescent or horn shape, roll dough between palms to form a rope, then bend it and pinch edges. Form pretzels and twists the same way.

5. Create ridges by pressing fork tines into the dough. Make a second impression at a right angle to the first, to create a crosshatch pattern.

icebox cookies

When making multiple batches, icebox cookies are ideal: Form the dough into logs, and then chill, cut, and bake as you desire—or store for later.

1. Start by forming the dough into a rough log shape on a sheet of parchment paper. Place the dough slightly off center, toward one end of the parchment. Fold the parchment paper over the dough.

2. Push with a ruler to mold the wrapped dough into a narrow cylinder about the diameter of a paper-towel tube (about 1½ inches). Press hard to remove air pockets and to keep the cylinder of dough even.

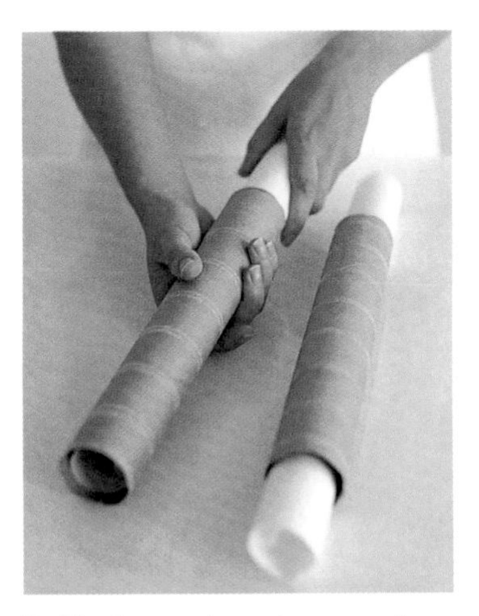

3. Slip the parchment-wrapped rolled dough into an empty paper-towel tube to maintain its shape as it chills. Refrigerate at least 3 hours, until very firm. Store in the refrigerator or freezer, if desired.

4. When ready to bake, roll the thoroughly chilled dough back and forth in a baking pan sprinkled with sanding sugar or another flavorful coating, such as chopped nuts, cocoa, candied fruit, or candied ginger.

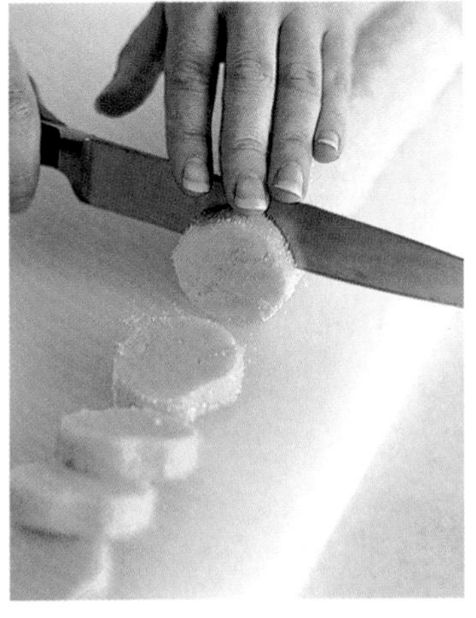

5. Slice the refrigerated or frozen logs, and bake the cookies as you need—or just want—them. Slice them into ¼- to ½-inch-thick rounds, depending on the recipe.

TIPS FOR SUCCESS

- Use cold hands to form the dough into a rough log.
- To prevent icebox cookies from flattening on one side, roll dough logs on a hard surface several times during the chilling process. Do the same after cutting every handful of slices.
- Even a single type of dough can become many kinds of cookies. Roll logs in chopped nuts, sanding sugar, or candied fruit for cookies with crunchy or chewy edges. Brush the perimeter of logs with water first, to help the coating adhere to the dough.
- Icebox cookies can be cut while still frozen. Use a long, sharp slicing knife for precision.
- Prepare several types of dough and keep them in your freezer for up to 1 month. Slice and bake a whole log, or cut a few slices from different logs for an assortment, returning unbaked dough to the freezer.

rolling

Beautifully rolled and cut cookies are extra special. Just a few basic techniques guarantee professional-looking results every time. Once the dough is prepared, chill it in the refrigerator until firm, at least 1 hour. For most recipes, divide the dough in half before rolling, for easier handling.

TIPS FOR SUCCESS

- To test chilled dough to see if it's ready for rolling, press it with your finger; if it presses easily, it isn't chilled enough. Pressing a finger into well-chilled dough will barely leave an indentation.
- Avoid pressing hard when rolling over dough edges, as this will thin them.
- Use only the amount of flour you need to reduce sticking, since the dough will incorporate the flour; too much added flour can toughen the cookies.
- For easy release, dip cookie cutters in flour before cutting.
- When moving shapes, pull scraps away so you can maneuver the spatula without damaging edges.
- Line baking sheets with parchment or have a nonstick baking mat (such as Silpat) ready before you begin so you can transfer shapes as soon as they are cut.
- Place baking sheets holding cut cookies in the refrigerator until dough firms up. Reduce chilling time by using the freezer instead.

1. Before chilling, wrap each half loosely in plastic wrap; roll once or twice to fill gaps and form an even, flat package. This reduces chilling time and helps dough to roll out more easily.

2. Roll out the chilled dough on parchment paper, keeping the rolling pin and the parchment under the dough dusted with flour to prevent sticking. Place the rolling pin in the center of the dough, and roll dough out toward the edges; decrease pressure at edges. Repeat process until dough reaches desired thickness.

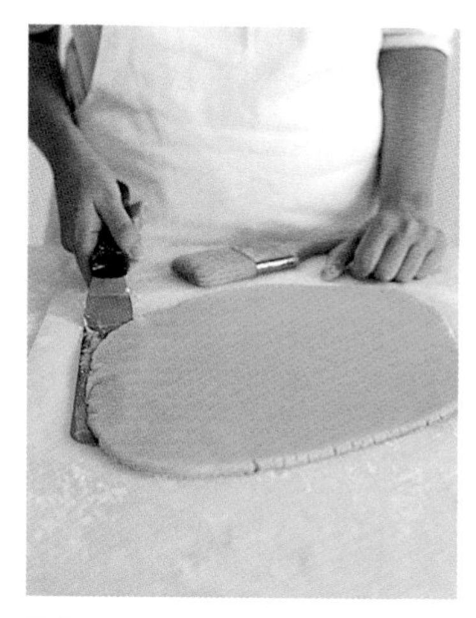

3. Frequently, use a long metal offset spatula to loosen the dough from the surface so it rolls freely; dust with more flour as needed. Keep a clean wide brush on hand to periodically remove excess flour from your work surface and the dough.

4. Cut cookie shapes from the outside edges of the dough into the center, arranging cookie cutters as close together as possible to minimize scraps. Chill scraps, reroll, and cut again.

5. Soft cookie dough (above right) loses its shape when moved; to retain crisp cut edges, refrigerate dough until firm (above left) before baking.

tools for baking dough

1. TIMER
Cookies, which usually bake quickly and are made in batches, require a close watch. A timer helps you to monitor their progress.

2. CAKE PANS
Round cake pans work well when making shortbread wedges; the dough is baked, removed from the pan, and then cut. A springform pan can also be used, and makes for easier release.

3. PARCHMENT PAPER
When placed in the oven, parchment will not burn. It is used to line baking sheets to prevent cookies from sticking and does not require greasing. Do not substitute waxed paper for parchment when lining sheets and pans.

4. LARGE OFFSET METAL SPATULA
The angled design and length of this tool make it indispensable for releasing rolled-out dough from a work surface.

5. LARGE FLAT SPATULA
A flat spatula is used similarly to an offset spatula and is also helpful in lifting rolled-out dough onto baking sheets, and removing large flat cookies, like graham crackers, from a baking sheet.

6. METAL SPATULA
A wide, thin-edged spatula slides easily under just-baked cookies to transfer them to cooling racks. It's also handy for removing cut bar cookies and squares from a baking pan.

7. NONSTICK BAKING MAT
These mats, which are used sometimes instead of parchment to line baking sheets, are washable, reusable, and made of heat-resistant silicone.

8. FLAT BAKING SHEET
Heavy-duty, shiny aluminum is best for even baking, and it will not curl or warp. Sheets have a lip on the short sides for easy gripping, and the flat edges allow you to slide cookies off parchment or a nonstick mat without disturbing their shapes.

9. RIMMED BAKING SHEET
Like flat baking sheets, rimmed sheets are best when made from heavy-duty, shiny aluminum. The rims are useful when you are making bar cookies.

10. THERMOMETER
One of the home baker's most invaluable tools, an oven thermometer will check the accuracy of your oven temperature.

11. COOLING RACK
Most often made of heavy-duty wire, cooling racks allow air to circulate around cookies after they are removed from the oven.

12. SMALL SPATULAS
Used mostly in the same way as large spatulas, the smaller ones are also handy for spreading icing onto small cookies for decorating.

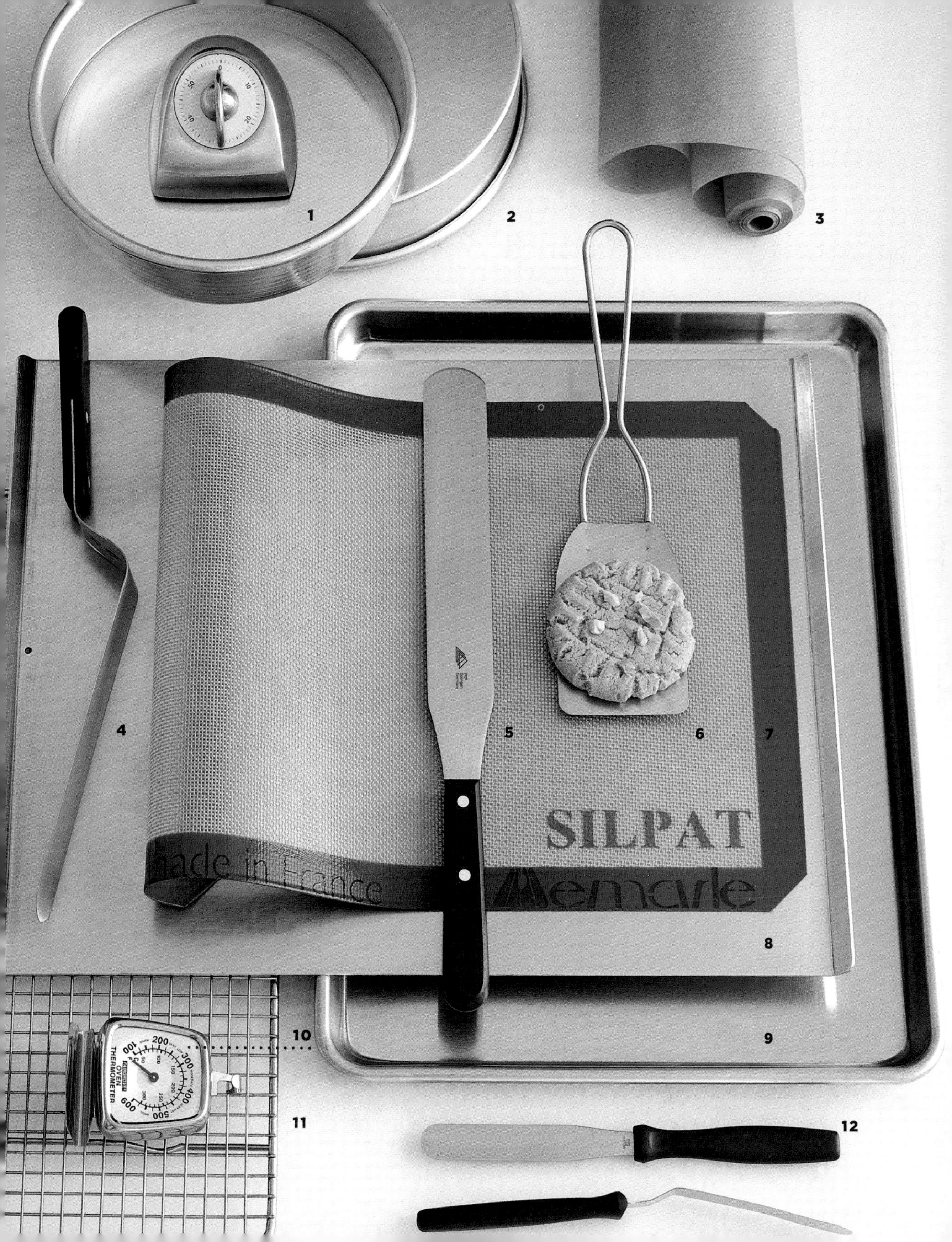
1
2
3
4
5
6
7
SILPAT
made in France
8
9
10
11
OVEN THERMOMETER
12

tools and ingredients for decorating

1. WOODEN SKEWERS
These are handy for drawing out wet icing in contrasting colors to create designs, and are easier to grip than toothpicks.

2. DRAGÉES
Use these tiny, round, hard candies, which are usually silver or gold, only as decoration, not on any cookies you plan to eat.

3. TWEEZERS
There is no better tool for putting tiny nonpareils and dragées in a specific place.

4. SPRINKLES
Candy bits add texture and color to cookies. Sprinkle over icing while still wet.

5. NARROW PASTRY BRUSH
Use the bristles to gently brush away stray sugar crystals from cookies after flocking (see page 327 for more on this technique).

6. SANDING SUGAR
Crystal sugar is available in a range of colors and grains, from fine to coarse; each will give a different sparkling effect.

7. SMALL OFFSET SPATULA
This angled tool's flat surface is perfect for spreading and smoothing out icing.

8. COLORING AND NONPAREILS
Liquid gel, gel-paste, and powdered food coloring add hues to icing; white nonpareils provide contrast.

9. ROUND TOOTHPICKS
If you don't have skewers, use these for drawing out wet icing. Also perfect for mixing color into small batches of icing, for cookie-decorating details.

10. PASTRY BAG
For easy handling, look for pastry bags that are flexible and lightweight. A few plain round tips will handle most piping jobs for cookies. And don't forget a set of plastic couplers, to hold tips securely in place.

1
2
3
4
5
PURE BRISTLES
6
7
8
9
10

decorating

Equip yourself with pastry bags, piping tips, and toothpicks—plus fresh-baked cookies and icing—and then follow our step-by-step instructions to apply the finishing touches.

TIPS FOR SUCCESS

- Royal Icing is perfect for decorating cookies. A mixture of confectioners' sugar, meringue powder, and water, it hardens as it dries, making it excellent for decorations that won't smudge or smear. Royal Icing can be mixed thin or thick; a thinner consistency is good for making a flat background (called floodwork), while thicker icing is best for piping designs. Thin the icing as needed by adding more water; to thicken it, add more confectioners' sugar or meringue powder.
- To tint icing, use gel-paste, liquid, or powdered food coloring. We prefer gel-paste, which is more concentrated than liquid. Add it a dab at a time with a toothpick, using a new toothpick each time, and blend the color well before adding more. It might take some experimentation to get the hue you want.
- Don't fret if your first decorations are less than perfect looking. You can always hide messy squiggles with well-placed dots, stripes, or other details. And remember, even your mistakes will be delicious.

1. Attach a tip to a pastry bag fitted with a coupler. Form a cuff with the top 3 inches of the bag. Set a damp paper towel in a glass; place the empty pastry bag upright in the glass. Spoon icing into the bag until it is two-thirds full; cinch with a rubber band so the icing won't seep out at the top.

2. Outline half a cookie using a #2 tip. Rotate the cookie about 180 degrees, and then pipe the other half. Let the icing set for 5 to 10 minutes. Using a #5 tip, draw several zigzags across the entire surface of the cookie (this is called flooding).

3. Spread icing evenly over the cookie with a small offset spatula. Allow the icing to dry overnight. Store unused Royal Icing in an airtight container at room temperature (as long as it's made with meringue powder). When ready to decorate, use a #2 tip to pipe your design.

4. To create a motif, pipe designs with Royal Icing in a contrasting color on each cookie, starting at the top. To make leaves such as those shown here, apply pressure to the pastry bag to make a leaf's base, and let up on the pressure as you move toward the tip. Stagger leaves along the stem. If you want to apply silver dragées, do so before the icing hardens.

5. Have ready a bowl of sanding sugar. While the icing is wet, hold the cookie over a clean paper towel; sprinkle liberally with sugar (this is called flocking). Let sit for 5 minutes before shaking off excess sugar. Let dry completely, for several hours, before gently removing stray crystals with a soft pastry brush. Shake the sugar from the paper towel back into the bowl to reuse.

6. Once decorated, allow cookies to dry in a single layer overnight. Arrange cookies in layers in an airtight container at room temperature, separated by sheets of parchment paper. Don't crowd cookies, or they might bump together and break. Decorated cutouts will keep for about 1 week.

packaging *and* giving

Even the simplest wrapping reinforces the heartfelt nature of a home-baked gift. Many of the materials for making cookie packages are probably in your home already: strips of ribbon or baker's twine can work wonders when tied around a cellophane bag, and a bit of decorative paper transforms an ordinary box into a charming container. With a little more crafting and a few more materials, an oatmeal carton can be recycled into a regal gift drum. Size up the packaging potential of other boxes, tins, patterned papers, and notions, and be sure to line containers with parchment or waxed paper before filling with cookies. Above all, allow cookies to cool completely before you pack them; any trapped steam will make cookies soggy. Happily, the warm spirit of the giver will remain when the present reaches its destination.

HOSTESS GIFTS Dividing bamboo or paper trays creates a way to carry a medley of flavors to a holiday party or open house. A liner and two tent-folded corrugated papers keep cookies from looking or tasting jumbled. Slip the tray into a self-sealing cellophane envelope and give it a gift tag.

SOMETHING FOR EVERYONE A mixed tin is a guaranteed crowd-pleaser. Line the bottom and sides of a square or rectangular airtight tin with corrugated paper and fold pieces in half for dividers. For this assortment, we wrapped delicate macaroons in polka-dotted tissue paper (top left), buffered sugar-topped tea cookies in corrugated paper tubes (middle left), protected two types of butter cookies with accordion-folds of red paper (bottom), and tied a stack of crackly chocolate cookies with baker's twine (middle right).

COOKIE DRUMS Here's a recycling project in the most festive spirit: After using the contents of an oatmeal container to make cookies, decorate the boxes to package the baked goods. We give instructions for making two drums out of each container; to make larger drums, skip the part about cutting the box in half crosswise.

HOW TO MAKE DRUMS You'll need a measuring tape, a cylindrical oatmeal container, a utility knife, scissors, heavy white paper, spray adhesive, a pencil, gold paper, decorative fabric (such as satin or silk), a ruler, vellum, a hot-glue gun, gold cording, and ribbon.

1. Cut box in half crosswise with the utility knife. Measure the circumference and height of the box. Cut a strip of heavy white paper to those dimensions. Fix the paper to the container with spray adhesive. Cut a disk of gold paper to cover the bottom of container (for a container made from the upper half, the lid serves as the bottom); attach with spray adhesive. Cut a length of fabric to the height and circumference of container. Before affixing, mark it where the cord zigzags will attach: Divide the fabric's length by 10, and make a small tick with a pencil at each of these points along one side of the strip. On the opposite edge, make pencil ticks midway between each pair of the first 10, to form a zigzag. Attach the fabric—marked side out—to the container with spray adhesive.

2. Cut a vellum disk about ¼ inch wider than the mouth of the drum. Make small cuts around the disk at regular intervals so the overhang will fold neatly. Fill the drum with cookies. Cover the mouth with the vellum disk; attach tabs to the drum with a glue gun.

3. Carefully run cording in a zigzag around the drum, hot-gluing it at each tick mark. Wrap ribbon around the top and bottom of the drum, covering zigzag ends.

1

2

3

For EMMA

DOUBLE DUTY Lovingly prepared cookies deserve packaging that befits their worth. Lidded or not, kitchen molds make attractive gift containers, and they will serve the recipient well long after the cookies are eaten. Brown moiré ribbon adorns a lidded pudding mold; colored waxed paper secured with bookbinder's tape covers a lidless mold (opposite). An ice cream mold (above left) filled with scallop-edged sugar cookies is dressed up with a wide band of military ribbon; fabric glue is used to attach gold rickrack just below the rim. Tied, the gauzy silver ribbon holds the cookies in place. Heavy-duty square cake pans (above right) have notched corners, which are perfect for securing the cording and rickrack that crisscross over the parchment-paper lids.

RECIPES FOR SUCCESS A collection of holiday recipes, accompanied by a sweet sample (left), is a gift that will be appreciated for years. The cheery presentation adds to its appeal. To make one booklet (above), cover the exterior of a blank greeting card with patterned wrapping paper using a glue stick. Remove the flap from an envelope that will accommodate 3 by 5-inch recipe cards. Glue the front of the envelope to the inner right-hand side of the greeting card. Stuff the envelope with recipe cards, printed by hand or on a computer. Finish by affixing a label to the front of the booklet.

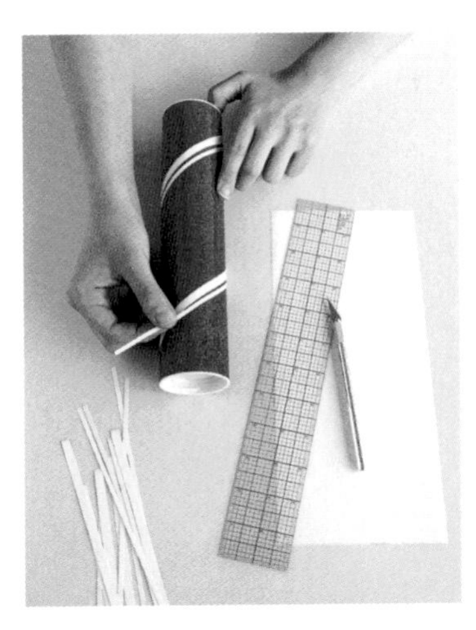

STACKING UP NICELY Just the right shape for mailing (or hand-delivering) cookies, bright-colored cardboard tubes look even more fetching when outfitted in red and white (opposite). Choose sturdy cookies, and gently but securely wrap decorative tissue paper around them before slipping them into the tube. To add stripes, cut strips of adhesive paper in different widths with a utility knife and a straightedge (right); using a glue stick, adhere them to bright mailing tubes from office-supply stores.

CATCH A GLIMPSE Tempt everyone with a peek at their gifts. Look for windowed boxes in a range of sizes at baking- and kitchen-supply stores (above). To make windows on plain boxes (left), first disassemble the boxes. With a pencil and a ruler, or a template, draw an oval, a circle, a square, or a rectangle on the top panel of the inside of the box. Cut it out with a utility knife. (Use the same method to add windows to the sides, if you like.) Cut out cellophane for the windows and add it inside with double-sided tape. Reassemble the box using double-sided tape. Before packing them, line the boxes with colorful glassine. Embellish the boxes with ribbon, yarn, or baker's twine, and add gift tags or adhesive labels.

PRETTY LITTLE BOXES Ordinary jewelry boxes make lovely receptacles for small batches of cookies, especially on Valentine's Day. We lined a long slender bracelet box with red linen trimmed with scalloping shears, then topped the liner with a half dozen mini cookies. A pink heart-shaped doily, secured with a knotted piece of waxed red twine, completes the endearing package.

THE WHOLE LOT Bar cookies are easy to make, and they stay fresher longer when delivered in the original baking dish. After the pan holding a batch of bars has cooled, cover the sides with a combination of wide and very narrow grosgrain ribbon. Next, place a sheet of glassine paper on top. Or wrap a pan, such as an 8-inch square aluminum one containing brownies, with an uncomplicated origami-style fold (see instructions below).

HOW TO MAKE ORIGAMI FOLD
1. Center pan on colored wax paper. Fold both sides over pan. 2. On ends, fold outer corners in (as with gift wrapping). 3. Join tapered ends over pan's center. Fold edges over twice. Wrap wide ribbon around packet, and staple. Punch a hole, and add thin ribbon and a tag.

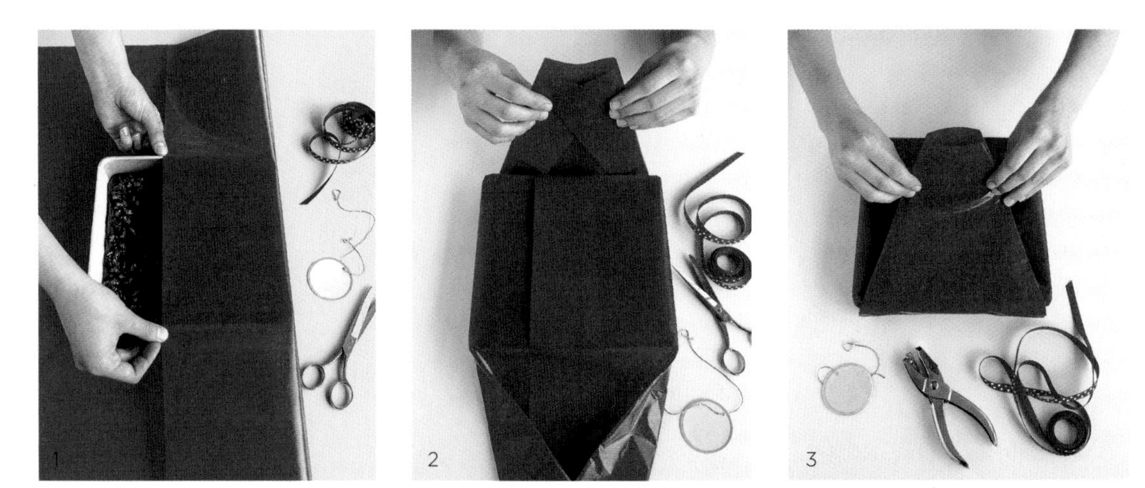

ONE AT A TIME Think outside the box and place a single oversize cookie in a CD envelope from a music or office-supply store. Wrap the cookie in glassine first, and slip it into the package; then secure with ribbon or cord, seal with a label, and mark with the recipient's name.

TIN FULL OF TREATS Fill an oversize tin to brimming with a batch of cookies for a whole family or a group of friends at work. Line the tin with colored corrugated paper cut to its circumference. We matched the spiral pinwheel cookies with this tin's swirly pattern for a playful presentation, but any sturdy vessel will do.

BY THE DOZEN A box of spritz wreaths festooned with tiny ribbon bows in an array of similar shades makes a perfect gift for a tree-trimming party. We lined a shallow necklace box from a jewelry supply store with textured paper to hold a single layer of wreaths.

SHOWING OFF Clear acetate boxes and cylinders in assorted shapes and sizes hold single varieties of a medley of cookies (top to bottom, left to right): Fruit and Nut Cookies, Cornmeal Thyme Cookies, Chocolate-Almond-Marsala Cookies, Lemon–Poppy Seed Crisps, Candy-Stripe Cookie Sticks, Mini Black-and-White Cookies, and Coconut Cream–Filled Cookies.

sources

INGREDIENTS

CHOCOLATE, SUGARS, CANDY, AND TOPPINGS

Royal Pacific Foods
800-551-5284
www.gingerpeople.com.

Sweet Celebrations
800-328-6722
www.sweetc.com

Sweet Life
212-598-0092
www.sweetlifeny.com

DRIED FRUITS AND NUTS

A. L. Bazzini
212-334-1280
www.bazzininuts.com

Russ & Daughters
800-787-7229 or 212-475-4880
www.russanddaughters.com

SPICES AND EXTRACTS

Adriana's Caravan
800-316-0820 or 617-649-4749
www.adrianascaravan.com

Kalustyan's
212-685-3451
www.kalustyans.com

EQUIPMENT

Bridge Kitchenware
800-274-3435 or 212-688-4220
www.bridgekitchenware.com

Broadway Panhandler
866-266-5925 or 212-966-3434
www.broadwaypanhandler.com

Candyland Crafts
877-487-4289
www.candylandcrafts.com

CopperGifts
620-421-0654
www.coppergifts.com

Roberts European Imports (for bratseli iron)
800-968-2517
www.shopswiss.com

Sugarcraft
513-896-7089
www.sugarcraft.com

Williams-Sonoma
800-541-2233
www.williams-sonoma.com

PACKAGING SUPPLIES

The Container Store
800-786-7315
www.containerstore.com

GlerupRevere Packaging
866-747-6871
www.glerup.com

Independent Can Co.
410-272-0090
www.independentcan.com

Kate's Paperie
800-809-9880
www.katespaperie.com

Masterstroke Canada
866-249-7677
www.masterstrokecanada.com

New York Cake & Baking Distributor
800-942-2539 or 212-675-2253
www.nycake.com

Paper Presentation
800-727-3701 or 212-463-7035
www.paperpresentation.com

Uline Shipping Supplies
800-295-5510
www.uline.com

photo credits

All photographs by
VICTOR SCHRAGER except:

ANTONIS ACHILLEOS 92 (left), 196 (right)

SANG AN 76 (right), 88 (left), 100 (right), 111, 203, 276, 283 (left)

CHRISTOPHER BAKER 327 (bottom right)

JUSTIN BERNHAUT 129 (right), 211, 302 (right)

ANITA CALERO 118

BEATRIZ DA COSTA 91

DANA GALLAGHER 72 (left), 158, 212

GENTL & HYERS 113 (right), 237 (left), 295, 332, 333

LISA HUBBARD 88 (right), 226 (right), 260 (right), 305, 336 (top right and left)

RICHARD GERHARD JUNG 308, 311–313, 315–321, 323, 325, 326, 327 (top left)

JOHNNY MILLER 6

NGOC MINH NGO 55 (inset)

CON POULOS 181, 268, 269, 277, 285

MARIA ROBLEDO 234, 334, 335

DEIDRE ROONEY 194

MATTHEW SEPTIMUS 327 (all except top left and bottom right)

ANNA WILLIAMS 95, 99, 113 (left), 131, 237 (right), 290 (left)

index